MW01121375

The Impact of the Subprime Crisis on Global Financial Markets, Banks and International Trade

The Impact of the Subprime Crisis on Global Financial Markets, Banks and International Trade: A Quest for Sustainable Policies

By

Indranarain Ramlall

CAMBRIDGE
SCHOLARS

P U B L I S H I N G

The Impact of the Subprime Crisis on Global Financial Markets, Banks and International Trade:
A Quest for Sustainable Policies,
by Indranarain Ramlall

This book first published 2013

Cambridge Scholars Publishing

12 Back Chapman Street, Newcastle upon Tyne, NE6 2XX, UK

British Library Cataloguing in Publication Data
A catalogue record for this book is available from the British Library

ISBN (10): 1-4438-4738-0, ISBN (13): 978-1-4438-4738-4

Dedicated to my parents, the reason for my existence, and to God for granting me the strength to write this book.

"Success is not final, failure is not fatal: it is the courage to continue that counts."
—Winston Churchill

TABLE OF CONTENTS

LIST OF FIGURES

LIST OF TABLES

PREFACE

With the occurrence of the US crisis, international focus has shifted from finance to financial stability, especially when vigorous efforts have been channelled worldwide to preserve financial stability. Financial stability constitutes a fascinating area by virtue of its inherent connection to a plethora of directly or indirectly related issues, including macroeconomic stability, debt sustainability and banking sector stability, amongst others. Interestingly, financial stability is so important that I strongly believe that the mandatory policy of any central bank in the world should be first and foremost to preserve financial stability, followed by price stability. The reason is that price stability is a necessary but not sufficient condition for financial stability. Beyond that, financial stability is more encompassing and hence best captures the whole intricacies of an economy's risks, let alone inflation risks.

I have written this book keeping in mind a broad audience. The book offers analyses of financial stability risk assessment at three main levels, namely international financial markets, banks and international trade. The research is innovative, timely and highly luscious in terms of policy implications. I believe that these three areas constitute the core fundamentals prerequisite for the smooth functioning of the global financial system. I coin the term "Egonomics" to label the wrong application of "Economics" in view of concentrating benefits to certain parties at the expense of deadweight losses to society. Many cases of "Egonomics" have been identified during the crisis and are reported in this book.

Today, the world is buffeted by three main crises, namely, debt crisis, ageing population and climate change. In that respect, it is utterly misleading to focus solely on policies to curb a debt crisis. Indeed, having too much emphasis laid upon debt sustainability issues signifies scaling up the level of Gross Domestic Product, even at the expense of witnessing a considerable increase in the level of CO^2 emissions. In a similar manner, issues relating to a growing ageing population are gaining momentum in developed economies; this gnaws at savings levels and subsequently ricochets into subdued future growth prospects. To deal with these crises, new policies have also been suggested.

I hope that the book will incite new thinking and open up possibilities for invigorating research. The book has been written for academicians, policy-makers, regulators and researchers. It can also be used as a research text in the area of financial stability. I welcome any comments from readers.

Indranarain Ramlall

November 2012

Email: i.ramlall@uom.ac.mu/iramamam@yahoo.com

CHAPTER ONE

INTRODUCTION

Today, financial stability lies at the heart of any financial system in the world. Financial system stability is demonstrated by the capacity of a financial system to bear external shocks without engendering significant impairments on its macroeconomic activities. Alternatively stated, financial stability signifies the ability of the financial system to be resilient against any unexpected shocks. Financial stability can also be defined as a situation whereby there is public trust in the financial system. Conversely, financial instability pertains to a situation where even a small negative shock can create drastic and adverse consequences. By default, financial stability is deemed to be a public good because any financial crisis is symptomatic of market failure. The US crisis constitutes a major lesson to humanity in terms of devising new policies to consolidate the resilience of the world financial system.

One of the most widely used methods of gauging financial stability pertains to systemic risk assessment, in view of sieving out any potential threat that can spark off detrimental consequences onto the real economy. For instance, in the case of households, a fall in the share prices of their stock holdings not only eats up their wealth but also undermines their consumption of goods and services. Based on the fact that a systemic financial risk constitutes a rather rare event, it is usually not easy for the financial authorities to fully gauge the impact of such a risk on their economies. Notwithstanding, regulatory authorities should be on constant guard and regularly perform stress testing exercises.

To obviate any financial crisis, authorities usually wield two main tools: a macroprudential approach to deal with systemic risk (such as in systemically important institutions) and a microprudential approach to cope with institution-specific risk. Whenever distortions are exerted on financial markets, they impair on the efficient allocation of funds and result in subsequent costs to taxpayers. The severity of any crisis is principally assessed via its effects on the real economy and is mainly determined by the extent of financial system interconnectedness. For example, the stronger the interconnection between banks, firms and households, the more pronounced the effects of financial instability tend to be. Larger financial systems constitute a double-edged sword. On one hand, it holds that the larger the financial system, the better its ability to absorb any given shock. On the other hand however, in the case of a large global shock, the larger the financial system, the stronger the transmission mechanisms are of the adverse effects.

The US subprime crisis, which started in 2007 with losses manifesting at two Bear Stearns hedge funds, left behind permanent scars on the financial system. Amongst all the financial crises that have buffeted the world, the US subprime crisis is considered unique. First, the amount of losses incurred were huge (estimated in October 2012 by Mark Adelson, former chief credit officer at Standard & Poor's, to hover around $15 trillion); it is considered the worst crisis since that of the Great Depression of the 1930s. Second, the crisis manifested itself in a period of free trade, whereby positive shocks induced positive growth effects, while negative shocks generated strong contagion effects. Above all, globalisation strengthened the speed at which the crisis could spread throughout the world, since many countries allowed entry to foreign banks under the globalisation philosophy. Third, the crisis did not seem to end even after the use of distinct policies such as government bailouts (which were used in the case of American Insurance Group) or unconventional monetary policies (Quantitative Easing).

This book is organised into seven chapters, all imbued with innovative research and policies. The second chapter focuses on the causes, consequences and policies to adopt with respect to the US subprime crisis. The author points out the need for a country Financial Stability Fund that would cater not only for systemically important institutions but also for those institutions imbued with a strong level of interconnectedness. Among other proposed solutions, the author argues for greening or socialising the "cost of capital" as the best way to hedge against erratic business cycles and thereby mitigate losses. Moreover, the author finds that Financial Stability Reports are not published by all central banks (only around 38 per cent of all central banks do publish Financial Stability Reports). Above all, for those reports which are published, there is still a lack of harmonised features, timeliness concerns and extent of authenticity in reporting and even divergence when compared to IMF country reports. Concerted efforts between central banks and IMF/BIS staff would undeniably leverage the quality and comparability of Financial Stability Reports worldwide. Ironically, some countries have utterly ceased reporting Financial Stability Reports post the onset of the crisis.

The third chapter of the book develops a Global Financial Stability Multifactor Arbitrage Pricing Theory model to uncover any crisis-induced irrational exuberance. This is executed through the investigation of 29 world assets, with findings confirming potential irrational exuberance for certain assets. The Global Financial Stability Multifactor Arbitrage Pricing Theory model is expected to be widely used by policy-makers when assessing international asset risk. The fourth chapter of the book probes into banks' specific and macroeconomic factors under a pre- and post-crisis investigation by using a unique database based on country-wise aggregate banks' data. Findings show that capital strength and funding costs constitute the most important drivers for banks' profitability, considering the fact that Portugal, Italy, Greece and Spain were all subject to problems even before the crisis. The fifth chapter develops a credit risk model that focuses on the repayment capacity of developing countries in the world with specific focus given to international trade. Results show that international trade has been particularly stimulating during the pre-crisis period with a positive effect noted on the debt repayment capacity of developing countries. However, post the crisis, no such effects prevail. Such a finding adds significant momentum to the fact that the crisis may already be curbing growth prospects via the trade channel for developing countries, with potential rekindling effects on protectionism.

In the sixth chapter of the book, the author draws attention to the need to enhance public debt management functions. Ironically, with the onset of the crisis, this can constitute the proper time for developing countries to leverage their debt management strategies. In the last chapter of the book, the author comments on global policies to be adopted to mitigate against not only the US subprime crisis (debt crisis) but also two other crises which have already taken firm grip on society, namely an ageing population and the adverse effects of climate change. The author argues that global policies should be trident in dimension to mitigate against any potential backfiring effects. For instance, the international community seems to be so focused on the financial crisis that efforts to leverage economic activities may further aggravate carbon emissions worldwide. Similarly, ageing populations increasingly impinging upon developed countries has the effect of triggering significant strains on savings and growth prospects. The author argues for the establishment of long-term approaches to policies; social banks; green finance; radical changes in the work environment; limits to speculation in derivatives; a shift from "Egonomics" to "Economics;" checks on growth of the artificial economy, as well as a re-engineering of bank loans approvals via inclusion of sustainability reports.

For academics, the crisis can be viewed in something of a positive light—perhaps possessing an element of spiritually ingrained wisdom for humankind, if you will—since it provides the opportunity to rethink the world of finance and propose new theories. Only a theory can kill a theory; dead theories cause new theories to develop, which can in turn be utilised until they fail. In essence, the efforts dedicated towards scaling up wealth for years went to waste as the US witnessed massive losses. This may imply that the concept of equilibrium may need to be revised in terms of having equilibrium as a balancing state between the material world and the spiritual world.

CHAPTER TWO

CAUSES, CONSEQUENCES AND SOLUTIONS TO THE US FINANCIAL CRISIS

2.0 Introduction

Three financial experts are widely acclaimed to have predicted the global financial crisis. Nouriel Roubini is considered to be the father of the crisis as he anticipated the coming collapse of the US housing market. Charles Morris, author of the book *Trillion Dollar Meltdown*, published in 2008, also predicted the crisis in early 2007. Finally, George Magnus foresaw that the US subprime crisis would result in recessions. However, to date, there still exists no single and clear-cut explanation as to the cause of the US financial crisis. The underlying consensus is that a mixture of factors contributed to the crisis, including falls in house prices, securitisation, information asymmetry, low interest rates, and leverage effects of hedge funds. This chapter is split into three sections; Section 2.1 addresses the causes of the US crisis, Section 2.2 deals with its consequences, while Section 2.3 focuses on possible solutions.

2.1 Explanation on the chart explaining the schema of the crisis

I identify three main factors/forces that paved the way towards the US subprime crisis: core structural weaknesses or cracks, domestic shocks and external shocks as illustrated in Figure 1. The structural weaknesses refer to existing inefficiencies that permeated the unregulated banking sector of the financial system, such as long periods of deregulation following the repeal of the Glass-Steagall Banking Act of 1933 (no distinction between commercial banking and investment banking), real estate bubbles, opaqueness in securities, existence of information asymmetry, and perverse remuneration mechanisms. Domestic shocks pertain mainly to the fall in house prices, which acted as the catalyst for the crisis. External shocks refer to the burgeoning difference in current account positions without proper adjustments in the exchange rates. For instance, despite the fact that China rejoiced over sustained current account surpluses, it strived even hard to maintain a low currency value. The crisis has also pointed out the importance of catering for endogenous risks, which had previously triggered harmful impacts onto the financial system via feedback effects.

(a) Macroeconomic liquidity risk: Large capital flows are usually associated with crisis periods. In the year 1973, oil-producing countries witnessed a significant rise in due to a fourfold hike in oil prices. These surplus countries channelled their monies to US banks that later lent them out to Latin American countries. However, the latter defaulted. Subsequently, Brady bonds were created to revamp the market debt instruments, allowing banks to alter their claims on developing countries into tradable instruments. Excess global liquidity coupled with limited assets usually constitutes the most germane conditions for the existence of asset price bubbles.

Ironically, the financial crisis appears to be something of a repetition of the above process. The source of the crisis emanated from macroeconomic imbalances at the international level based on current accounts imbalances and exchange rates misalignments; for example, China had been clinging to undervalued exchange rates for many years to boost exports and thereby accumulate burgeoning surpluses which then flew to the US economy. Based on the need to generate higher returns on these funds, US banks channelled these funds to local credit markets linked to mortgages. As cheap funds were present, this income boosted up the demand for mortgages, thereby engendering house price bubbles.[1] These price bubbles fed on themselves chiefly when higher house prices enshrined collateral values so as to induce more lending, which in turn led to higher house prices based on rising demand for houses.

(b) Securitisation: Credit risk transfer instruments consist of credit derivatives like Credit Default Swaps and credit securitisation like Collateralised Debt Obligations. Securitisation can be technically defined as the transformation of illiquid nonmarketable assets into liquid marketable ones, such as the pooling up of mortgage loans into liquid Collateralised Debt Obligations, which are then sold to investors. Without securitisation, banks would rely on deposits to provide loans to borrowers endowed with sound collaterals and repayment capacities. With securitisation, banks were

---

[1] Technically speaking, a bubble can be defined as a consistent and sustained divergence of an asset market price from its fundamental or intrinsic value.

able to transform the loans into securities that could be offloaded to investors. However, the issue of concern about securitisation pertains to a system whereby in lieu of effectively transferring the risks, banks were taking back the risks again via investments in the mortgage-backed securities—synonymous to pulling the gun's trigger upon oneself. This is depicted in Figure 1 as the red thick arrow connecting banks to mortgage-backed securities.

One of the causes of the crisis was improper use of securitisation. Securitisation was devised mainly for credit risk transfer to investors willing to bear credit risk. However, this innovative financial tool was misused by banks, who neglected their initial purpose by employing them principally to increase their leverage to such an extent that a negative shock would convert these off-balance sheets onto on-balance sheet modes.[2] This utilisation thereby substantially increased the exposure of banks. Consequently, securitisation camouflaged the separation of market and credit risk since banking book positions could be hedged using trading book instruments. Banks had strong incentives to scale up their components of asset-backed securities because the latter involved low capital weights based on their high ratings by rating agencies. These off-balance sheet instruments consisted mainly of asset-backed commercial paper and structured investment vehicles. Once the quality of these assets deteriorated, investors would have recourse to the banks, which would then provide both liquidity and credit enhancements.

As long as things remained rosy, banks would avail of such leverage to spur profits. However, once a negative shock emerged, it would have devastating consequences for both the bank, in terms of eroding away its' capital base, as well as the economy as a whole via the ripple effect. Consequently, banks were exposed to significant latent risks not truly captured by their capital base, which evidently burst into larger losses for banks having greater exposure to asset-backed securities. The irony of this is that latent risks built subsequent burgeoning latent risks which fed upon themselves, since by having lower risk weights for risky assets, the implicitly saved capital could be employed towards further leverage activities. The process was accentuated on the back of rising house prices, which acted as a real catalyst to the securitisation process. Consequently, once the bedrock component was affected, i.e. falling house prices, this engendered explosion in all parts of these intricate processes with direct

---

[2] All three types of conduits, whether fully supported conduits, partially supported conduits or structured investment vehicles, have recourse to the bank balance sheet.

effect on banks' balance sheets in the form of insufficient capital base. This clearly explained why those banks which had considerable exposures to asset-backed commercial paper suffered the most from the crisis.

(c) Securitisation and credit boom: Securitisation has been implemented in view of alleviating the credit risk of banks by transferring credit risk to those willing to bear it. Since these securitised transactions were recorded as off-balance sheet items as long as collaterals value (house prices) remained in the comfort zone, it signifies that no strong capital requirements were needed for these securitisation transactions. Securitisation enabled banks to leverage up as much as they could and in the process they provided credit to bad borrowers. Excessive leverage bred inefficient allocation of capital. Above all, this provided an opportunity for banks to offload bad borrowers' risks onto the market—a blatant instance of adverse selection. Bad borrowers were provided with credit as they were made to pay higher interest rates, and these signified higher profits for banks. In this process, securitisation was amplified in lieu of mitigating credit risk, which assisted in rendering the crisis to a mountainous scale. Central banks acted as central bombs as they clung to excessively low interest rates, which induced robust speculative forces so as to accentuate the process. When things remained positive, this booming state stimulated not only an appetite for leveraging but also asset bubbles in the housing market. However, once things turned sour, the bubble burst, thereby unleashed deleveraging and company collapses. Indeed, once the collateral value fell below the loan value, lenders started to undertake forced sales to recoup on funds and this significantly drove down values of other houses, which thereby negatively impacted on loans along with massive defaults.

(d) Characteristic of subprime loans: The nature or feature of subprime loans was such that their refinancing hinged mainly on the appreciation of mortgages' values so that these loans generated large-scale macroeconomic effects. Indeed, these loans were fixed in interest rates for the first two or three years and thereafter were subject to adjustable rates so that the borrowers either defaulted or refinanced their loans once the fixed interest rate period was over. Substantial increase in subprime loans was caused by easy credit, low interest rates and the securitisation process, which was stimulated by high ratings on assets.

(e) Hedge funds, leverage and shadow banking: Leverage signifies getting funds by increasing debt to amplify investment returns. Hedge funds[3] along with private equity firms have mostly been the catalytic components behind leverage investments. However, leverage constitutes a double-edged sword with strong asymmetric effects; it amplifies not only profits during good times but also losses, thereby scaling up the probability of going bankrupt during bad times. For instance, a highly geared company can enhance its profits by taking on more debt during periods of low interest rates. However, should interest rates be subject to drastic hikes, this would imply rising interest rates, which directly unleash concerns about the company's repayment capacity.

The shadow banking system inherent in the financial systems of developed countries such as the US also played an important role in inducing the crisis. In principle, shadow banks operate like normal banks by borrowing short-term but investing the proceeds into long-term assets. However, compared to the conventional banking system, shadow banks are not regulated and thereby do not respect any capital requirements. Most importantly, hedge funds, a component of shadow banking, cling to excessive leveraging. This results in a strong systemic risk, chiefly when hedge funds tend to demonstrate correlated positions, which poses substantial negative externalities to the financial system.

(f) Interbank market and liquidity risk: Liquidity risk can be defined in three ways. First, liquidity risk, if understood in its market definition, is when an asset can easily be sold without being subject to major costs. Such a definition also implies the inability to find funds despite having high quality assets on the balance sheets. Second, liquidity risk refers to the extent of assets-liabilities mismatch and is usually captured under the risk management section of most financial statements in the form of gap analysis. A third way to classify liquidity risk involves the type of focus—local or global. At a local level, liquidity pertains to the extent to which the bank can easily fund itself from the interbank market. During the crisis, interbank markets were frozen, which led to rising spreads and meant that banks found it costly to refinance their interbank liabilities. These also generated negative externalities since, despite the fact that some banks were not exposed to toxic assets, they were still subject to financing difficulties. At the global level, macroeconomic liquidity risks manifest themselves in the form of a "savings glut" like that of China, other Asian countries, and oil-producing countries channelling monies to the US, the latter of which is distributed as cheap credit to uncreditworthy borrowers, as well as funding projects of companies which may not be

---

[3] Effectively speaking, hedge funds are well-known for selling volatility.

endowed with positive NPV projects. In a parallel manner, macroeconomic liquidity lies at the basis for carry trades, which further increase risk.

It is important to bear in mind that ordinarily, liquidity tends to work perfectly without any constraint; however, during stressful conditions, liquidity tends to dry up and thereby engenders heightened volatility; an inverse relationship exists between liquidity and volatility. This explains the need to consider liquidity stress testing exercises in view of sieving out any feasible liquidity risks, chiefly in the banking sector.

It can be argued that the US financial crisis originated from macroeconomic liquidity risk, which then transformed into a bank liquidity crisis, thus engendering the need for Basle III.

(g) Credit derivatives and credit boom: Credit Default Swaps were employed to mitigate risk exposures related to the Collateralised Debt Obligations. With credit derivatives, banks were able to shift credit risk to other players, which allowed them to provide more loans to borrowers. This helped in the creation of the credit boom.

(h) Traders and herd behaviour: Traders followed the "herd behaviour," thereby ignoring the importance of clinging to fundamental or intrinsic values, and hence amplifying the bubble's effects. Short-term investment strategies are heavily tilted towards technical analysis tools which utterly fail to capture fundamentals; this means that an investment is made purely on the basis of high short-term profits, independent of whether the company is sound in terms of financial ratios. In principle, any sound investment undertaken should be based on three important elements: fundamental analysis, technical analysis and intuition.

(i) Extremely accommodative monetary policy and central bombs: Calm water is very deep as to induce drowning—this is also the truth in financial markets. As central banks espoused low interest rates, the latter induced strong speculation in view of making higher and higher profits without any checks made onto how the artificial economy was growing with respect to the real economy. In the process, this triggered considerable leveraging (asset bubbles) which when pricked, released deleveraging and vicious circles of falling prices and defaults. **Central banks were implicitly acting like central bombs** with low interest rates inducing carry trades, characterised as going long position in high-yielding currencies and short position in low yielding currencies. Above all, the Libor scandal showed that the Bank of England did not take any concrete measures, despite being aware of the Libor manipulations.

The Libor scandal revealed deceptive activities undertaken by banks which adjusted the Libor rates as and when required to generate profits from trades, with low Libor rates reflecting heightened confidence in the financial system and high Libor rates being symptomatic of high levels of risk aversion. When the Libor scandal broke, it transpired that Libor manipulations had been a common practice since 1991. Such Libor manipulations directly impacted on the US derivatives markets and thereby engendered negative spillover effects. In June 2012, Barclays Bank was forced to pay $200 million to the Commodity Futures Trading Commission, with total payments of $453 million to both UK and US regulators.

(j) **Poor regulatory structures:** Lax regulatory policy prevailed since the capital base of banks was found to be underestimated with respect to the level of risk assumed. This was also due to regulatory authorities not creating the proper demarcation line between commercial banking and investment banking.

(k) **Opaqueness in instruments:** It should also be stressed that the asset-backed commercial paper and structured investment vehicles were opaque in nature; banks had no knowledge of the potential losses, should the asset-backed commercial paper market be subject to stressful conditions.

(l) **Guarantees:** Both direct guarantees in the case of deposit insurance schemes and indirect guarantees in the case of certain banks being "too big to fail," ironically triggered distortions in the financial system in terms of increasing the costs to taxpayers.

(m) **Lax credit policies and credit boom:** Imprudent credit policies were also in place, such as increases in loan-to-value ratios due to easy credit flows, which led to poor lending standards. Banks also practised vigorous lending so that securitised products were sold to investors who did not understand the true nature of these products. Above all, it is a pity to note that financial institutions lacked not only knowledge of the loans that they securitised, with most securitised products being highly complex and not transparent, but also knowledge of who was holding these complex products. Ultimately, the craving for profits acted as a blindfold to proper risk management.

(n) International trade: The positive effects of globalisation have tapered as bruised economies begin to rekindle their own economic activities; a useful analogy in this instance is that if everybody's house was on fire, each homeowner would strive hard to save their own house first. This can be simply captured by the basic Aggregate Demand function whereby if (X-M) component does not work, stress would have to be laid upon C, I and G components to stimulate demand and rekindle local economic activities.

(o) Derivatives ironically inducing higher risks: Derivatives markets have been particularly helpful in the risk management activities of many companies in the world for distinct types of risks like credit risk, interest rate risk, liquidity risk and currency risk. By luring hedgers, speculators and arbitrageurs, derivatives markets also induce liquidity and thereby reduce transaction costs. Moreover derivatives (in particular options) help to sieve out volatility (implied) and thereby improve on analysis that would rely solely on historical volatility.

There are two types of derivatives markets: Over The Counter markets and Exchanges. Exchanges have recourse towards standardised contracts which induce liquidity, transparency and well-contained counterparty risk since the Clearing House acts as a buyer to every seller and as a seller to every buyer. However, in the case of Over The Counter markets, counterparty risks are significantly increased by virtue of customised and non-standardised products. Above all, there is a higher level of counterparty risks since each market player directly deals with another market player (bilateral system) rather than trading with a centralised player (like the Clearing House in an exchange market). The statement made by Warren Buffet (2002) whereby "Derivatives are financial weapons of mass destruction, carrying dangers that, while now latent, are potentially lethal," undeniably holds true.

Finally, the true meaning of "Economics" has not been applied in practice but simply moulded to suit the specific needs of distinct parties, and is properly renamed as "Egonomics," as captured in Table 2.1. This table depicts the differences between "Economics" and "Egonomics" on several fronts such as securitisation, financial derivatives, central banks, and rating agencies, among others.

Table 2.1: Establishing the demarcation line between Economics and Egonomics

Specific Focus	Economics	Egonomics
Securitisation	Credit risk transfer	Offload risk from bad borrowers
Financial derivatives	Risk-sharing	OTC-opaqueness/Complex
Balance of payments imbalances	Surplus countries—appreciating currencies; Deficit countries —depreciating currencies	China keeping undervalued currency
Information	Free flow of information	Asymmetric information-Market players having no access to timely and accurate information
High Foreign Reserves	Portfolio Diversification-spread between both real and financial assets	Skewed towards financial assets to generate high short-term profits
Trading philosophy	Fundamentals	Herd Behaviour-Traders acting like frantic ants
Central Banks	Sound regulators	Central Banks = Central Bombs-Bank of England aware of Libor manipulations well before the Libor Scandal. Extremely accommodative monetary policy stance induced excessive risk-taking. Allowed regulatory arbitrage
Banks	Well-capitalised	Shadow banking like hedge funds; regulatory arbitrage
Rating Agencies	Risky assets should be given low ratings	Risky assets given higher ratings; Rating agencies acting as both driver and traffic controller
Credit Processing	Sound repayment capacity and proper collateral values	"No Income, No Job and No Assets" (NINJA) borrowers

2.2 Consequences and implications

(a) Moral hazard and frantic bailouts

The crisis has shown increased moral hazard problems as governments intervened to save important institutions like the Federal National Mortgage Association (Fannie Mae) and the Federal Home Loan Mortgage Corporation (Freddie Mac). It can be argued that the failures of these institutions would have entailed major costs to the financial system, let alone strong negative effects onto the real side of the economy. However, by saving these institutions, the government indirectly increased the scope for moral hazards in the case of systematically important institutions.

(b) Central Bank Balance Sheets as Shock Absorbers

Central banks' balance sheets for both developed and developing countries have undergone drastic changes following the crisis. This signifies that the risks have now been transferred to central banks (as shock absorbers) which are now subject to new challenges in terms of balance sheet restructuring. In that respect, empirical studies are further needed at the central bank level to gauge the level of risks borne by central banks. For instance, one of the recurring aspects among most central banks' balance sheets pertains to a considerable rise in Special Drawing Rights under the IMF. The benefit that central banks avail of is that their liabilities side does not involve major costs based on their sole vested power in the issuance of notes and coins.

(c) Considerable deadweight losses

It is no wonder that the rising number of households who defaulted on their loans triggered significant deadweight losses to the financial system. Above all, selling pressures on mortgages further drove down the prices in a vicious spiral which could also affect households, who despite having sound repayment capacity, were still subject to negative net worth.

(d) Burgeoning Public Debt and declining private debt

During the period of the financial crisis, massive government expenditures led to escalating government debts. As far as private debts (household debt makes up a large proportion of the components of private debts) were concerned, they declined on the back of dwindling economic activities and incomes. Moreover, burgeoning public debt levels compelled governments to resort to taking austerity measures, which adversely impacted upon growth, which was already feeble.

(e) Countries operating under Fixed Exchange rate regimes bear more pressures

It is widely accepted that countries subject to fixed exchange rate regimes have to sacrifice internal balance to maintain external balance, meaning that an inherent conflict of objectives prevails. Above all, under crisis conditions, there is a need for a higher level of reserves to maintain external balance. For instance, the Namibian dollar is linked to the South African rand so that despite experiencing sluggishness in demand, Namibia is compelled to cling to a similar inflation rate as that prevailing in South Africa so as to ensure exchange rate parity. In that respect, Namibia is forced to sacrifice its internal policy of boosting demand under crisis conditions merely to ensure exchange rate parity. This can feasibly account for the very high unemployment rate in Namibia, chiefly if it happens to be of a frictional nature.

(f) Decline in remittances, Foreign Direct Investments Portfolio Investments and aid flows

The crisis has engendered significant declines in remittances to developing countries, some of which heavily relied on them to spur growth. This signifies that countries have to source funds elsewhere to be able to maintain growth prospects. In a parallel manner, Foreign Direct Investments and Portfolio Investments have undergone downward trends. The crisis has also undermined the level of aid flows to African countries which indirectly bear the adverse effects of the crisis, despite having no or fewer exposures to toxic assets—a glaring instance of negative spillover effects.

(g) Implicit costs of higher public debt due to poor central banks' profitability

One important element, which has been utterly overlooked in the aftermath of policies taken to deal with the crisis, pertains to the profitability of central banks. Indeed, the era of very low interest rates has significantly undermined the net interest income of central banks. This results in vital repercussions on public debt since central banks' profits in most countries go to the government purse. Such a state serves to considerably lower the ability of governments to finance themselves from central banks' profits; this can therefore be considered as implicit costs in terms of higher public debt.

(h) Fair Value Accounting—Curtailing excessive risk-taking

Had fair value accounting been overlooked, this could have caused more risk to the financial system in the US. Indeed, by marking to market, fair value accounting depicted the extent of financial damage to institutions. If cost accounting were to be maintained, institutions would be urged to undertake even higher levels of risks in view of making good for past losses and thereby significantly scaling up the upside risks to financial stability.

(i) Lack of Regulation increases taxpayers' costs

Lack of regulation induced perverse incentives and generated negative externalities. The crisis has clearly shown the necessity of creating a proper demarcation line between commercial banking and investment banking. Authorities now mourn having repealed the Glass-Steagall Banking Act of 1933 in 1999.

(j) Level of Financial Development: Trade-off between Resilience and Contagion

The financial crisis has clearly demonstrated that the more financially developed a country, the quicker the transmission is of shocks throughout its whole financial system. Financial innovation helps to scale up resilience of the financial system with respect to shocks but they also quickly spread to the whole system. This is the inherent trade-off imbued with financial development: resilience versus contagion. In a parallel manner, the presence of foreign-owned banks helps to diversify the provision of credit but ironically it represents one of the key transmission channels of outside shocks onto the local financial system.

(k) Impotency of Portfolio Diversification

Modern Portfolio Theory points out the benefits of diversification in reducing risks. However, when the US crisis broke out, portfolio diversification benefits faded away. In essence, as the crisis engulfed global markets, assets commoved strongly as to wipe out potential diversification benefits, thereby rendering Modern Portfolio Theory impotent. This signifies that portfolio diversification constitutes a double-edged sword; when things are going well, diversification does work but when things go sour, no benefits can be derived from portfolio diversification. Under the same perspective, the strategy used by multinational banks to enhance their value by diversifying their activity base is unlikely to pay off during crisis times.

(l) Ponzi Schemes Unveiled and Tragedies

The crisis has unveiled the existence of ponzi schemes, which would have otherwise remained hidden. The longest and largest ponzi scheme ever disclosed in history pertained to Bernard Madoff, who was later sentenced to 150 years of imprisonment for hiding a fraud of $65 billion. Unfortunately, such fraud also left behind human tragedies. The son of Madoff, Mark Madoff, who was running a separate division at Madoff Securities, committed suicide by hanging himself in 2010. Jeremy Friehling, son of Madoff's accountant also killed himself after his father, David Friehling, pleaded guilty in 2009. Although there is no clear indication as to whether Jeremy Friehling's suicide is linked to the fraud scandal, it does appear that such things do not occur out of thin air. These examples provide robust evidence that excessive greed leads to bleed and not to bliss.

(m) Macroeconomic evils
The crisis occasioned unwanted macroeconomic evils such as loss of GDP, rising unemployment with corresponding human sufferings and loss in wealth. In addition, by increasing the capital base of banks to enshrine their resiliency levels, the authorities ironically reduced the level of loanable funds. Alternatively stated, as banks maintained a higher capital base to cushion any potential losses, this signified constraint on credit creation process. Moreover, rising sovereign risks in certain countries signified that banks found it difficult to obtain short-term funding. To scale down funding pressures, some euro-area banks sold liquid assets, including equities, which contributed towards further equity price declines.

(n) Vicious circles of rising yields
Countries like Portugal, Italy, Greece and Spain underwent vicious circles of rising yields. As debt levels rose, this led to downward credit ratings. Consequently, whenever these countries needed to raise funds, they were subject to higher costs to compensate investors for the higher risks involved in investing in the issued bonds. Consequently, these rising costs led to even higher public debt which in turn induced further downgradings, all sparking off vicious circles of higher debts and rising costs of issuances. Downgradings to junk bonds have also been noted for certain countries. The standard benchmark used for capturing European sovereign spreads is via the difference between a given 10-year European government bond yield with respect to its German counterpart.

(o) Gold as the best hedge against uncertainty
Prior to the onset of the crisis, investors purchased gold to harness maximum benefits from portfolio diversification. The crisis triggered a comeback for gold, so much so that gold is now viewed as an alternative

monetary market, in addition to a reference point for inflation expectations. Above all, gold constitutes the best hedge against uncertainties. Moreover, the very fact that interest rates are very low signifies that the costs of holding gold in terms of forgone interest rates do not matter significantly, unleashing additional impetus to hold gold.

(p) Vulnerable Capital Inflows
The low interest rates in the advanced economies, combined with the earlier and stronger recovery in a number of emerging economies, help to drive significant capital inflows into emerging markets. However, a quick reversal can also manifest itself, as the developed economies require more funds to spur their own economic growth on the back of the crisis. Consequently, risks loom large on feasible reversal in capital inflows to emerging markets, which could increase their vulnerabilities to capital flows shocks.

2.3 Solutions

(a) System-wide risk analysis
The best approach to regulation consists of both a system-wide risk analysis and institution-specific risk analysis, both of which complement each other. The chief benefit of system-wide analysis is that it fosters financial stability by explicitly accounting for interconnectedness among the distinct units of the financial system. The microscopic approach to regulation does not provide a true picture of the whole risk of the financial system as it fails to identify the interconnectedness (and hence extent of externalities) among units of the financial system. Nonetheless, microscopic analysis is crucial when it comes to assessing systemically important institutions. Technically speaking, network analysis can be applied as the appropriate tool to identify the extent of interconnectedness.

(b) Leveraging risk management processes via improving data and models
One of the vital avenues that can be employed to promulgate financial stability worldwide is to leverage the risk management processes. This can be accomplished via three main channels. First and foremost, it is of paramount significance to have timely, accurate and comprehensive data so that modelling processes trigger reliable results. Otherwise, this will simply take after the GIGO (Garbage In Garbage Out) system. Second, it is important that human efforts are confined solely to modelling issues and not to the collection of data, so as to minimise errors and distortions.

Above all, the application of automation/mechanisation of the data collection processes ensures that data is both timely and accurate. Third, it is imperative that all results generated in terms of models or any other assessments are done under a broader perspective, with all systemic risks given due consideration. This is achievable if and only if risk management processes are communicated throughout all units of a given financial institution. Above all, risk management processes need to be simple, well understood and effectively embedded in system controls, allowing risk to be demystified and all members in an organisation to perfectly converse with the risk management culture in terms of disciplined decisions.

The best credit risk management approach that can be taken by banks is to always cling to a diversified credit portfolio in view of mitigating loan risks. In the event that banks are practising securitisation, it is imperative that they do not close the system by investing into products that they themselves create. Last but not least, proactive risk management is essential to ensure that negative effects of the crisis are properly dealt with ex-ante measures in lieu of ex-post policies which embody considerably higher costs of intervention. This concurs well with the saying, "prevention is better than a cure."

(c) Re-engineering the credit processing approach
To deal with the problem of foreclosures and defaults, both short-term and long-term strategies should be considered, all impregnated with the same proactive risk management flavour.

(i) Long-term strategies
To curb the problem of foreclosures and defaults by households, it is necessary to establish long-term household contracts whereby mutual benefits prevail—banks obtain sound profits for the risks they assume while households are able to secure homes. The values for collaterals encumbered in favour of loans are automatically adjusted as per the diverse states of the business cycles, which pose the major source of risks to banks. In that respect, I suggest banks adhere to a maximum and minimum house price policy to mitigate against major risks. This should be implemented from the outset of loan processing. For instance, during downturn parts of the business cycles, it would be appropriate for banks to compute minimum house prices to ensure that applied margin covers are still sustainable. Otherwise, in the case of crisis times when price declines are correlated, the latter not only gnaw at the balance sheet of banks but also signify the need for additional capital to ensure business continuity. Conversely, in the case of booming periods, it is important that banks are

not blinded by excessive house prices as to induce excessive risk-taking. Banks can also cling to average house prices in lieu of low/high house prices during these extreme periods to obviate any risks of foreclosures/asset bubbles. In a nutshell, whenever granting loans, it would be better if banks did not use actual house prices which may reflect overshooting/undershooting effects in housing markets, chiefly when prices mainly reflect the speculative forces rather than fundamentals. A long-run rational expectations path for house prices can also be contemplated. It would also be interesting if central banks set up a special house price unit to undertake that task, as they would best serve the purpose of consolidating financial stability chiefly when house prices are key drivers for household performance.

(ii) Short-term strategies

Under short-term strategies geared towards ensuring a prudent repayment capacity, lengthening of the loan maturities under crisis conditions undeniably constitutes a form of sound credit risk management policy. Consider an example. A borrower contracts a mortgage of $100,000 over a period of 10 years at an interest rate of 10% payable every month with an Equal Monthly Instalment (EMI) hovering around $1,322. The house costs $120,000 with $20,000 representing the down payment. The buyer's repayment capacity emanates from his net disposable income. As a considerate banker, the latter should adopt a prudent rule, for example that the EMI should represent around 60% of net disposable income. Effectively, the buffer induces counter-cyclicality with respect to the economic conditions. Should conditions deteriorate, the buyer may still be able to pay. Should there manifest a real drastic fall in the net disposal income of the borrower; it would be wise for the banker to lengthen the loan maturities to prevent correlated mortgage defaults. This is one aspect of proactive risk management geared towards consolidating the borrower's repayment capacity. Alternatively stated, based on stressful periods, it is wise for the bankers to further increase their loan maturities to generate breathing scope for the borrowers so that they do not default.

(d) Greening or socialising the cost of Capital—the best hedge against cycles

Considered as one of the basic tenets in finance, the cost of capital has widely been explored. For instance, under the famous Pecking Order Theory of capital structure, the cost of internal funds is always lower than that of debt which is in turn lower than that of equity. This is explained by a hierarchy in the financing structure whereby firms prefer to use internal funds first, then debt and equity only as a last resort. Technically speaking, the crisis is not expected to impact on the Pecking Order Theory since its structure will remain unchanged. However, the crisis will affect the extent of the difference, as illustrated in the table below.

Table 2.2: Crisis impact on cost of capital under Pecking Order Theory

	Before Crisis	Post-Crisis	Long-Term Cost of Capital
Internal cost of funds	2%	2%	2%
Cost of Debt	4%	7%	5.5%
Cost of Equity	6%	10%	8%

The internal cost of funds relates to the minimum required rate of return for existing shareholders of the company—this can be deemed at least equal to the best alternative forgone, for example, the savings rate. Prior to the crisis, there seems to be a difference of around 2% between each of the distinct financing mediums. However, post the crisis, the difference is subject to major hikes in light of rising uncertainties and mounting risk aversion levels that permeate the financial markets. The increase in the cost of debt and equity imply that projects that formerly generated positive Net Present Value (say a return of 6.5%) tend to lose their attractiveness and this may unleash considerable losses. Subsequently, it seems sensible to adhere to a long-term approach to cost of capital (lower cost of capital relative to cost of capital under crisis conditions) and this is where social banks and green finance are called to induce long-term sustainability in finance.[4] In the above table, the long-term cost of capital has simply been computed as average values of both up and down conditions. Other approaches can also be employed to compute the long-term cost of capital like using past periods of data and generating the general trend. The main benefit of using the long-term cost of capital is that it alleviates the adverse effects of the crisis so as to secure sales and ongoing business activities, with the whole focus being laid on long-term sustainability. In essence, finance should be more geared towards a longer-term approach to smooth out shocks, so as to induce equanimity of the international financial system against both positive and negative shocks.

---

[4] This is addressed in Chapter 7 of the book.

(e) Enhancing Corporate Governance—a naturally ingrained business philosophy

I believe that a sound corporate governance system should not only be imposed by regulators but should also be practised on an ongoing basis in the form of a normal/inherent process of business risks. Staff should be made both responsible and accountable and information should flow freely at all levels of the organisation. Corporate governance should be further consolidated in all financial institutions to mitigate feasible bubbles and corresponding upside risks to financial stability. For instance, to further align the managers, employees and shareholders' interests, employees could be partly paid in shares to induce higher productivity; this would simultaneously benefit all the stakeholders concerned. The compensation mechanism should also be reviewed in view of stopping excessive bonus payments to CEOs who are then induced to take higher levels of uncalculated business risks.

(f) Risk-enshrining Remuneration Mechanisms

Traders should be deterred from undertaking excessive risk-taking in view of generating high short-term profits on which their short-term bonuses are based upon. The best channel to remedy such a situation would be the introduction of a longer-term approach to bonus payments. A bonus account should be kept whereby bonuses paid are tied to long-term profits which are more sustainable relative to high spikes in profits, which would in turn constitute the germane conditions for inducing perverse incentives. This will obviously ward off excessive risk-taking because traders, who previously behaved like casino players, will now be less willing to do so when bonuses are tied to long-term sustainable profits. In a parallel manner, salaries/compensations to CEOs of all financial institutions should be made more transparent in order to really gauge the extent of excessive payment packages that camouflage excessive risk-taking at upper management level. The most recent example is given in the words of Jerome Kerviel, who incurred three years of imprisonment and a fine of €4.9 billion as damages for the January 2008 Société Générale trading loss. During a TV interview, Jerome Kerviel claimed that his superiors were perfectly aware of the risks that he was taking during trading.

(g) Fair Value Accounting

Under fair value accounting, assets and liabilities are reported at values that they would seek directly in the market, à la marked-to-market philosophy. The main benefit attached to fair value accounting pertains to its more realistic nature, in terms of reflecting the true prices of assets and liabilities at the balance sheet reporting date. However, assessing the other side of coin, fair value accounting does not work well in case of extreme conditions like bubbles and crisis conditions. During bubbles, fair value accounting tends to trigger too much optimism, thus inducing further leverage and risk-taking. In a parallel manner, during crisis times, fair value accounting generates significant systemic risk as losses precipitate towards interlinked units of the financial system. Hence, fair value accounting works best under normal conditions. Alternatively stated, fair value accounting induces systemic risk during crisis times[5] and euphoria during credit boom periods, both of which scale up the divergence between fair values and actual values.

In that respect, it is considerate to adopt cost accounting during crisis/bubbles times to prevent any misjudgements. However, this will be problematic from the perspective of comparing yearly values, say for example, one done under cost accounting while another under fair value accounting. By reporting both fair and cost values, this will assist in showing the extent of deviation and hence the true level of risk undertaken by a company. In that respect, it may be better that companies report twice, once under fair value accounting and once under cost accounting. To provide them incentives for such dual reporting, it would be apt to use the tax rate as a motivating tool—those reporting both will be subject to a fall in the tax rate, the amount of which would be determined by the required authorities, such as the Financial Accounting Standard Board in the US. Indirect benefits may also manifest. For instance, under the Financial Accounting Standards Board Statement No. 133, Accounting for Derivative Instruments and Hedging Activities, fair values are used and this hinders researchers in deriving nominal values of a derivatives contract used for hedging to capture the extent of hedging undertaken by a company.

(h) Augmenting the quality of risk management in banks
The core functions of banks worldwide consist of linking deficit units to surplus units, providing an efficient payment system, encouraging maturity transformation in terms of converting savings into loans, and asset management (chiefly under investment banking). It is therefore important to properly measure, monitor and control risks which prevail in various forms like credit risk, liquidity risk, interest rate risk, currency risk and operational risk, so as to ensure that banks properly undertake their

---

[5] However, by disclosing the true value of assets, fair value accounting can prevent crisis-induced excessive-risk-taking, geared towards reducing past losses.

functions as engines of growth in lieu of increasing the costs to taxpayers. Banks should also set up proper ex-ante (right when they take decisions) and ex-post (in terms of sound monitoring devices). However, in practice, risk management is not an easy task, as risk also exists in latent forms which can be converted into losses at any point in time.

Risk can be defined as probability assigned to uncertain events that can lead to losses. Independent of the type of banks under focus, risk can be quantified into two main categories. First, risk hinges on the probability of losses manifesting. Second, risk also depends on the value of collaterals to gauge on the potential amount that can be recovered. Hence, banks should put in place proper mechanisms that regularly compute the likelihood of losses and recoveries values to eventually gauge the exact level of losses susceptible to eat up their capital.[6] It is also vital that banks establish proper risk modelling mechanisms. For instance, to properly gauge the impact of interest rate risk on the banks' bottom line, it is of utmost significance to model the yield curve.[7] In a parallel manner, to generate sound credit risk models, Merton (1974) options models can be applied, along with sound credit-scoring systems. However, apart from properly measuring risks and their associated losses, it is also important to know the major drivers for higher risks so that proper actions can be taken at distinct levels to mitigate them.

Regulatory bodies should be wary of the basic banking equation whereby risk and return are inherently linked and represent two sides of the same coin. Consequently, high profit-making banks should be properly scrutinised in order to unveil any major risk-taking. Beyond that, regulatory bodies should be cautious about those innovations[8] which are initially geared towards enhancing efficiency, but which then tend to be used incorrectly by banks to camouflage leverage risks.

(i) Mandatory role of Central Banks-Shift from Inflation Targeting to Financial Stability

The mandatory role associated with central banks worldwide pertains to price stability. This has usually been best captured in the form of inflation

---

[6] Tier 1 capital or core capital constitutes the most easily available capital to absorb loses. Tier 2 capital pertains to additional capital, which is less enduring in nature.

[7] Modelling the yield curve is not an easy task in case of developing countries, which are usually buffeted by irregular issuances at longer maturity levels.

[8] Credit Securitisation and Credit Derivatives are particularly interesting but dangerous financial instruments that enable banks to transfer or off-load credit risks. These contingencies or off-balance sheet items can at any point be converted into on-balance sheet items and hence pose substantial latent risks.

targeting based on a myriad of benefits that it confers. First, inflation targeting enhances transparency and accountability of monetary policy, making it highly effective. Second, inflation targeting is widely acclaimed to anchor inflation expectations so as to heighten the credibility of monetary policy. Third, inflation targeting reduces inflation volatility and hence scales up confidence in the economy.

However, such inflation targeting as a role of central banks should now be reviewed. The reason is that inflation simply constitutes a necessary but not a sufficient condition for financial stability. The mandate of central banks has been too narrow in terms of exclusive focus on price stability in lieu of broader issues of financial stability. In that respect, the mandatory role of central banks should be primarily to ensure financial stability, since it is more encompassing of inherently incorporate elements of price stability. For instance, what is the use of having low inflation[9] but high unemployment, a factor that not only damages the economic state of a country but also generates negative social repercussions, such as riots? Coupled with the latter, central banks should also be wary of feasible asset prices bubbles which possess the power to jeopardise the future macroeconomic soundness indicators of the country. They should thereby ensure that asset bubbles are burst beforehand and not at a stage where substantial credit booms/leverage effects already characterise the economy; fundamentally, it is vital to dissipate any negative latent forces.

(j) Building a Financial Stability Fund

It is important to bear in mind that the risk of any given financial institution to the overall financial system hinges not only on the size of the financial institution (like "Too Big to Fail" or "Systemically Important Institutions") but also on the level of interconnectedness. A financial institution may not be big enough to trigger direct collapse of the financial system, but due to robust interconnectedness through major units of the financial system, it can pose considerable risks to financial stability. In that respect, it will be appropriate to create a Financial Stability Fund. Based on the fact that financial institutions do pose systemic risks, there is a need to internalise these latent negative externalities by taxing institutions as per the level of risk they trigger. These funds will then be

---

[9] Unfortunately, some countries are compelled to have low inflation rates chiefly when they adhere to a fixed exchange rate system. For instance, the Namibian dollar is pegged to the South African Rand so that Namibian inflation rates fluctuate in relation to those prevailing in South Africa. This is the drawback under a fixed exchange rate as it generates the sacrifice of internal policies in order to maintain external ones.

used judiciously to endorse any bruised financial institution. For instance, systemically important institutions will be compelled to provide larger chunks of funds to the Financial Stability Fund so that in the case of problems, they will also avail of higher level of funds—ultimately, cutting the coat according to the cloth. Such an approach undeniably assists in guarding against feasible moral hazard effects. In a parallel manner, institutions imbued with robust interconnectedness will be compelled to contribute larger amounts to the Financial Stability Fund. The Bank for International Settlements (BIS) could be called upon to manage these Financial Stability Funds, so as to ensure transparency.

To implement this approach, the very first step will be geared towards measuring each financial institution's risk to the total risk of the financial system. In this process, all channels of connections should be properly scanned to identify spillover effects into the real sector (trade and production). A network analysis would be appropriate for such a task. Above all, there may be incentives for these larger financial institutions to scale down their systemic risk via proper insurance techniques that would help them in reducing the amount they need to contribute to the Financial Stability Fund.

(k) Highly Accommodative Monetary Policy Stance

One of the major structural cracks in the international financial system has been the era of excessively low interest rates in view of scaling down the cost of servicing debt. This has been implemented in view of consolidating economic activities following major events like the burst of the dotcom bubble and the terrorist attacks of 2001, as well as under the inflation targeting approach of central banks in view of enhancing the credibility of monetary policy. Unfortunately, the low interest rates era provided opportunist incentives for speculators who could leverage their gains by borrowing at low interest rates and investing in high-yielding risky assets. This was further accentuated by the presence of bonuses being tied to short-term profits. With low interest rates, bad borrowers could also borrow, thereby increasing the credit risk level. Ironically, banks adopted vigorous lending for easy profits instead of making lending predominantly based on the borrower's ability to repay and sound security values. Consequently, banks' activities also increased financial instability.

(l) Leveraging the Quality of Financial Stability Reports

Information flow worldwide is still a hurdle to proper risk assessments. It is disappointing to note that only about 38 per cent of the world's 183 central banks publish Financial Stability Reports/Reviews. These reports underwent a major boost following the crisis when many central banks began their publication. The following propositions are therefore aimed at leveraging the quality of Financial Stability Reports, so as to enshrine global financial stability.

Financial Stability Reports should be dynamic, timely and unbiased. "Dynamic" implies generating proactive solutions to mitigate financial stability risks. Very few reports cater for such a need since the lion's share of reports merely cling to information reporting. As aforementioned, risks pertaining to large institutions and those having high interconnectedness should be properly established and commented along with required measures/actions being taken.

Not all central banks in the world publish Financial Stability Reports yet, and those that publish them suffer from the problem of lagged effects in reporting. Usually, if a Financial Stability Report is to be issued in June, the information contained therein refers to the period ending March of the same year; a lag of three months is usually considered acceptable. Unfortunately, for some countries, the issuance date and reported information date tends to exceed three months. Above all, some countries have ceased to publish their Financial Stability Reports after the onset of the crisis; for example, as of 2012, the latest report by Greece was published in June 2010.

Biased reporting also characterises some Financial Stability Reports. In the event that the central banks do not want to create mounting risk aversions under a self-fulfilling prophecy channel, it seems rational to avoid the disclosures of sensitive information susceptible to jeopardise the financial system. However, too much divergence is particularly dangerous for a country, chiefly when the Financial Stability Reports depict a highly rosy picture while its corresponding IMF country report points out a gloomy state of affairs. In that respect, I suggest that Financial Stability Reports should constitute a joint work of the central bank staff along with the BIS/IMF staff, not only to enhance the level of authenticity of information reported but also in terms of consistency of information reported; this would be helpful for inter-country comparisons. By including the IMF in the Financial Stability Report task, this would also bring out a formalised way to report a country's Financial Stability Maps and induce inter-country comparisons. For instance, different countries report distinct forms of Financial Stability Maps. In the Figure 2, different metrics[10] of financial stability are considered to have a full-fledged financial stability map.

---

[10] The list of metrics used is however not exhaustive.

In a parallel manner, it would be appropriate if all countries were called on to stick to one report in lieu of having a multitude of separate reports such as Inflation reports and Financial Stability Reports. Since financial stability is more important than price stability, it is better to make it the report's main focus and then include a chapter for inflation. The main benefit of this would be to reduce costs and also release staff efforts, which can then be channelled towards other productive areas like more policy-oriented research. Indeed, central banks should also promote high-quality ongoing research papers based on risks to financial stability which can be incorporated in the report either as a full paper or in brief versions as case studies.

(m) Properly aligned Exchange Rates

The crisis has clearly shown the need to have balanced current accounts to improve on global prosperity and growth sustainability. In order to foster global financial stability, it is vital that nations forge an agreement over differences in terms of policies to be adopted in the case of current account imbalances. For instance, the US subprime crisis was caused by China's channelling of surpluses to the US, which then faced significant unchecked credit booms. Indirectly, the crisis showed the extent of damage done under misaligned exchange rates. International institutions like the IMF, World Bank and Bank for International Settlements should see to it that exchange rate misalignments are duly condemned, with countries liable to fines and penalties.

(n) Enhancing Regulation

The aim of banking supervision is principally directed towards ensuring financial system stability. Apart from that, banking supervision also consists of other aims like cushioning depositors, ensuring the safe operation of banks and ensuring compliance with the law. The key components of supervision encompass the following; proper licensing, sound capital adequacy, proper risk management frameworks (chiefly in terms of proactive risk management policies), proper mixture of on-site and off-site supervision, adherence to international standards in terms of internal controls and audit, regular contacts with CEOs/ top management of banks to ensure good coordination with the banking industry, and regular monitoring of banking sector financial soundness indicators like capital adequacy, asset quality, earnings and profitability, liquidity and market risks.

A more proactive approach would be to regularly monitor the banking sector stress index, a continuous measure to assess risk. The interesting feature of the banking sector stress index relates to its ability to capture distinct conditions prevailing in the banking sector, such as banks' stock prices, banks' bond yield spreads, returns on assets, returns on equity, and inter-bank deposits, among others. However, the banking sector stress index does not constitute a foolproof approach, since it does not represent an early warning sign of crisis, nor does it constitute a fully robust measure or indicator of financial crisis. Consequently, regular stress testing exercises should be carried out. Stress testing assesses the extent of resiliency of banks to any exogenous shocks susceptible to buffeting the financial system. Besides, regulators should incorporate not only exogenous risks but also feasible endogenous risks while implementing stress testing exercises. The quality of regulatory metric should also be improved with the need to re-engineer the whole regulatory framework in terms of spanning possibilities into whole economy-wide risk analysis. Finally, regulation should be improved, in order to distinguish between commercial banking and investment banking.

(o) Mergers and Acquisitions
Since the onset of the crisis, many companies now face dwindling demand and have found that the best way to survive is to reduce costs. Mergers and acquisitions can be used to optimise on revenues and thereby enhance the state of the weaker banks.

(p) Structural problems calling forth Structural Adjustment Programmes
In the case of structurally ingrained problems, structural policies will be required to effectively reduce risks. The only way out is to gradually weed out these structural problems. For instance, the widely recognised structural problem in the eurozone pertains to a monetary union without sound coordinated fiscal policies which are capable of guaranteeing the long-term sustainability of public finance. Alternatively stated, the crisis has clearly made a call for a credible fiscal consolidation programme to secure public debt sustainability. Another problem under the European Monetary Union pertains to flexibility of policies for countries subject to major debt problems. It would be inappropriate to increase tax levels at a stage whereby growth is practically nonexistent. Ironically, being in the European Monetary Union appears to be something of a curse; countries are not able to adjust policies to enhance growth because maintaining the same inflation rates under a common currency is vital, even at the expense of having high levels of unemployment. One suggested change would be to force the exit of either the badly bruised countries or the very strong

economies, so that the feeble economies can start to re-engineer their
economic activities to boost economic growth. A clustering policy can
also be contemplated; this would entail maintaining the Euro but under
different values for three distinct categories that would consist of strong
economies, average economies and poor economies.

(q) Shift from Financial Assets to Real Assets by Surpluses Countries
Real assets comprise of fixed assets like buildings, factories and land,
while financial assets consist of claims on the real assets. If countries that
run surpluses had channelled their funds mainly towards real assets like
factories and the construction of companies, this would have mitigated the
extent of the credit boom in the form of cheap credit flowing to the US.
The underlying rationale is that higher prices of financial assets induce
higher demand based on robust speculative forces. Following the
aftermath of the crisis, many countries are now looking for investments in
real assets. For example, China has now poised itself as a major investor in
projects involving real assets in different African countries in a bid to
diversify its reserves base and also mitigate against financial risks related
to financial assets—a really sound and sustainable long-term investment
strategy.

(r) Planned bailouts
Bailouts should be properly planned and not executed in a frantic or ad-
hoc basis as to induce mounting levels of moral hazards that thereby lead
to higher costs for the taxpayer. Indeed, with the crisis, the US government
shifted from a capitalist society to a communist one with massive
injections of funds. Just as companies practice fire drills, in the same vein,
stress testing exercises should be practiced regularly to gauge the level of
both exogenous and endogenous risks.

      To end this chapter, I would like to lay stress upon the current
conjecture of world affairs and the required policies to be applied. Too
much focus has been laid upon the effects of the US crisis and debt crisis,
which has led to the two other crises which are simultaneously affecting
man—namely the ageing population and climate change—being ignored.
In that respect, univariate policies geared towards a specific crisis are
highly likely to backfire. I address these pertinent issues in the last chapter
of the book.

Figure 2.1: Broad Overview-Schema of the Crisis

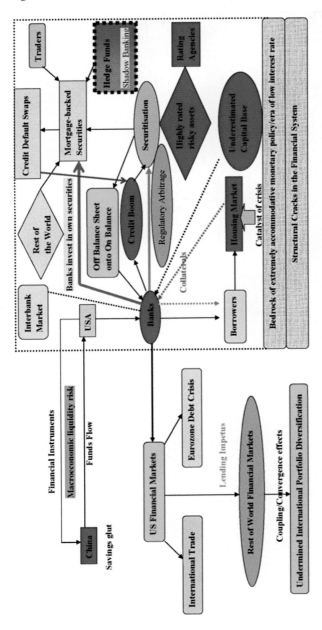

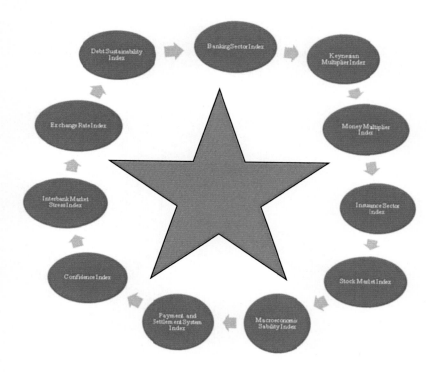

Figure 2.2: Harmonising Financial Stability Risk Maps

References

1. Merton, Robert C., 1974, On the Pricing of Corporate Debt: The Risk Structure of Interest Rates, *Journal of Finance*, 29 (2), 449-470.
2. Warren, Buffet, 2002, Shareholders Letters to Berkshire Hathaway Incorporation

CHAPTER THREE

IS THE WORLD HEADING
TOWARDS CRISIS-INDUCED IRRATIONAL
EXUBERANCE IN INTERNATIONAL ASSETS?
INVESTIGATING UNDER GFS-APT-GARCH
MODEL

This chapter develops a GFS-APT-GARCH model to uncover any looming risks to global financial stability with respect to crisis-induced irrational exuberance for twenty-nine world major assets. Findings suggest that the crisis has unleashed substantial post betas increases for ASX All Ordinaries Index, Indian Rupee, Russian Ruble, Corn, Wheat and Platinum, as well as significantly pronounced leverage effects in currencies. Furthermore, under inter-assets linkages, strong evidence of "waiting for dead men's shoes" irrational exuberance effects prevail in the case of Platinum, Australian Dollar, New Zealand Dollar, Nasdaq Composite Index and ASX All Ordinaries Index. Strong substitution impacts of MSCI and DXY on BRICS countries' currencies are also noted. Evidence is found for equities markets in advanced economies operating like value generators, those in emerging countries behaving like growth propellers, as well as many cases of crisis-induced structural shifts in parameters. The GFS-APT-GARCH model is expected to be widely used by policy-makers worldwide in gauging international asset risk.

3.0 Introduction

Capital Asset Pricing Model (CAPM) constitutes a well-founded theoretical model widely used in financial research and industry applications. A number of researchers are usually associated with the development of CAPM, namely Sharpe (1964), Lintner (1965), Mossin (1966) and Black (1972). The basic tenet of CAPM presumes that expected returns constitute fair compensation for the level of risk borne by a security. This study adopts a modelling approach to sieve out any feasible risks to overheated global assets.

In this chapter, I develop a Global Financial Stability-Arbitrage Pricing Theory-GARCH (GFS-APT-GARCH) model to uncover any feasible irrational exuberance in world major asset classes, namely equities, currencies and commodities. As financial markets are enthralled by the US subprime crisis spectre, there tends to be a massive switch towards certain assets deemed to be relatively less risky by international investors. These assets thereby witness significant price hikes, mostly explained by heightened risk aversion and lesser on fundamentals.[1] The newly developed GFS-APT-GARCH model is geared towards uncovering any irrational bubbles sparked off by the crisis as bruised market players shift towards assets perceived to be less risky. In essence, this chapter sheds light on potential asset price reversal, another looming risk to financial markets crisis with important implications for policy-makers. The study undertaken is comprehensive as it captures 29 world major assets classified under three main asset classes, namely 11 equities markets, 11 currencies and 7 commodities, all widely coveted by international investors. To the author's best knowledge, no study has investigated the impact of financial crisis on APT, let alone devised an APT model that weaves through all the vital aspects of financial stability at the global level.[2]

Many benefits emanate from the GFS-APT-GARCH model. Apart from uncovering the possible existence of irrational exuberance, this chapter also highlights spillover effects among the three major asset classes. For instance, currencies tend to impact on equities and commodities. Besides, under the umbrella of financial stability, the equities side of the study can also enable country risk evaluation by virtue of equities markets reflecting the economic barometer of their corresponding countries. In addition, the study introduces a new economically sensible asset-specific risk aversion metric to capture the extent of risk aversion prevailing in a particular asset. In fact, this is the very first study that adopts a dual approach to risk aversion by incorporating both a general risk aversion metric and an asset-specific risk aversion metric. In addition, the findings of the chapter are particularly vital for fund managers, investment bankers and central bankers in view of implementing sound portfolio diversification. Focus is

---

[1] I describe this as the "waiting for dead men's shoes" effect, since the price of assets increases in response to the decline of the price of other assets.

[2] Previous studies have also used the words "Global CAPM" like O'Brien (1999), despite the fact that, unlike the current study, such work does not really model CAPM at the global level. For instance, O'Brien (1999) focuses specifically on a UK multinational company.

also afforded as to whether leverage-induced effects have been brought about by the crisis.

Findings show that ASX All Ordinaries Index demarcates itself with a substantial beta increase of 76.57 per cent under equities beta analysis, reflecting potential irrational exuberance of Shiller (2005). Under currencies betas, findings suggest a shift mainly towards BRICS[3] countries' currencies in the post-crisis period. In the same vein, it is found that the crisis has engendered increasing substitution effects away from international equities markets to BRICS countries' currencies. Moreover, commodities betas for Wheat, Corn, Platinum and Sugar register significant increases. Overall, considerable beta increases for ASX All Ordinaries Index, Indian Rupee, Russian Rouble, Corn, Wheat and Platinum can foreshadow potential risks to global financial stability.

The study also finds evidence in favour of value premium whereby equities of developed economies behave like value generators while those of emerging countries work more as growth propellers. Findings further reveal significant leverage effects in currencies. Evidence is also found as to the newly developed asset-specific risk aversion metric working well and resulting in positive momentum in the case of the Indian Rupee, Gold and Silver. Conversely, VIX is found to significantly weigh down on the commodities in the post-crisis era.

Under inter-asset spillover effects, strong evidence is found of DXY affecting hard commodities on the back of predominating purchasing power effects. Some bouts of MSCI effects are also noted on commodities but with positive effects before the crisis, due to equities related wealth effects and negative impacts post the crisis on account of investors' hedging motives. In the case of MSCI and DXY impact on currencies, irrational exuberance tends to permeate AUD.

The chapter is organised as follows: Section 3.1 provides a brief review of the empirical literature on CAPM/APT; Section 3.2 describes the data and estimation methodology; Section 3.3 presents the empirical results; and finally Section 3.4 concludes.

3.1 Brief Literature Review and Motivations

Independently developed by Sharpe (1964), Lintner (1965), Mossin (1966) and Black (1972), CAPM constitutes the workhorse of finance, as corroborated by the findings of Graham and Harvey (2001) and Welch (2008) whereby around 75 per cent of chief financial officers and finance

---

[3] BRICS stands for Brazil, Russia, India, China and South Africa.

professors, respectively, have recourse towards CAPM when it comes to calculating the cost of capital for capital budgeting purposes. Apart from computing the cost of capital, CAPM has also been used to compute abnormal returns and evaluate the performance of managed portfolios. In addition, beta has also been used for assessing the extent of market integration (Bruner et al. 2008).

Over time, CAPM has been subject to major challenges, usually encompassed in form of anomalies:

    (a) Firm size (Banz, 1981; Reinganum, 1981)
    (b) Long-term price reversal (DeBondt and Thaler, 1985)
    (c) Post-Earnings-Announcement-Drift (Foster et al. 1984; Bernard and Thomas, 1989)
    (d) Book-to-market (Fama and French, 1992)
    (e) Momentum (Jegadeesh and Titman, 1993)
    (f) Liquidity (Pastor and Stambough, 2003)
    (g) Earnings Information Uncertainty (Kim, 2006, 2010)
    (h) Asset growth (Yao et al. 2011)

The above criticisms/shortcomings have given birth to distinct variants of CAPM.

To obviate the failure of CAPM in accounting for a cross-section of average returns, the literature contains the shift from static single-period to continuous multi-period models. The continuous CAPM models comprise of the Consumption-based CAPM (CCAPM) (Rubinstein, 1976; Lucas, 1978; Breeden, 1979) and the Intertemporal CAPM (ICAPM) of Merton (1973). One variant of CCAPM has been the world CAPM, which posits that goods and financial markets are perfect substitutes so that investors have access to similar investment sets. Merton (1973) comes up with ICAPM in which an asset's return is a function of its covariance with the market portfolio along with state variables that reflect changes in the investment opportunity set. Merton's (1973) ICAPM provides a positive relationship between conditional first and second moments of excess returns on the market portfolio. Later, Merton (1980) points out that the expected return of an asset should be related to its conditional risk which hinges not only on the market portfolio but also on individual stocks. However, the empirical literature is still not conclusive in terms of the direction between risk and expected return following works of Abel (1988), Backus and Gregory (1993), and Gennotte and Marsh (1993), who find a negative relation between expected return and risk.

With time, other different variants/extensions of CAPM have been suggested. Pettengill et al. (1995) argue for a split beta analysis: one pertaining to up markets analysis and one referring to down markets analysis. Their technique has permeated various studies undertaken for different countries: Fletcher (1997) for the UK stock market, Isakov (1999) for the Swiss stock market, Theriou et al. (2010) for the Greek market and Durand et al. (2011) for the emerging markets of Asia. Bodnar et al. (2003) present a hybrid model with both local and global indexes. Additionally, third-moment CAPM of Hull et al. (2004) factor in both downside risk and co-skewness to explain anomalies. Bekaert et al. (2009), Acharya and Pedersen (2005) and Iqbal and Brooks (2007) focus on the illiquidity aspects to see whether illiquid stocks do compensate for illiquidity risk. Post and Vliet (2006) find that downside risk is related to both size and value effects. Adrian et al. (2009) augment the CAPM by incorporating a learning process which scales down the pricing error by around 45 per cent. Hwang et al. (2010) use an option-risk version of CAPM based on bond-credit-spread data as a proxy for default risk and show that excess credit-spread can account for CAPM anomalies.

Most importantly, the shortcomings of CAPM in terms of its inability to explain the cross-sectional spread in average returns have given birth to the Arbitrage Pricing Theory (APT) of Ross (1976). Unfortunately, the theory contains no information as to the number of factors and the identification of factors. Campbell (1996) introduces a five-factor dynamic APT model that caters for both changing investment opportunities and human capital. Perhaps, the greatest variant of CAPM or most prominent APT-inspired models has been that of the Fama and French (1993) three-factor model (market factor, SMB, HML[4]) and a five-factor model (market factor, SMB, HML, Term spread and Default spread). In addition, Kim (2006) points out that his two-factor model, which consists of the market factor and the earnings information uncertainty risk factor, perform well in accounting for both the firm size and the January effect.

However, the CAPM/APT literature is usually geared towards specific asset analysis. At the current juncture of rising fears of recession, it becomes interesting to develop a model that focuses on the world's major financial assets like currencies, equities and commodities, instead of the feasible interactions among these three asset classes. In essence, the objective is to gauge on the extent of risk embodied in each major international equity, currency and commodity asset. The chief benefit of the study is to bring to light any feasible irrational exuberance, a sort of

---

[4] SMB and HML stand for small minus big and high minus low, respectively.

crisis-induced euphoria. In that respect, the study develops a multifactor APT model in view of safeguarding financial stability at the international level. The newly developed GFS-APT-GARCH model is explored with all globally important asset classes.

3.2 Data and Estimation Methodology

3.2.1 Data part

Weekly data spanning the period from January 2000 to December 2011 are used for the empirical investigation. To sieve out the effects of the US financial crisis,[5] two estimation periods are used: January 2000 to July 2007[6] and August 2007 to December 2011.[7] Andersen et al. (2005) provide evidence that equity market betas change as per macroeconomic indicators. In the same vein, Groenewold and Fraser (1999) and Ghysels (1998) point out that betas do exhibit significant variations over time. Consequently, all our results are reported for two periods, one before the crisis and one post the crisis. The focus on major categories of asset classes not only shuns off any feasible bias introduced by thinly traded assets but also assists in having global wide analysis. The study resorts towards weekly analysis since it constitutes the best time horizon. While daily data may be erratic or excessively noisy, monthly data may be hiding important information.[8] Above all, in the arena of financial markets, most investors tend focus on weekly news in view of altering their active investment strategies. Finally, weekly analysis helps to avoid problems related to infrequent and non-synchronous trading. Three distinct models are developed, one model relating to each specific asset class, namely, equities, currencies and commodities.

---

[5] Financial crisis is used despite the fact that this constitutes merely the first stage of the crisis, which developed into an economic crisis and eventually a debt crisis.

[6] August 2007 is used as the cut-off point that demarcates the pre- and post-crisis periods.

[7] It can be argued that the term "post-crisis" is a misnomer since the US crisis effects still permeate international financial markets. However, the motive of using post-crisis is to demarcate from the pre-crisis period and clearly uncover any major structural changes that could feasibly pose a risk to global financial stability.

[8] Moreover, GARCH analysis is particularly convenient for higher frequency data relative to monthly data.

To capture equities international markets, recourse is made towards Dow Jones Industrial Average (DJIA[9]), Nasdaq Composite Index, S&P 500 Index, Shanghai Stock Exchange Composite Index, Nikkei Stock Average 225 Index, BSE 30 Index, CAC-40 Index, DAX Index, Hang Seng Index, FTSE 100 Index and ASX All Ordinaries Index. The following 11 currencies[10] are considered: Japanese Yen (JPY), British Pound (GBP), Euro (EUR), Swiss Franc (CHF), Brazilian Real (BRL), Russian Ruble (RUB), Indian Rupee (INR), Canadian Dollar (CAD), Australian Dollar (AUD), South African Rand (ZAR) and New Zealand Dollar (NZD). Finally, the following commodities (both soft and hard) have been considered: Sugar, Wheat, Coffee, Corn, Platinum, Silver and Gold. These commodities form part of ten of the most traded commodities in the world. Data for equities have been gleaned from Yahoo Finance while currencies and commodities data have been obtained from Reuters and Bloomberg. In general, the analysis is comprehensive with twenty-nine distinct assets involved in the investigation.

In a world buffeted by uncertainty, rational agents have to infer about the feasible factor loadings. For the multifactor APT model considered, for any given asset class, a corresponding asset is required to reflect the global market index with respect to that specific asset type. For equities, the MSCI World Index is employed. The MSCI World Index constitutes a widely used international equity tool to gauge on general equity indices performance of 24 countries from the developed world, namely: Australia, Austria, Belgium, Canada, Denmark, Finland, France, Germany, Greece, Hong Kong, Ireland, Israel, Italy, Japan, Netherlands, New Zealand, Norway, Portugal, Singapore, Spain, Sweden, Switzerland, the United Kingdom, and the United States. In the same vein, to capture global market trends for currencies, the US Dollar Index (DXY) is used, since the US dollar is the base currency with which other currencies are usually quoted. Launched in 1973 by the New York Board of Trade, the DXY is calculated based on the exchange rates of six major world currencies[11]: the Euro, Japanese yen,

---

[9] While DJIA constitutes an index based on stock prices of 30 of the largest companies, S&P 500 and Nasdaq Composite Index represent 500 companies and thousands of companies (start-up and technology companies), respectively.

[10] The Chinese Yuan has been overlooked on the grounds that China has a policy of keeping its yuan/renmimbi artificially low under a fixed exchange rate system to boost its exports. As per IMF De Facto Classification of Exchange Rate Regimes, China is classified under "other conventional fixed peg arrangements."

[11] Effectively, the DXY represent the currencies for 22 countries: 17 countries of the European Union, with the addition of Japan, Great Britain, Canada, Sweden, and Switzerland. DXY is made up of Euro (57.6%), Japanese Yen (13.6%),

Canadian dollar, British pound, Swedish krona and Swiss franc. An increase in DXY signifies a rise in US dollar value/appreciating US dollar. Because the composition of the DXY is heavily tilted towards the Euro, DXY is sometimes referred to as the anti-Euro Index. For the last asset class, recourse is made towards the Thomson Reuters/Jefferies CRB Index. Introduced in 1957 by the Commodity Research Bureau, the CRB Index is the most widely watched barometer of the general commodity price level and comprises of 19 distinct commodities with adjustments made over time to ensure accurate representation of general commodities trends.

In this paper, I use beta shifts for equities, currencies and commodities asset classes to capture changing market expectations at the global level and the level of riskiness associated with the US financial crisis.

3.2.2 Modelling of GFS-APT-GARCH model

The conventional CAPM/APT model presumes a linear relationship between an individual stock's excess return (return beyond the risk-free rate) and the market portfolio's excess return. The basic CAPM/APT relies heavily on normal distribution so that its relevance requires investors either possessing quadratic utility functions or caring only about the first two moments. In practice, returns are non-normal. Indeed, due to presence of heteroscedasticity in assets' returns which can result in inaccurate rejection or non-rejection of the distinct hypotheses on the econometric modelling, recourse is made towards GARCH models. The variance part of the multifactor APT model is characterised by a TGARCH model of Engle (1990) and Engle and Ng (1993) with the appropriate parameter constraints. The best model is selected based on the value of log likelihood function, which is taken for three distinct distributions, namely normal distribution, student-t distribution and Generalized Error Distribution. Our revised model of APT provides a more intuitive explanation for global assets evaluation.

3.2.3 Equity Part

The GFS-APT-GARCH equity model is specified as follows:

Pounds Sterling (11.9%), Canadian Dollar (9.1%), Swedish Krona (4.2%), and Swiss Franc (3.6%).

$[E(r_t)-r_{ft}] = \beta^S [E(MSCI_t-r_{ft})]+$

$\delta_1 HLC_t + \delta_2 Gold_t + \delta_3 CRB_t + \delta_4 DXY_t + \delta_5 VIX_t + \varepsilon_t$ (1)

$\sigma^2_t = \lambda_0 + \lambda_1 \sigma^2_{t-1} + \lambda_2 \varepsilon^2_{t-1}$ (2)

$\lambda_0 > 0, \quad \lambda_1, \lambda_2 \geq 0, \quad \lambda_1 + \lambda_2 < 1$

$\sigma^2_t = \lambda_0 + \lambda_1 \sigma^2_{t-1} + \lambda_2 (\varepsilon - \omega)^2_{t-1}$ (3)

$\omega > 0$ confirms presence of leverage effects

Where:

$[E(r_t)-r_{ft}]$:   Expected return of the selected stock market index over risk-free rate

r_{ft} :   Weekly return on 90 day Treasury Bills

β^S: Beta coefficient for the selected stock market index

$MSCI_t$:   Return on MSCI World Index

HLC_t: Difference between highest and lowest values scaled by the closing value of the considered equity asset

$Gold_t$:   Return on Gold

CRB_t: Return on the Reuters/Jefferies CRB Index

DXY_t: Return on the US Dollar Index

VIX_t: Return on CBOE Volatility Index

Equation (1) relates the mean equation of the GARCH model. The model befits the work of Bos and Newbold (1984) in terms of incorporating both microeconomic and macroeconomic factors when modelling beta, but here is based on a truly worldwide analytical framework compared to O'Brien (1999). The dependent variable for equity returns reflects realised excess returns which is regressed on the conditioning variables. Based on the fact that each country's main stock market index is analogous to a security/stock component under the APT, the market portfolio used represents the MSCI World Index. Alternatively stated, the first independent variable pertains to the usual market factor component (MSCI World Index) susceptible to impact on a country's main equity index performance. To capture the risk-free rate, the 90 days government Treasury bill is employed. Our model suppresses the intercept term in equation (1) as this constitutes one of the main assumptions of CAPM/APT, similar to the model of Adrian et al. (2009) which also reinforces a robust analysis of the null hypothesis. Returns data are used for the non-market state factors to directly capture sensitivity effects or non-market betas. The non-market factor can be deemed as a vector of state variables, which spells out the investment opportunity set and consists of Gold, CRB, DXY and VIX. Indeed, Fama and French (1992) provide evidence in favour of other factors besides that of beta itself that can account for returns. The rationale for incorporating each of the non-market factors is explained below.

To gauge on feasible inter-asset linkages emanating from currencies and commodities channels, the US Dollar Index and CRB Index are considered. The DXY reflects the general value of the US dollar against a basket of world major currencies and is thereby appropriate to assess any feasible impact of the US dollar on equities performance. Indeed, international investors have dual returns whenever they invest in foreign markets; core returns emanating from the equities and peripheral returns emanating from currency movements. It is therefore important to factor in currency movements. Similarly, the CRB Index is considered as an additional independent variable by virtue of potential spillover effects from the commodities channel onto the equities channel.

Gold has also been included based on the recent events whereby the crisis may have induced considerable demand for gold. The latter has become world's most coveted asset in light of uncertainty about world growth. Above all, the substantial demand for gold has been motivated by quantitative easing which has spread lingering fears of rising inflation; gold is undeniably perceived as the best hedge against inflation. In that respect, gold is expected to act as a substitute to equities holdings. Among all commodities, gold is expected to engender considerably stronger effects, thereby warranting its inclusion as a separate variable.

During crisis times, investors demonstrate heightened levels of risk aversion which exerts significant pressures on distinct assets. Technically speaking, any APT model which does not incorporate risk aversion, particularly during the US financial crisis, is expected to be wrongly specified. Risk aversion has also been used to moot on the long-standing puzzle in the field of financial economics, in particular, the existence of high equity premium. Hwang et al. (2010) point out that expected excess returns are countercyclical due to higher risk/risk aversion in recessions. Bali and Engle (2010) restrict the risk aversion coefficient to be the same for all assets compared to the methodology employed here, effectively cutting the coat according to the cloth. The current study not only includes risk aversion metrics into the APT model but also adopts an utterly new approach to modelling risk aversion. In essence, to yield consistent and unbiased betas, both asset-specific and general risk aversion metrics are incorporated into the model. To capture investors' level of risk aversion, the model incorporates the HLC variable which reflects the difference between the highest and lowest value divided by the closing value of the same asset under consideration. Essentially, it is expected that the larger the difference between the highest and lowest values, the greater the extent of market uncertainty and thereby the higher the level of risk aversion inherent in that specific asset type. To capture the general risk aversion level, the Chicago Board of Options Exchange (CBOE) Volatility Index (VIX[12]) is included. A priori, we expect pronounced effects of the risk aversion metrics in the post-crisis era relative to the pre-crisis period.

In line with Chen and So (2002), I expect beta values to change considerably in the post-crisis period. Jegadeesh and Titman (1993) point out the significance of past returns in predicting the cross-sectional and time series variation in future returns on individual stocks. However, the current study presumes a weekly contemporaneous relationship between the dependent and various explanatory factors, since a weekly horizon leaves ample manoeuvre time for any international portfolio adjustments. The above model is considered particularly important at evaluating worldwide risk, especially from the perspective of global financial stability.

3.2.4 Currency part

The GFS-APT-GARCH currency model is specified as follows:

$$E(FX_t) = \beta^F_t \, [E(DXY_t \,] + \kappa_1 HLC_t + \kappa_2 VIX_t + \kappa_3 CRB_t + \kappa_4 MSCI_t + \varepsilon_t \qquad (4)$$
$$\sigma^2_t = \pi_0 + \pi_1 \, \sigma^2_{t-1} + \pi_2 \, \varepsilon^2_{t-1} \qquad (5)$$
Where $\pi_0 > 0, \quad \pi_1, \pi_2 \geq 0, \quad \pi_1 + \pi_2 < 1$
Or in case of leverage effects
$$\sigma^2_t = \pi_0 + \pi_1 \, \sigma^2_{t-1} + \pi_2 \, (\varepsilon - \xi)^2_{t-1} \qquad (6)$$
$\xi > 0$ confirms presence of leverage effects

Where:
$E(FX_t)$:   Expected return on the selected currency with respect to the US Dollar
β^F: Beta coefficient for the selected currency asset
DXY_t: Return on the US Dollar Index
HLC_t: Difference between highest and lowest values scaled by the closing value of the specific currency under consideration
VIX_t: Return on CBOE Volatility Index
CRB_t: Return on the Reuters/Jefferies CRB Index
$MSCI_t$:   Return on MSCI World Index

---

[12] VIX is a widely recognised risk aversion metric among global investors.

Compared to the equities specification, the currencies specification assumes zero interest rates since currencies can be traded anywhere in the world based on a 24-hour market. To capture the component for market return, recourse is made to the US dollar index. The underlying rationale emanates from the US dollar representing the globally accepted currency relative to which other currencies are usually referenced. Like its equity counterpart, risk aversion is proxied twice, a general level of risk aversion in the form of VIX and an asset-specific risk aversion in the form of HLC.

Finally, to reflect the feasible effects of commodities and equities on currency returns, CRB and MSCI are inserted into the model as additional state variables. Should commodities influence demand for currencies, κ_3 is expected to be both economically and statistically significant. The impact of commodities on currencies is expected result mainly from speculative actions of traders in international assets. MSCI is also considered since international equity markets' performances are also likely to impact upon currencies' performance. For instance, in the case that international investors demand more stocks in a specific country, this will initiate a simultaneous burgeoning demand for that country's currency, increasing its propensity of appreciation. Conversely, in the case that a country's risk assessments are negative, fleeing investors will dispose of that country's equities, making its currency liable to depreciating pressures.

Leverage effects, under the currency model, are captured by the coefficient ξ. It is widely recognised that leverage effects permeate the world of finance in both equities and commodities markets. The famous explanation used to rationalise the equity leverage effects pertains to the debt-to-equity ratio. When the stock price falls, this unleashes a higher debt-to-equity ratio synonymous to a higher bankruptcy probability of the company so that there is massive equities sell-off; this thereby generates higher volatility. In that respect, a negative shock triggers off a higher volatility relative to a positive shock of the same magnitude. For commodities, a positive shock triggers off higher volatility relative to a negative shock of the same magnitude due to adverse impact on consumers' purchasing power. However, in the case of currencies, the empirical literature is still not fully developed in terms of an explanation to account for leverage effects. I believe that currencies markets also share leverage effects in the sense that a negative shock occasions a higher volatility than a positive shock of the same magnitude. The reason is that, when a currency witnesses a negative return, this incites speculators to sell more of that currency in expectation of further negative momentum, to the effect that a negative shock elicits higher volatility than a positive shock of the same magnitude. Such a sale is triggered by virtue of most disciplined speculators adhering to stop losses. Focus is exclusively laid on speculators since they account for more than ninety per cent of total transactions undertaken in international foreign exchange markets on any given trading day.

3.2.5 Commodity part

$$E(COM_t) = \beta^C_t \, E(CRB_{tt}) + \varphi_1 HLC_t + \varphi_2 VIX_t + \varphi_3 DXY_t + \varphi_4 MSCI_t + \varepsilon_t \qquad (7)$$

$$\sigma^2_t = Y_0 + Y_1 \, \sigma^2_{t-1} + Y_2 \, \varepsilon^2_{t-1} \qquad (8)$$

Where $Y_0 > 0$, $Y_1, Y_2 \geq 0$, $Y_1 + Y_2 < 1$
Or in case of leverage effects

$$\sigma^2_t = Y_0 + Y_1 \, \sigma^2_{t-1} + Y_2 \, (\varepsilon - \varphi)^2_{t-1} \qquad (9)$$

$\varphi < 0$ confirms presence of leverage effects

Where:
$E(COM_t)$: Expected return on the selected commodity (soft and hard)
B^C: Market beta coefficient for the selected commodity asset
CRB_t: Return on the Reuters/Jefferies CRB Index
HLC_t: Difference between highest and lowest values scaled by the closing value of the considered currency
VIX_t: Return on CBOE Volatility Index
DXY_t: Return on the US Dollar Index
$MSCI_t$: Return on MSCI World Index

In the case of the commodity APT, the CRB index is used to capture the market return. Both specific and general risk aversion metrics are again employed. Finally, to sieve out the potential effects of the currency and equity markets, DXY and MSCI are incorporated to generate a full-fledged assessment. In fact, many analysts around the world consider commodities to gain momentum based on a forex-fuelled price rally, which is usually propelled by a weak dollar. Similarly, MSCI is incorporated to probe into any potential spillover effects of equities markets on commodities. Positive impacts can manifest as investors channel part of their profits from equities towards commodities in view of harnessing maximum portfolio diversification benefits. This could be particularly true in light of the crisis as equities markets tend to trigger coupling effects among themselves.

A conspicuous difference in the case of commodities pertains to reverse position in the leverage effects, whereby a positive shock triggers higher volatility relative to a negative shock of the same magnitude, since a price rise in commodities represents bad news for consumers (see Carol Alexander, 2008).

The exponential GARCH (EGARCH), introduced by Nelson (1991) and shown in equation (10), is used in the case of parameter violation under TGARCH. The leverage impact is captured by parameter ϱ, which is expected to be negative for equities and currencies but positive for commodities.

$$\text{Log } (\sigma^2_{\text{st}}) = \Pi + \sum_{j=1}^{q} \vartheta_j \log (\sigma^2_{\text{st}-j}) + \sum_{i=1}^{p} \tau_i \mid \varepsilon_{t-i} / \sigma_{\text{st}-j} \mid + \sum_{k=1}^{r} \varrho_k \ (\varepsilon_t / \sigma_{\text{st}-k})$$

$$(10)$$

For each of the 29 assets under consideration, eight regressions are run, four regressions in the pre-crisis episode and four regressions in the post-crisis era. In each period, the four regressions respectively represent the symmetric GARCH model with and without the asset-specific risk aversion variable and the asymmetric GARCH models with and without the asset-specific risk aversion variable. The regression coefficient values are derived as an average of all the statistically significant values under each period, with an imposed condition of having at least two statistically significant values when computing the average values. By averaging values of the statistically significant values using both symmetric and asymmetric GARCH models, the results are expected to be robust.

3.2.6 Irrational Exuberance

It can be posited that Shiller (2005) is the father of irrational exuberance based on behavioural finance whereby excessive price increases beyond true fundamentals can foreshadow potential bubbles. In this study, I resort to three avenues to capture any crisis-induced irrational exuberance in light of the worst crisis since the Great Depression of the 1930s. First, significant market beta increases above 50 per cent is considered as potential exuberance. Second, recourse is made towards VIX, general risk aversion impact on assets' returns. Third, I integrate inter-assets linkages to identify any positively induced momentum emanating due to another's assets contagion effects. This is synonymous with the "waiting for dead men's shoes" effect.

3.2.7 Benefits of GFS-APT-GARCH model

This study generates a myriad of benefits, which are as follows:

1. The newly developed GFS-APT-GARCH model is particularly interesting from the perspective of financial stability in terms of analysing risk across a plethora of the world's major assets. The GFS-APT-GARCH model attempts to uncover any potential risks to financial stability with respect to crisis-induced irrational exuberance. As the crisis unfolded and adversely affected international assets, this model could re-channel significant investments towards certain assets which thereby underwent exaggerated price hikes purely due to shifting effects in lieu of robust fundamentals. This paper sheds light on a potential reversal in asset prices and thereby another looming risk to financial markets stability.
2. The study innovates from all previous APT studies by resorting to a dual approach to risk aversion: a general risk aversion metric (VIX) and an asset-specific risk aversion metric (HLC).
3. The GFS-APT-GARCH model is also valid for gauging on the level of country risk chiefly in the case of equities since equities markets are usually deemed the economic barometer of their corresponding countries. Beta is made conditional on two major market states, a pre-crisis and a post-crisis state. Such a distinction is vital in light of bringing out any major shifts/structural changes in international betas of the world's major asset classes.
4. The GFS-APT-GARCH model also caters for inter-assets spillover effects among the currencies, equities and commodities indices.
5. Leverage effects are also explored, not only for equities and commodities but also for currencies.
6. In general, there is explicit recognition of globalisation and market integration via the use of the newly proposed GFS-APT-GARCH model. This helps to analyse as to whether international portfolio diversification has been significantly affected by the crisis. Such a state of affairs is particularly important for individual members of the international investment community such as fund managers, investment bankers and central bankers.

3.3 Empirical Results

Table 3.1 in Appendix A reports the summary statistics of the variables used in the GFS-APT-GARCH model. All series have excess kurtosis, which is a well-known feature when working with financial data. Strong ARCH effects are observed in almost all the assets under consideration.[13] Appendix B contains all the empirical results for the three asset classes. Tables 3.2 to 3.12 provide results for the distinct equities markets. For currencies results, Tables 3.13 to 3.23 apply, while for commodities, results are shown in Tables 3.24 to 3.30.

3.3.1 Beta analysis

All beta coefficients behave properly in all asset cases under scrutiny. In terms of equities beta changes, Nasdaq Composite Index, Dow Jones Industrial Average, DAX Index, Nikkei Stock Average 225 Index and BSE 30 Index undergo negative changes. On the other hand, positive equities beta changes are noted for S&P 500 Index, FTSE 100 Index, CAC-40 Index, Hang Seng and ASX All Ordinaries Index. However, compared to all positive or negative changes, ASX All Ordinaries Index demarcates itself with a substantial beta increase of 76.57 per cent. It can be argued that fundamentals do account for such a state of affairs. As per Reserve Bank of Australia's Financial Stability Report 2011, Australia has not been affected by the crisis on the back of a robust banking sector, low levels of Non-Performing loans, sound growth, a strong capital base which has been able to absorb any unexpected losses, and practically no exposure to toxic assets. However, it can still be contended that, overall, the increases noted appear to be exaggerated. For instance, India has also not been significantly affected by the crisis but has not suffered the same fate as Australia, reflecting potential irrational exuberance for ASX All Ordinaries Index. Shanghai Composite Index registers no impact before the crisis but post the crisis, its' beta value hovers around 0.2208, glaringly demonstrating a crisis-induced structural shift.

Brazilian Real posts no beta impact before the crisis but after the onset of the crisis, it shows a beta value of 0.2513. Indian Rupee and Russia Rouble are subject to substantial upward changes of 600.85 per cent and 385.04 per cent, respectively. These findings plainly suggest a crisis-induced shift mainly towards emerging economies coined as BRICS (Brazil, Russia, India, China and South Africa) based on investors' exceptional appetite for these countries' currencies. Australian Dollar, Canadian Dollar, Swiss Franc, British Pound, New Zealand Dollar and South African Rand post negative changes in the betas. Besides, negative beta values are noted for some currencies in the case of the US dollar,

---

[13] Results are not reported to save space but are available on request.

Euro, British Pound and New Zealand Dollar. Such a finding implies that these four currencies are usually considered substitutes, rather than complements, to the US dollar. This clearly manifests in the case of Euro and British Pound, which form part of the basket of currencies in DXY composition. Australian Dollar and New Zealand Dollar also post negative relationships with DXY but with less pronounced effects conspicuously noted in the post-crisis period, plausibly attributable to investors demanding more of these currencies in light of the crisis. Finally, for the commodities asset class, Wheat, Corn, Platinum and Sugar depict beta increases of 172.93%, 136.19%, 72.01% and 68.68%, respectively. The excessive increases in sensitivity with respect to the overall market trend manifest not principally due to sound fundamentals but chiefly on the back of investors moving away from risky assets.

From the perspective of global equities portfolio composition, betas are also analysed in terms of aggressive/defensive states. S&P 500 Index, Nasdaq Composite Index, DAX index and CAC-40 Index maintain aggressive betas and this holds independent of the period under investigation, while all the rest of the equities depict defensive betas.[14] This can potentially reflect the finding of Arisoy (2010) in which case value stocks earn higher average returns than growth stocks, coined as value premium, but here on a country-wise equities market perspective. Equities markets of advanced economies can be viewed as value generators, while those of emerging markets are seen as growth propellers. Furthermore, probing deeper, Nasdaq Composite Index and DAX Index depict negative falls in the aggressive betas. This can be attributed to "flight-to-quality" effects at the global level in which value stocks underperform and are riskier than growth stocks, analogous to the findings of Barinov (2008) and Arisoy (2010) but who base themselves on stocks analysis.

Among commodities, only soft commodities such as Corn, Sugar and Wheat report aggressive betas in the post-crisis era, while only Sugar preserves a beta value above one in the pre-crisis period. Currency wise, only Euro and Swiss Franc exhibit aggressive betas, though the signs are different. For Euro, this is explained by the fact that Euro constitutes the lion's share of basket weight under DXY composition. However, for Swiss Franc, a positive sign is obtained, which could be attributed to the fact that Swiss Franc accounts for less than 5 per cent in the DXY

---

[14] Though DJIA and FTSE 100 Index do not exhibit beta values above one, they are pretty much close to one, relative to the emerging economies.

composition. The systematically positive betas noted for all commodities add further strength to their coveted investment asset nature.

3.3.2 Gold impact on equities

The findings do not show that Gold has generally triggered an adverse impact on equities markets during the crisis period. Indeed, all equities markets post impotent effects from Gold, apart from DJIA, which is subject to a negative impact of 5.20%. Also in the pre-crisis period, bearish Gold effects permeated S&P 500 Index (-4.04%), Nasdaq Composite Index (-6.21%) and DJIA (-4.84%). Interestingly, prior to the outbreak of the crisis, Gold acted as a bullish force to BSE 30 Index and ASX All Ordinaries Index by unleashing positive returns of 22.08% and 13.09%, respectively. Such a finding consolidates the fact that India constitutes one of the largest purchasers of Gold in the world and that Australia's equity market is inherently linked to commodities performance. In essence, the general impotency of Gold on equities in the post-crisis episode can be due to Gold being perceived as a less risky asset in itself, so that there is a systematic break in terms of Gold's spillover effects onto the equities markets.

3.3.3 Leverage effects analysis

The reported signs under EGARCH and TGARCH terms are consistent with our a priori expectations for all assets, with exception of one anomaly noted for Brazilian Real. Out of the three asset classes, conspicuously pronounced leverage effects are noted for currencies in the post-crisis era. It can therefore be conjectured that the crisis has indeed caused higher volatilities in currencies markets on the back of negative shocks. Nonetheless, some bouts of leverage effects prevail for Nasdaq Composite Index, FTSE 100 Index and DAX Index in the pre-crisis period and for Shanghai Stock Exchange Composite Index and Hang Seng Index in the post-crisis era. Another interesting finding pertains to dissipating leverage effects in the case of commodities markets, which demonstrate leverage effects for more assets in the pre-crisis period relative to the post-crisis period; this holds mainly for soft commodities like Coffee, Corn and Sugar. A plausible explanation is that following the crisis, commodities price rises were no longer considered as bad to consumers based on very low interest rates that prevailed in most advanced economies. In addition, while Wheat and Gold maintain their leverage effects in both the pre- and post-crisis periods, leverage effects are altogether absent in the case of

Silver and Platinum. Interestingly, the size of Gold leverage effects undergoes a decline in the post-crisis episode. This implies that though a positive shock generates higher volatility relative to negative shock of the same magnitude, the size of the volatility has declined in the post-crisis era, substantiating Gold's appeal as a crisis-induced coveted international asset.

3.3.4 Asset-Specific Risk aversion

Results show satisfactory performance of the newly developed asset-specific risk aversion variable. Focusing exclusively on the post-crisis period, the newly developed asset-specific risk aversion metric HLC generates negative returns of 10.30%, 25.60%, 11.77% and 16.63% on Nikkei Stock Average 225 Index, ASX All Ordinaries Index, British Pound and Japanese Yen, respectively. Ironically, HLC also result in positive impacts in the case of S&P 500 Index, Nasdaq Composite Index, DJIA, Indian Rupee, South African Rand, Gold and Silver post the crisis. But, delving deeper, it transpires that Indian Rupee, Gold and Silver emerge among the formerly cited assets with the highest impacts of 22.44%, 16.19% and 16.69%, respectively, while the rest of the assets post positive returns in the range of 4% to 7%. The significant increases noted for Indian Rupee, Gold and Silver are interesting, since they show that rising asset-specific risk aversion during the US subprime crisis period unleashed positive momentum for these three assets. Such a finding is of paramount significance as it also shows that asset-specific risk aversion can spark off bullish forces in the case of certain assets, a factor so far utterly overlooked in prior empirical research.

Furthermore, even before the crisis, the asset-specific risk aversion variable works well for FTSE 100 Index, BSE 30 Index, ASX All Ordinaries Index, Russian Rouble and Corn with a negative impact. However, DAX Index, Japanese Yen, South African Rand and Silver witness positive increases of 6.11%, 11.64%, 17.19% and 15.23%, respectively. Such a finding also shows that the crisis has brought about structural changes in forces that determine the returns. This is mainly observed in the case of Japanese Yen, which registers a shift from 11.64% to -16.63%. Again, significant structural changes are noted in the case of S&P 500 Index, Japanese Yen and South African Rand. Overall, findings do corroborate the need to include the newly developed asset-specific risk aversion metric in the model to avoid model misspecification.

3.3.5 General risk aversion (VIX)

It transpires that in the post-crisis episode, VIX exerts negative pressures on Dow Jones Industrial Average, Swiss Franc, Russian Rouble, Coffee, Corn, Sugar and Wheat, with the soft commodities conspicuously posting pronounced effects ranging from -22.47% to -34.75%. In fact, VIX significantly weighs down on the commodities with significant increases in post VIX values noted for Corn and Wheat. The negative impact of VIX on soft commodities may imply that higher VIX is synonymous with higher discount rates to investors, which thereby gnaw at the demand for soft commodities. However, post the crisis, VIX influence on hard commodities utterly fades away, most probably due to flight towards hard commodities during the crisis period as constituting the best hedge not only against uncertainty but also against lingering concerns of rising inflation. Moreover, remarkable drifts in the case of positive momentum of VIX are noted between the two periods; prior to the crisis, VIX triggered positive impacts on FTSE 100 Index, BSE 30 Index and Indian Rupee, while post the crisis, ASX All Ordinaries Index, Euro and British Pound witnessed similar positive momentum.

3.3.6 Inter-Assets Linkages

3.3.6.1 MSCI & DXY Impact on Commodities

Compared to MSCI, DXY engenders robust impacts on commodities. This finding suggests that the purchasing power argument predominates over spillover effects. DXY unleashes negative impacts on commodities, supporting the fact that the higher the general value of the US dollar, the lower the demand for commodities. A noticeable finding pertains to DXY mainly affecting hard commodities except for some effects noted in the case of Corn (in both periods) and Wheat (only in the post-crisis period), with Silver witnessing the highest rise in negative impact post the crisis. Some spurts of MSCI effects are also manifest but with mostly positive impacts occurring prior to the crisis and negative effects post the crisis. Two main reasons can be cited for such a state of affairs. First, some potential negative spillover effects can run from equities markets to commodities markets during stressful times while during good times, equities markets in general (as captured by MSCI) act as positive catalyst to commodities, presumably due to wealth effects emanating from positive equities performances. Second, the negative effect encountered during the crisis period could also herald the hedging signal of investors' investment set as they cling to commodities assets to hedge against uncertain states, so that lower equities prices automatically draw higher investments towards commodities. Only Platinum preserves a positive impact from equities, irrespective of the period under analysis, let alone a hefty increase noted in the impact.

3.3.7 MSCI & CRB on Currencies

A priori, in all currencies which bear statistically significant relationships under MSCI and DXY, the post-crisis episode records significant increases in the impacts (except for the Kiwi under CRB). MSCI is found to have significantly increased its positive impact in the case of Australian Dollar and New Zealand Dollar, while a similar finding only exists for Australian Dollar under CRB. This result plainly shows that the crisis has been particularly bullish for Australian Dollar and New Zealand Dollar, which could possibly witness some irrational exuberance. However, higher MSCI performances trigger bearish performances for Brazilian Real, Canadian Dollar, Indian Rupee, Russian Rouble and South African Rand, independent of whether the focus is laid on pre- or post-crisis periods, but with stronger magnitude impacts witnessed after the crisis. In a parallel manner, similar findings are noted in the case of CRB on BRL and CAD. Such a finding is of paramount significance as Brazilian Real, Canadian Dollar, Indian Rupee, Russian Rouble and South African Rand, in general reflect the currencies of the BRICS countries. It can therefore be conjectured that the crisis has trailed behind mounting substitution effects away from international equities markets to currencies of BRICS countries with Indian Rupee (Brazilian Real), registering the highest increase under MSCI (DXY). A prominent finding pertains to substantially higher impacts of MSCI relative to CRB on currencies in the post-crisis episode, forcefully demonstrating that global equities rather than global commodities have a considerable grip over currencies movements. This adds luster to the fact that equities markets do reflect any country's state of economic health.

3.3.8 DXY and CRB on Equities

Overall, results suggest that CRB effect on international equities markets is very limited. In utter contrast, DXY systematically unleashes positive impacts on equities with Nasdaq Composite Index and ASX All Ordinaries Index posting the highest positive changes (beyond a 50% increase) in values from the pre-crisis era to the post-crisis period. Positive but lower changes are also noted in the case of S&P 500 Index, FTSE 100

Index and BSE 30 Index. Only DAX Index registers a slight fall in the post-crisis impact. The positive impact of DXY can be explained by the fact that as the US dollar gains value relative to other major currencies, this moots on the level of concerns about the US economy and thereby generates positive momentum to equities investments, not only in the US but also in other countries. This follows from the fact that the US economy tends to lead international financial markets. No impacts manifest for Shanghai Stock Exchange Composite Index and Hang Seng Index because China adheres to a crawling peg exchange rate system while Hong Kong clings to a currency board system.[15] An eye-opening finding pertains to the impotency of DXY on Nikkei Stock Average 225 Index in the post-crisis period, while prior to the onset of the crisis, DXY entailed the highest positive effect of 42.03% on Japanese equity market.[16] This can be explained by the fact that before the crisis, a higher US dollar value enshrined Japanese exports, while after the crisis, the yen has been subject to upward pressures which incite the Japanese authorities to intervene in order to preserve their competitiveness level. This has been conspicuous in the aftermath of the earthquake and tsunami which hit Japan in March 2011. Such a finding again depicts that both structural changes induced by the crisis and natural phenomena influence equity performance of the Japanese stock market.

3.4 Conclusion

The US subprime crisis has left the whole financial world stunned. To the author's best knowledge, there are presently no studies that have undertaken an analysis of looming risks to instability based on crisis-induced irrational exuberance. The current study attempts to fill such a vacuum by developing a GFS-APT-GARCH model. The study captures irrational exuberance via three main avenues, namely significant change in market betas, risk aversion effects and inter-asset linkages. Many benefits emanate from the GFS-APT-GARCH model. Apart from its ability to analyse irrational exuberance across a plethora of world's major assets, the GFS-APT-GARCH model is very powerful in catering for inter-assets spillover effects among the currencies, equities and commodities asset

---

[15] De Facto Classification of Exchange Rate Regimes and Monetary Policy Frameworks under IMF, April 31, 2008.
[16] It is found that for most equities markets, if a statistically significant result is obtained in the pre-crisis period, the same re-occurs in the post-crisis period. Similarly, in the case of no effects encountered in the pre-crisis period, impotency again prevails in the post-crisis era.

classes. Finally, the GFS-APT-GARCH model supports the rational asset pricing theory. The study also innovates by resorting to a dual approach to risk aversion analysis: an asset-specific risk aversion metric coupled with a general risk aversion metric, as captured by VIX to reflect the broad level of risk aversion. Moreover, leverage effects are also explored for equities, commodities and currencies. The study also assists in bringing out any major structural changes/shifts in betas of international assets.

Results show that the crisis has significantly scaled up the market betas of ASX All Ordinaries Index, Indian Rupee, Russian Rouble, Corn, Wheat and Platinum, which can feasibly foreshadow latent bubbles build-ups. The study also finds evidence in favour of value premium of Arisoy (2010) but here at a global level. By exhibiting aggressive betas, advanced economies can be viewed as value generators, while emerging markets can be viewed as growth propellers. From the perspective of leverage effects, currencies markets demonstrate a higher level of leverage effects relative to equities or commodities markets. Such a finding can signify that speculators are more active in currencies markets than in equities or commodities markets. Some Asian markets also witness leverage effects but only in the post-crisis era. Interestingly, dissipating leverage effects are noted for soft commodities.

The newly developed GFS-APT-GARCH model brings to light structural changes in betas for some assets which could potentially herald possible crises in international financial markets. For instance, for the Shanghai Stock Exchange Composite Index, there has been a drift from no impact before the crisis to a beta value of 0.2208 in the post-crisis era. Brazilian Real also posts no impact before the crisis but after the onset of the crisis, it depicts a beta value of 0.2513. Prior to the outbreak of the crisis, Gold triggered bullish forces to BSE 30 Index and ASX All Ordinaries Index. Such a finding confirms the fact that India constitutes the largest purchaser of gold, chiefly during wedding seasons. Similarly, Australia is often associated with being a commodity-related country. No effects of Gold are observed post the crisis, except for a slight negative impact on DJIA. Hence, Gold does not seem to cause adverse repercussions onto equities markets worldwide, again adding luster to structural shifts induced by the crisis.

In terms of risk aversion, the newly developed asset-specific risk aversion variable appears to be working fairly well with significant positive values noted for Indian Rupee, Gold and Silver in the post crisis episode. Such a finding implies that the higher the uncertainty in these markets, the better it is in terms of positive momentum, sending bouts of irrational exuberance. The implication of this finding is that during crisis times, assets deemed as less risky by the international investment community tend to experience bullish forces. The positive values noted for the abovementioned three assets can be explained by the fact that India is reputed for its significant contribution to world economic growth, while Gold and Silver constitute hard commodities widely lured by virtue of heightened upside risk to inflation, ensuing massive fiscal stimulus packages. Crisis-induced structural change is clearly recognisable in the case of JPY, which posts a change in sign between the two periods under investigation. Overall, the findings do suggest the need to explicitly incorporate the newly developed variable when modelling asset returns to shun off any model misspecification.

Under the general risk aversion level (VIX), findings suggest that VIX entails significantly pronounced effects in the case of soft commodities in the post-crisis episode. For hard commodities, negative impacts of VIX manifest only in the pre-crisis era, while no such effects prevail in the post-crisis period. Such impotency on hard commodities implies that investors have clung to hard commodities under periods of uncertainty so that VIX no longer exerts any downward influence on this asset type. Such mounting interest in hard commodities can also be caused by massive liquidity injections which favour commodities as the best inflation hedge. Finally, in terms of potential irrational exuberance, no major positive impacts of VIX manifest in the post-crisis period since findings show marginal positive influence in the range of 3% to 6% in the case of ASX All Ordinaries Index, Euro and British Pound.

Under inter-asset linkages based on DXY and MSCI influence on commodities, it surfaces that DXY triggers considerable negative impacts on hard commodities in both pre- and post- crisis periods, attributable to purchasing power effects. MSCI is found to unleash some negative effects (but lower in magnitude than the effects of DXY) in the case of Corn, Sugar and Gold but only after the crisis, most plausibly due to hedging motives. Before the crisis, MSCI generates positive effects based on prevalence of wealth effects. Overall, purchasing power effects predominate over both wealth and hedging motives based on robust impacts of DXY. In the case of MSCI and CRB effects on currencies, the former mainly affects currencies. In addition, strong evidence prevails as to a crisis-induced substitution effect, away from global equities/ commodities towards BRICS countries' currencies. Above all, some possible euphoria could exist for Australian Dollar and New Zealand Dollar based on the considerable rise in post-crisis impact of MSCI on these two specific assets. Strong evidence also exists as to MSCI mainly influencing currencies so that global equities rather than global commodities have considerable grip over currencies movements. Finally, with regards to DXY and CRB impact on equities, no major effect of CRB on equities is identified while DXY generates considerable positive impact on equities. As the US dollar gains value it encourages positive world growth, which in turn triggers positive momentum to equities markets performance. Impotency effects for Hang Seng Index and Shanghai Stock Exchange Composite Index can be explained by the fact that they cling to pegged currency regimes. Structural changes induced by the crisis, along with natural phenomena, are also noted in the case of the Japanese stock market, which registers a very strong positive impact of DXY, although only in the pre-crisis era.

Overall, findings do suggest the existence of crisis-induced irrational exuberance, but only in certain assets. However, it can be argued that such overshooting effects manifest based on the world's limited assets, so that inter-repercussions are most susceptible to manifest. In that respect, the crisis-induced irrational exuberance, uncovered for some assets, can be regarded as being rational. The flip side of the coin is that the existence of these irrational exuberances can be a double-edged sword. Indeed, if the world economic recovery gains significant momentum, this can re-channel a drastic reversal chiefly for the crisis-induced coveted assets. Such an event would definitely generate painful adjustments. Policy-wise, this suggests that sustained and consistent growth is better than erratically excessive growth which may encapsulate latent instability risks.

Appendix A. Summary Statistics

Table 3.1: Summary Statistics

Table 3.1: Summary Statistics							
	Mean	Median	Maximum	Minimum	Std. Dev.	Skewness	Kurtosis
ASX All Ordinaries Index	0.0007	0.0025	0.0844	-0.1623	0.0222	-0.9258	8.8051
BSE 30 Index	0.0023	0.0050	0.1408	-0.1595	0.0354	-0.3618	4.9908
CAC-40 Index	-0.0004	0.0014	0.1324	-0.2216	0.0329	-0.5335	7.3299
DAX Index	0.0004	0.0033	0.1612	-0.2161	0.0358	-0.2797	6.6952
Dow Jones Industrial Average	0.0005	0.0021	0.1129	-0.1815	0.0267	-0.5636	8.4385
FTSE 100 Index	0.0001	0.0017	0.1341	-0.2105	0.0269	-0.6104	11.3560
Hang Seng Index	0.0009	0.0011	0.1243	-0.1632	0.0342	0.0172	4.7828
Nasdaq Composite Index	0.0001	0.0009	0.2575	-0.2530	0.0394	-0.0809	9.6676
Nikkei Stock Average 225	-0.0007	0.0009	0.1698	-0.2433	0.0327	-0.6113	9.4366
S&P 500 Index	0.0002	0.0008	0.1203	-0.1820	0.0280	-0.3978	7.7894
Shanghai Stock Exchange Composite Index	0.0012	0.0000	0.1496	-0.1384	0.0354	0.2303	4.9063
Australian Dollar	0.0009	0.0024	0.0641	-0.1590	0.0196	-1.2005	11.3552
Brazilian Real	0.0003	-0.0018	0.1485	-0.0870	0.0235	1.0865	8.3907
Canadian Dollar	-0.0005	-0.0007	0.0993	-0.0567	0.0140	0.9374	9.4693
Swiss Francs	-0.0007	-0.0001	0.1212	-0.0621	0.0160	0.6065	8.0813
Euro	0.0005	0.0003	0.0512	-0.0571	0.0148	-0.2271	3.7790
British Pound	0.0000	0.0005	0.0534	-0.0833	0.0139	-0.4853	6.3866
Indian Rupee	0.0004	-0.0002	0.0458	-0.0458	0.0081	0.3423	8.5360
Japanese Yen	-0.0004	-0.0001	0.0465	-0.0718	0.0146	-0.2559	4.1558
New Zealand Dollar	0.0009	0.0032	0.0650	-0.1022	0.0199	-0.6743	5.1870
Russian Rouble	0.0003	-0.0001	0.1149	-0.0454	0.0114	2.6527	26.9941
South African Rand	0.0008	-0.0005	0.1132	-0.1219	0.0251	0.5201	5.6999
Coffee	-0.0009	-0.0032	0.1750	-0.1400	0.0402	0.1314	3.6180
Corn	0.0007	0.0000	0.2022	-0.1538	0.0389	0.0569	5.0887
Gold	0.0032	0.0058	0.1347	-0.0931	0.0264	-0.2150	4.8169
Platinum	0.0025	0.0046	0.1152	-0.1438	0.0331	-0.4391	5.4564
Silver	0.0039	0.0063	0.2208	-0.2721	0.0464	-0.8281	7.6153
Sugar	0.0036	0.0031	0.1839	-0.1748	0.0497	-0.0641	3.5745
Wheat	-0.0001	-0.0027	0.1554	-0.1501	0.0422	0.2046	3.7689
CRB	0.0019	0.0035	0.0880	-0.1483	0.0261	-0.7243	5.9353
DXY	-0.0003	-0.0011	0.0810	-0.0406	0.0127	0.6492	5.9563
MSCI	0.0001	0.0020	0.1234	-0.2005	0.0270	-0.7329	9.3895
VIX	0.0038	0.0064	0.3310	-0.2034	0.0515	-0.0881	6.2533

Appendix B. Results

Notes to Table 3.2:
***, ** and * denote statistical significance at the 1, 5 and 10 per cent, respectively. In the pre-crisis periods, the ARCH term under symmetric GARCH has been negative so that recourse has been made towards IGARCH. Similarly, due to negative ARCH term under asymmetric GARCH models in the pre-crisis analysis, EGARCH has been used. Under EGARCH, there are no such ARCH and GARCH terms, since the coefficient for the log variance in EGARCH has some correspondence with the sum of the ARCH and GARCH terms in TGARCH (See Carol Alexandra, 2008, Practical Econometrics). In that respect, only leverage terms have been reported.

Notes to Table 3.3:
***, ** and * denote statistical significance at the 1, 5 and 10 per cent, respectively. In the pre-crisis periods, due to negative ARCH term under asymmetric GARCH analysis, EGARCH has been used. Under EGARCH, there are no such ARCH and GARCH terms since the coefficient for the log variance in EGARCH has some correspondence with the sum of the ARCH and GARCH terms in TGARCH (See Carol Alexandra, 2008, Practical Econometrics). In that respect, only leverage terms have been reported.

Notes to Table 3.4:
***, ** and * denote statistical significance at the 1, 5 and 10 per cent, respectively. In the pre-crisis periods, the ARCH term under symmetric GARCH has been negative so that recourse has been made towards IGARCH. Similarly, due to negative ARCH term under asymmetric GARCH models, EGARCH has been used in the pre-crisis period. Under EGARCH, there are no such ARCH and GARCH terms, since the coefficient for the log variance in EGARCH has some correspondence with the sum of the ARCH and GARCH terms in TGARCH (See Carol Alexandra, 2008, Practical Econometrics). In that respect, only leverage terms have been reported.

Notes to Table 3.5:
***, ** and * denote statistical significance at the 1, 5 and 10 per cent, respectively. Due to negative ARCH term under asymmetric GARCH models in the pre-crisis period, recourse is made towards EGARCH. Under EGARCH, there are no such ARCH and GARCH terms, since the coefficient for the log variance in EGARCH has some correspondence with the sum of the ARCH and GARCH terms in TGARCH (See Carol Alexandra, 2008, Practical Econometrics). In that respect, only leverage terms have been reported.

Notes to Table 3.8:
***, ** and * denote statistical significance at the 1, 5 and 10 per cent, respectively. In the post-crisis periods, the ARCH term under asymmetric GARCH has been negative, so that recourse has been made towards EGARCH. Under

EGARCH, there are no such ARCH and GARCH terms, since the coefficient for the log variance in EGARCH has some correspondence with the sum of the ARCH and GARCH terms in TGARCH (See Carol Alexandra, 2008, Practical Econometrics). In that respect, only leverage terms have been reported.

Notes to Table 3.9:
***, ** and * denote statistical significance at the 1, 5 and 10 per cent, respectively. In the post-crisis periods, due to negative GARCH term under symmetric and asymmetric GARCH analysis, IGARCH and EGARCH have been used, respectively. Under EGARCH, there are no such ARCH and GARCH terms, since the coefficient for the log variance in EGARCH has some correspondence with the sum of the ARCH and GARCH terms in TGARCH (See Carol Alexandra, 2008, Practical Econometrics). In that respect, only leverage terms have been reported.

Notes to Table 3.10:
***, ** and * denote statistical significance at the 1, 5 and 10 per cent, respectively. In the pre-crisis periods, the ARCH term under symmetric GARCH has been negative, so that recourse has been made towards IGARCH. Similarly, due to negative ARCH term under asymmetric GARCH analysis, EGARCH has been used in the pre-crisis period. Under EGARCH, there are no such ARCH and GARCH terms, since the coefficient for the log variance in EGARCH has some correspondence with the sum of the ARCH and GARCH terms in TGARCH (See Carol Alexandra, 2008, Practical Econometrics). In that respect, only leverage terms have been reported.

Notes to Table 3.11:
***, ** and * denote statistical significance at the 1, 5 and 10 per cent, respectively. In both the pre- and post-crisis periods, due to negative ARCH term under both symmetric and asymmetric GARCH analysis, IGARCH and EGARCH have been used, respectively. Under EGARCH, there are no such ARCH and GARCH terms, since the coefficient for the log variance in EGARCH has some correspondence with the sum of the ARCH and GARCH terms in TGARCH (See Carol Alexandra, 2008, Practical Econometrics). In that respect, only leverage terms have been reported.

Notes to Table 3.12:
***, ** and * denote statistical significance at the 1, 5 and 10 per cent, respectively. GARCH models have been used in case of symmetric analysis and TGARCH applied to capture any asymmetric effects.

Notes to Table 3.13:
***, ** and * denote statistical significance at the 1, 5 and 10 per cent, respectively. In the pre-crisis period, EGARCH models have been used due to violation of GARCH terms under TGARCH model. Under EGARCH, there are no such ARCH and GARCH terms, since the coefficient for the log variance in

EGARCH has some correspondence with the sum of the ARCH and GARCH terms in TGARCH (See Carol Alexandra, 2008, Practical Econometrics). In that respect, only leverage components have been reported.

Notes to Table 3.14:
***, ** and * denote statistical significance at the 1, 5 and 10 per cent, respectively. In the pre-crisis period for symmetric GARCH model, the sum of ARCH and GARCH terms exceeded one so that IGARCH have been used. Similarly, in the case of asymmetric GARCH models in the pre-crisis period, EGARCH models have been used due to same violation. Under EGARCH, there are no such ARCH and GARCH terms, since the coefficient for the log variance in EGARCH has some correspondence with the sum of the ARCH and GARCH terms in TGARCH (See Carol Alexandra, 2008, Practical Econometrics). In that respect, only leverage components have been reported.

Notes to Table 3.15:
***, ** and * denote statistical significance at the 1, 5 and 10 per cent, respectively. In the post-crisis period, the ARCH term under asymmetric GARCH has been negative so that recourse has been made towards EGARCH. Under EGARCH, there are no such ARCH and GARCH terms, since the coefficient for the log variance in EGARCH has some correspondence with the sum of the ARCH and GARCH terms in TGARCH (See Carol Alexandra, 2008, Practical Econometrics). In that respect, only leverage components have been reported.

Notes to Table 3.16:
***, ** and * denote statistical significance at the 1, 5 and 10 per cent, respectively. For pre-crisis period, due to negative GARCH terms, IGARCH has been used for symmetric GARCH analysis while EGARCH has been employed for asymmetric GARCH analysis. Due to negative sign obtained under ARCH term for TGARCH in the post-crisis period, EGARCH models have thereby been used. Under EGARCH, there are no such ARCH and GARCH terms, since the coefficient for the log variance in EGARCH has some correspondence with the sum of the ARCH and GARCH terms in TGARCH (See Carol Alexandra, 2008, Practical Econometrics). In that respect, only leverage components have been reported.

Notes to Table 3.28:
***, ** and * denote statistical significance at the 1, 5 and 10 per cent, respectively. IGARCH has been used in case of symmetric GARCH for both periods. TGARCH has been used to capture the asymmetric effects in the pre-crisis era while EGARCH has been employed for the post analysis case. Under EGARCH, there are no such ARCH and GARCH terms, since the coefficient for the log variance in EGARCH has some correspondence with the sum of the ARCH and GARCH terms in TGARCH (See Carol Alexandra, 2008, Practical Econometrics). In that respect, only leverage terms have been reported.

Table 3.2: Equity Market Analysis under APT-GARCH models: US- S&P 500 Index

	Pre-Crisis Period: US-SP					Post-Crisis Period: US-SP				
	GARCH	GARCH.HL	AGARCH	AGARCH.HL	Average	GARCH	GARCH.HL	AGARCH	AGARCH.HL	Average
Beta	1.0286 (73.3452)***	1.0224 (73.1779) ***	1.0282 (76.1763) ***	1.0264 (77.3841) ***	1.0264	1.0321 (53.8193) ***	1.0366 (53.4925) ***	1.0308 (53.8467) ***	1.0406 (53.3229) ***	1.0350
DXY	0.2289 (9.2189) ***	0.2264 (9.2310) ***	0.2329 (9.6948) ***	0.2457 (10.2191) ***	0.2335	0.3397 (7.3532) ***	0.3375 (7.4399) ***	0.3384 (7.3379) ***	0.3413 (7.5101) ***	0.3392
GOLD	-0.0442 (-3.5699) ***	-0.0436 (-3.5448) ***	-0.0400 (-3.2811) ***	-0.0339 (-2.8490) ***	-0.0404	-0.0154 (-0.7470)	-0.0234 (-1.1287)	-0.0160 (-0.7707)	-0.0228 (-1.1076)	Impotent
CRB	-0.0392 (-2.3036) **	-0.0366 (-2.1708) *	-0.0336 (-1.9384) *	-0.0328 (-1.8821)*	-0.0356	0.0166 (0.5304)	0.0246 (0.7628)	0.0170 (0.5403)	0.0249 (0.7717)	Impotent
VIX	-0.0023 (-0.2905)	-0.0024 (-0.3165)	-0.0050 (-0.6403)	-0.0056 (-0.7195)	Impotent	-0.0192 (-0.9915)	-0.0230 (-1.1591)	-0.0195 (-1.0006)	-0.0228 (-1.1360)	Impotent
HL		-0.0366 (-1.8717)*		-0.0297 (-1.5924) *	-0.0332		0.0448 (1.9722) **		0.0506 (2.0439) **	0.0477
Adj. R²	0.9156	0.9153	0.9157	0.9156	0.9156	0.9406	0.9411	0.9406	0.9410	0.9408
ARCH	0.0412 (3.0632) **	0.0387 (2.9650) **			0.0400	0.1448 (2.1312) **	0.1476 (2.1307) **	0.1344 (1.6236)	0.1795 (1.7334) *	0.1571
GARCH	0.9588 (71.3150) ***	0.9613 (73.6429) ***			0.9601	0.8079 (9.8712) ***	0.8057 (9.9794) ***	0.8016 (8.6794) ***	0.8184 (10.0912) ***	0.8084
LEVERAGE			-0.0063 (-0.4113)	0.0088 (1.3985)	Impotent			0.0288 (0.1816)	-0.0706 (-0.4841)	Impotent
Log likelihood	1449.24	1450.74	1458.050	1460.63		778.49	779.91	778.51	780.05	
Distribution	Student-t	Student-t	Student-t	Student-t		Student-t	Student-t	Student-t	Student-t	

Table 3.3: Equity Market Analysis under APT-GARCH models: US- Nasdaq Composite Index

	Pre-Crisis Period: US-NAS					Post-Crisis Period: US-NAS				
	GARCH	GARCH.HL	AGARCH	AGARCH.HL	Average	GARCH	GARCH.HL	AGARCH	AGARCH.HL	Average
Beta	1.2758 (36.5924)***	1.2731 (35.9017)***	1.2750 (36.9727)***	1.2680 (35.9859)***	1.2730	1.1071 (38.0092)***	1.1193 (36.3320)***	1.1086 (38.4378)***	1.1188 (36.3786)***	1.1135
DXY	0.2956 (4.2331)***	0.2939 (4.1622)***	0.3021 (4.4690)***	0.3043 (4.4729)***	0.2990	0.4646 (7.4378)***	0.4704 (7.5620)***	0.4632 (7.3147)***	0.4697 (7.4458)***	0.4670
GOLD	-0.0635 (-1.9010)**	-0.0628 (-1.8718)**	-0.0642 (-1.9661)*	-0.0579 (-1.6425)*	-0.0621	0.0072 (0.2459)	-0.0085 (-0.2866)	0.0036 (0.1251)	-0.0087 (-0.2931)	Impotent
CRB	-0.0636 (-1.1475)	-0.0634 (-1.1404)	-0.0516 (-1.1632)	-0.0528 (-0.9862)	Impotent	-0.0335 (-0.7021)	-0.0189 (-0.3853)	-0.0325 (-0.6751)	-0.0191 (-0.3880)	Impotent
VIX	-0.0206 (-0.8632)	-0.0200 (-0.8354)	-0.0289 (-1.5672)	-0.0274 (-1.1817)	Impotent	0.0028 (0.1020)	-0.0023 (-0.0830)	0.0034 (0.1230)	-0.0019 (-0.0707)	Impotent
HL		-0.0198 (-0.4592)		-0.0341 (-0.8042)	Impotent		0.0758 (2.2054)**		0.0708 (1.8154)*	0.0733
Adj. R^2	0.6025	0.6027	0.6017	0.6027	0.6024	0.8794	0.8799	0.8792	0.8799	0.8796
ARCH	0.0009 (0.1281)	0.0001 (0.0162)				0.1961 (2.2913)***	0.2111 (2.3582)**	0.1830 (1.8052)*	0.2006 (1.9023)*	0.1977
GARCH	0.9847 (102.752)***	0.9857 (102.9405)***			0.9852	0.7519 (7.8493)***	0.7364 (7.2206)***	0.6573 (5.3590)***	0.7175 (6.4512)***	0.7158
LEVERAGE			-0.0503 (-4.7195)***	-0.0467 (-2.2626)**	-0.0485			0.2135 (1.0822)	0.0501 (0.3048)	Impotent
Log likelihood	1032.66	1032.74	1035.04	1035.70		688.49	690.47	689.03	690.52	
Distribution	Student-t	Student-t	Student-t	Student-t		Student-t	Student-t	Student-t	Student-t	

Table 3.4: Equity Market Analysis under APT-GARCH models: US- Dow Jones Industrial Average

	Pre-Crisis Period: US-DJI					Post-Crisis Period: US-DJI				
	GARCH	GARCH.HL	AGARCH	AGARCH.HL	Average	GARCH	GARCH.HL	AGARCH	AGARCH.HL	Average
Beta	0.9724 (52.4057)***	0.9752 (51.8946)***	0.9680 (56.9868)***	0.9784 (54.7927)***	0.9735	0.9351 (39.6703)***	0.9343 (45.8248)***	0.9281 (40.4065)***	0.9313 (44.6357)***	0.9322
DXY	0.2359 (6.3693)***	0.2383 (6.4737)***	0.2517 (7.0277)***	0.2455 (6.6605)***	0.2429	0.2604 (4.7522)***	0.2375 (4.8069)***	0.2399 (4.5687)***	0.2323 (4.6186)***	0.2425
GOLD	-0.0507 (-2.8549)***	-0.0512 (-2.8975)***	-0.0443 (-2.6241)***	-0.0474 (-2.7682)***	-0.0484	-0.0298 (-1.3204)	-0.0518 (-2.4140)**	-0.0303 (-1.3628)	-0.0521 (-2.4005)**	-0.0520
CRB	-0.0629 (-2.7222)***	-0.0659 (-2.8575)***	-0.0626 (-2.4961)**	-0.0650 (-2.5733)**	-0.0641	0.0377 (0.9646)	0.0379 (1.0313)	0.0432 (1.1417)	0.0398 (1.0807)	Impotent
VIX	-0.0142 (-1.4148)	-0.0139 (-1.3690)	-0.0114 (-1.0614)	-0.0125 (-1.1592)	Impotent	-0.0519 (-2.4032)**	-0.0503 (-2.2104)**	-0.0560 (-2.7157)***	-0.0527 (-2.2836)**	-0.0527
HL		0.0170 (0.9663)		0.0254 (1.4985)	Impotent		0.0724 (3.9417)***		0.0692 (3.2715)***	0.0708
Adj. R²	0.8181	0.8180	0.8179	0.8182	0.8181	0.9025	0.9026	0.9015	0.9024	0.9023
ARCH	0.0403 (3.0012)***	0.0368 (2.8546)***			0.0386	0.1361 (2.1447)**	0.1605 (2.3565)**	0.0994 (1.6501)*	0.1259 (1.4078)	0.1320
GARCH	0.9597 (71.4402)***	0.9632 (74.7646)***			0.9615	0.8280 (9.9822)***	0.8073 (9.8254)***	0.8153 (10.6349)***	0.8115 (9.9082)***	0.8155
LEVERAGE			-0.0086 (-0.6441)	-0.0093 (-0.5737)	Impotent			0.1257 (1.4362)	0.0572 (0.5878)	Impotent
Log likelihood	1313.32	1313.72	1323.25	1324.13		743.69	749.56	744.69	749.78	
Distribution	Student-t	Student-t	Student-t	Student-t		GED	GED	GED	GED	

Table 3.5: Equity Market Analysis under APT-GARCH models: FTSE 100 Index

	Pre-Crisis Period: UK					Post-Crisis Period: UK				
	GARCH	GARCH.HL	AGARCH	AGARCH.HL	Average	GARCH	GARCH.HL	AGARCH	AGARCH.HL	Average
Beta	0.8995 (40.9050)***	0.8936 (37.4300) ***	0.8730 (39.3801) ***	0.8607 (34.6187) ***	0.8817	0.9618 (38.1985) ***	0.9622 (37.5799) ***	0.9616 (38.2958) ***	0.9593 (37.5512) ***	0.9612
GBP	-0.3583 (-5.3520) ***	-0.3560 (-5.3124) ***	-0.3738 (-5.5946) ***	-0.3579 (-5.7043) ***	-0.3615	-0.2973 (-5.3304) ***	-0.2960 (-5.1108) ***	-0.2885 (-4.9421) ***	-0.2953 (-5.0066) ***	-0.2943
DXY	0.2637 (3.8960) ***	0.2633 (3.8941) ***	0.2228 (3.2077)***	0.2241 (3.8494) ***	0.2435	0.2905 (4.2657) ***	0.2912 (4.1968) ***	0.2989 (4.3727) ***	0.2954 (4.2878) ***	0.2940
GOLD	0.0329 (1.3031)	0.0329 (1.2906)	0.0395 (1.7212) *	0.0244 (0.9919)	Impotent	0.0263 (1.0818)	0.0257 (0.9632)	0.0178 (0.7229)	0.0205 (0.7770)	Impotent
CRB	-0.0302 (-0.8548)	-0.0279 (-0.7877)	-0.0445 (-1.3044)	-0.0362 (-1.0136)	Impotent	0.0537 (1.3869)	0.0543 (1.3372)	0.0566 (1.4805)	0.0532 (1.3401)	Impotent
VIX	0.0217 (1.2870)	0.0213 (1.2612)	0.0263 (1.6270)*	0.0285 (1.7740) *	0.0274	0.0111 (0.5410)	0.0107 (0.5072)	0.0112 (0.5698)	0.0132 (0.6483)	Impotent
HL		-0.0268 (-0.8308)		-0.0751 (-2.1935) **	-0.0510		0.0028 (0.0902)		-0.0143 (-0.4613)	Impotent
Adj. R²	0.7219	0.7220	0.7229	0.7226	0.7224	0.9025	0.9021	0.9029	0.9021	0.9024
ARCH	0.0466 (2.1481) **	0.0502 (2.0512) **			0.0484	0.2837 (2.6431) ***	0.2813 (2.6189) ***	0.1777 (1.5974)	0.1721 (1.5813)	0.2287
GARCH	0.9262 (35.0964) ***	0.9218 (30.3493) ***			0.9240	0.6227 (5.2000) ***	0.6218 (5.1838) ***	0.6248 (5.4162) ***	0.6255 (5.4395) ***	0.6237
LEVERAGE			-0.1067 (-2.1122) **	-0.0979 (-1.6030) *	-0.1023			0.2256 (1.2879)	0.2535 (1.3355)	Impotent
Log likelihood	1232.26	1232.54	1233.21	1233.21		732.85	732.85	733.98	734.08	733.44
Distribution	Student-t	Student-t	Student-t	Student-t		Student-t	Student-t	Student-t	Student-t	Student-t

Table 3.6: Equity Market Analysis under APT-GARCH models: DAX Index

	Pre-Crisis Period: DAX					Post-Crisis Period: DAX				
	GARCH	GARCH.HL	AGARCH	AGARCH.HL	Average	GARCH	GARCH.HL	AGARCH	AGARCH.HL	Average
Beta	1.3135 (40.2746)***	1.3244 (37.9031)***	1.2961 (39.8250)***	1.3089 (37.0056)***	1.3107	1.1309 (32.2521)***	1.1335 (31.8742)***	1.0909 (34.4616)***	1.0917 (33.8327)***	1.1118
EUR	-0.6586 (-11.2461)***	-0.6693 (-11.2760)***	-0.6449 (-11.0489)***	-0.6565 (-11.0378)***	-0.6573	-0.3970 (-4.9000)***	-0.3950 (-4.6676)***	-0.3954 (-5.8865)***	-0.3989 (-5.8522)***	-0.3966
GOLD	-0.0239 (-0.7064)	-0.0242 (-0.7174)	-0.0237 (-0.6886)	-0.0245 (-0.7157)	Impotent	-0.0025 (-0.0605)	-0.0057 (-0.1351)	0.0261 (0.8372)	0.0237 (0.7375)	Impotent
CRB	-0.0440 (-0.8955)	-0.0465 (-0.9467)	-0.0477 (-0.9477)	-0.0475 (-0.9490)	Impotent	0.0685 (0.9509)	0.0725 (1.0057)	0.0402 (0.6661)	0.0450 (0.7356)	Impotent
VIX	0.00008 (0.0045)	-0.0002 (-0.0113)	0.0030 (0.1536)	0.0014 (0.0724)	Impotent	-0.0613 (-1.5967)	-0.0635 (-1.6527)*	-0.0437 (-1.4283)	-0.0455 (-1.4630)	Impotent
HL		0.0611 (1.8225)*		0.0484 (1.3430)	0.0611		0.0268 (0.7049)		0.0150 (0.3883)	Impotent
Adj. R^2	0.7474	0.7462	0.7467	0.7461	0.7466	0.8627	0.8621	0.8595	0.8588	0.8608
ARCH	0.1346 (3.1370)***	0.1393 (3.0214)***	0.1090 (2.0889)**	0.1113 (1.8959)*	0.1236	0.0788 (2.0044)**	0.0792 (1.8196)*			0.0790
GARCH	0.8374 (17.2424)***	0.8325 (16.1459)***	0.7889 (13.9164)***	0.7999 (14.0545)***	0.8147	0.8077 (6.2770)***	0.8039 (5.9537)***			0.8058
LEVERAGE			0.1396 (1.6724)*	0.1040 (1.2511)	0.1396			-0.0560 (-0.6820)	-0.0516 (-0.6041)	Impotent
Log likelihood	1092.19	1093.47	1093.45	1094.19		631.32	631.52	638.36	638.42	
Distribution	Student-t	Student-t	Student-t	Student-t		Student-t	Student-t	Student-t	Student-t	

***, ** and * denote statistical significance at the 1, 5 and 10 per cent, respectively. DXY has been overlooked since it has been found to be highly correlated with EUR. In the post-crisis periods, the ARCH term under asymmetric GARCH has been negative, so that recourse has been made towards EGARCH. Under EGARCH, there are no such ARCH and GARCH terms since the coefficient for the log variance in EGARCH has some correspondence with the sum of the ARCH and GARCH terms in TGARCH (See Carol Alexandra, 2008, Practical Econometrics). In that respect, only leverage terms have been reported.

Table 3.7: Equity Market Analysis under APT-GARCH models: CAC-40 Index

	Pre-Crisis Period: France					Post-Crisis Period: France				
	GARCH	GARCH.HL	AGARCH	AGARCH.HL	Average	GARCH	GARCH.HL	AGARCH	AGARCH.HL	Average
Beta	1.310 (41.0441)***	1.1358 (39.2898) ***	1.1259 (41.2602) ***	1.1323 (39.4429) ***	1.1323	1.1643 (36.2465) ***	1.1552 (35.3286) ***	1.1694 (36.1831) ***	1.1592 (35.2591) ***	1.1620
EUR	-0.6657 (-14.8923) ***	-0.6689 (-14.7123) ***	-0.6598 (-14.7902) ***	-0.6652 (-14.3884) ***	-0.6649	-0.2993 (-5.0972) ***	-0.2955 (-5.1080) ***	-0.2970 (-5.0901) ***	-0.2933 (-5.0869) ***	-0.2963
GOLD	-0.0018 (-0.0619)	-0.0018 (-0.0615)	-0.0025 (-0.0871)	-0.0022 (-0.0774)	Impotent	-0.0390 (-1.2189)	-0.0327 (-0.9871)	-0.0393 (-1.1988)	-0.0335 (-0.9847)	Impotent
CRB	0.0038 (0.1116)	0.0006 (0.0184)	0.0039 (0.1123)	0.0014 (0.0409)	Impotent	0.0398 (0.7695)	0.0374 (0.6965)	0.0391 (0.7313)	0.0369 (0.6709)	Impotent
VIX	0.0027 (0.1815)	0.0030 (0.2026)	0.0037 (0.2532)	0.0033 (0.2238)	Impotent	-0.0333 (-1.1795)	-0.0294 (-1.0139)	-0.0340 (-1.1642)	-0.0298 (-0.9994)	Impotent
HL		0.0294 (0.9915)		0.0249 (0.7477)	Impotent		-0.0506 (-1.4442)		-0.0478 (-1.3437)	Impotent
Adj. R²	0.7789	0.7783	0.7787	0.7783	0.7786	0.8800	0.8797	0.8798	0.8796	0.8798
ARCH	0.1679 (2.6374) ***	0.1774 (2.6408) ***	0.1627 (1.6775) *	0.1706 (1.5899)	0.1693	0.1177 (1.3284)	0.1114 (1.2725)	0.1433 (1.0536)	0.1255 (1.0898)	Impotent
GARCH	0.7599 (10.4611) ***	0.7475 (9.8990) ***	0.7059 (8.2087) ***	0.7238 (8.6495) ***	0.7343	0.8087 (6.2365) ***	0.8137 (6.2165) ***	0.8198 (6.225) ***	0.8253 (6.3320) ***	0.8169
LEVERAGE			0.0807 (0.6855)	0.0416 (0.3248)	Impotent			-0.0777 (-0.6292)	-0.0608 (-0.5671)	Impotent
Log likelihood	1182.25	1182.61	1182.44	1182.66		659.51	660.45	659.83	660.65	
Distribution	Student-t	Student-t	Student-t	Student-t		Student-t	Student-t	Student-t	Student-t	

***, ** and * denote statistical significance at the 1, 5 and 10 per cent, respectively. DXY has been overlooked since it has been found to be highly correlated with EUR.

Table 3.8: Equity Market Analysis under APT-GARCH models: Shanghai Stock Exchange Composite Index

	Pre-Crisis Period: China					Post-Crisis Period: China				
	GARCH	GARCH.HL	AGARCH	AGARCH.HL	Average	GARCH	GARCH.HL	AGARCH	AGARCH.HL	Average
Beta	0.0941 (1.4056)	0.0928 (1.3869)	0.0958 (1.4292)	0.0944 (1.4108)	Impotent	0.2784 (2.9928) ***	0.2802 (3.0148) ***	0.1467 (1.6205) *	0.1778 (2.0089) **	0.2208
CNY	-3.9669 (-4.6495)***	-4.1886 (-4.7893) ***	-4.0482 (-4.7241) ***	-4.2810 (-4.8631) ***	-4.1212	2.6513 (3.0059) ***	2.7087 (2.9328) ***	2.5262 (2.7689)***	2.2700 (2.5086) **	2.5391
DXY	-0.1627 (-1.2114)	-0.1612 (-1.2045)	-0.1586 (-1.1854)	-0.1569 (-1.1778)	Impotent	0.0975 (0.4422)	0.0921 (0.4166)	0.0091 (0.0444)	0.0500 (0.2318)	Impotent
GOLD	0.0797 (1.0501)	0.0811 (1.0717)	0.0820 (1.0805)	0.0837 (1.1060)	Impotent	0.1453 (1.6588) *	0.1457 (1.6649) *	0.0919 (1.0676)	0.1115 (1.2661)	0.1455
CRB	0.0203 (0.2138)	0.0199 (0.2099)	0.0187 (0.1974)	0.0182 (0.1925)	Impotent	0.1765 (1.0888)	0.1799 (1.1041)	0.2225 (1.4781)	0.2036 (1.2604)	Impotent
VIX	0.0010 (0.0245)	0.0011 (0.0273)	0.0008 (0.0212)	0.0009 (0.0243)	Impotent	-0.0137 (-0.1601)	-0.0177 (-0.2046)	0.0129 (0.1622)	0.0074 (0.0861)	Impotent
HL		-0.0255 (-0.3749)		-0.0286 (-0.4162)	Impotent		0.0172 (0.2671)		-0.0453 (-1.4142)	Impotent
Adj. R²	0.0028	-0.0039	0.0022	0.0010		0.0471	0.0455	0.0465	0.0291	
ARCH	0.0911 (1.9754) **	0.0929 (1.9752) **	0.0830 (1.7430) *	0.0847 (1.7592) *	0.0879	0.0579 (1.8830) *	0.0575 (1.8750) *	0.2225 (1.4781)	0.2036 (1.2604)	0.0577
GARCH	0.8041 (9.3260) ***	0.8009 (9.2081) ***	0.8016 (9.3526) ***	0.7980 (9.2473) ***	0.8012	0.9319 (26.8923) ***	0.9323 (26.8819) ***	0.0129 (0.1622)	0.0074 (0.0861)	0.9321
LEVERAGE			0.0286 (0.4202)	0.0310 (0.4348)	Impotent			-0.0638 (-2.3370)**	-0.0739 (-2.5701)**	-0.0689
Log likelihood	828.56	828.60	828.65	828.70		428.06	428.13	433.98	434.07	
Distribution	Student-t	Student-t	Student-t	Student-t		Student-t	Student-t	Student-t	Student-t	

Table 3.9: Equity Market Analysis under APT-GARCH models: NIKKEI Stock Average 225 Index

	Pre-Crisis Period: Japan					Post-Crisis Period: Japan				
	GARCH	GARCH.HL	AGARCH	AGARCH.HL	Average	GARCH	GARCH.HL	AGARCH	AGARCH.HL	Average
Beta	0.8136 (16.0284)***	0.8089 (15.6857)***	0.8403 (16.3964)***	0.8319 (16.0214)***	0.8237	0.7591 (11.5451)***	0.7606 (11.5711)***	0.7449 (11.7252)***	0.7478 (12.0742)***	0.7531
JPY	-0.0127 (-0.1337)	-0.0057 (-0.0602)	-0.0196 (-0.2040)	-0.0131 (-0.1370)	Impotent	0.6084 (5.4146)***	0.5795 (4.9824)***	0.6245 (6.2740)***	0.5741 (5.3691)***	0.5966
DXY	0.4067 (3.3577)***	0.4004 (3.2986)***	0.4423 (3.6900)***	0.4317 (3.5903)***	0.4203	-0.0064 (-0.0374)	0.0258 (0.1465)	-0.1156 (-0.7169)	-0.0701 (-0.4283)	Impotent
GOLD	0.0408 (0.6964)	0.0440 (0.7472)	0.0421 (0.7003)	0.0436 (0.7266)	Impotent	-0.0567 (-0.9823)	-0.0443 (-0.7573)	-0.0753 (-1.4358)	-0.0600 (-1.1644)	Impotent
CRB	0.0744 (0.9512)	0.0756 (0.9699)	0.0760 (0.9667)	0.0784 (1.0012)	Impotent	0.0135 (0.1480)	0.0077 (0.0852)	0.0097 (0.1151)	-0.0046 (-0.0559)	Impotent
VIX	0.0060 (0.1806)	0.0066 (0.1982)	0.0092 (0.2793)	0.0089 (0.2645)	Impotent	-0.0336 (-0.7346)	-0.0317 (-0.6945)	-0.0364 (-0.8550)	-0.0268 (-0.6349)	Impotent
HL		-0.0927 (-1.3844)		-0.0717 (-1.0479)	Impotent		-0.0974 (-1.4897) *		-0.1086 (-1.8630) *	-0.1030
Adj. R^2	0.2293	0.2299	0.2248	0.2260	0.2275	0.7125	0.7131	0.7126	0.7129	0.7128
ARCH	0.1757 (2.5628) ***	0.1760 (2.5214) ***	0.2719 (2.5080) ***	0.2481 (2.4689) ***	0.2179	0.0235 (1.5851)	0.0240 (1.5088)			Impotent
GARCH	0.6781 (5.4216) ***	0.6696 (5.1972) ***	0.6176 (3.7790) ***	0.6261 (3.8287) ***	0.6479	0.9765 (65.7320)***	0.9760 (61.2927)***			0.9763
LEVERAGE			-0.2029 (-1.5728)	-0.1702 (-1.3076)	Impotent			-0.1012 (-0.8708)	-0.1456 (-1.2008)	Impotent
Log likelihood	905.92	906.63	906.92	907.32		562.43	563.29	565.52	566.82	
Distribution	Student-t	Student-t	Student-t	Student-t		Student-t	Student-t	Student-t	Student-t	

Table 3.10: Equity Market Analysis under APT-GARCH models: BSE 30 Index

	Pre-Crisis Period: India					Post-Crisis Period: India				
	GARCH	GARCH.HL	AGARCH	AGARCH.HL	Average	GARCH	GARCH.HL	AGARCH	AGARCH.HL	Average
Beta	0.5907 (8.6926)***	0.5823 (8.4737)***	0.5785 (9.6902)***	0.5706 (9.3728)***	0.5805	0.5438 (7.5823)***	0.5523 (7.5638)***	0.5410 (7.5910)***	0.5485 (7.5784)***	0.5464
INR	-1.3003 (-4.9947)***	-1.3326 (-4.9317)***	-1.3324 (-4.4721)***	-1.3776 (-4.4817)***	-1.3357	-1.1162 (-6.3336)***	0.0533 (0.8003)	-1.1175 (-6.2766)***	-1.0746 (-5.9932)***	-1.1028
DXY	0.3023 (2.5187)**	0.2963 (2.4926)**	0.2167 (1.8406)*	0.2307 (1.9687)**	0.2615	0.3577 (2.4447)**	0.3683 (2.5139)**	0.3552 (2.4161)**	0.3655 (2.4808)**	0.3617
GOLD	0.2261 (3.5721)***	0.2268 (3.5514)***	0.2143 (3.3352)***	0.2158 (3.3290)***	0.2208	0.0380 (0.5688)	0.0533 (0.8002)	0.0387 (0.5674)	0.0549 (0.8122)	Impotent
CRB	-0.1114 (-1.3002)	-0.1030 (-1.1946)	-0.1627 (-1.8419)*	-0.1436 (-1.6195)*	-0.1532	0.0094 (0.9419)	0.0102 (0.0801)	0.0066 (0.0510)	0.0058 (0.0456)	Impotent
VIX	0.0631 (1.6027)*	0.0600 (1.5259)	0.0754 (2.1553)**	0.0715 (2.0385)**	0.0700	0.0025 (0.0466)	-0.0031 (-0.0578)	0.0037 (0.0676)	-0.0017 (-0.0303)	Impotent
HL		-0.0989 (-1.7582)*		-0.0968 (-1.7560)*	-0.0979		-0.0814 (-0.1868)		-0.0844 (-1.3498)	Impotent
Adj. R²	0.2104	0.2220	0.2150	0.2253	0.2182	0.5169	0.5143	0.5167	0.5140	0.5155
ARCH	0.0283 (2.3774)**	0.0302 (2.3988)**			0.0293	0.1234 (1.8591)*	0.1265 (1.8767)*	0.1192 (1.6818)*	0.1215 (1.7636)*	0.1227
GARCH	0.9717 (81.5296)***	0.9698 (76.9328)***			0.9708	0.8561 (12.5808)***	0.8523 (12.0313)***	0.8517 (12.3408)***	0.8450 (11.6513)***	0.8513
LEVERAGE			-0.0064 (-0.1414)	0.0020 (0.0447)	Impotent			0.1192 (1.6818)*	0.0322 (0.3413)	Impotent
Log likelihood	857.88	858.98	854.11	863.41		496.85	497.85	496.89	497.56	
Distribution	Student-t	Student-t	Student-t	Student-t		Student-t	Student-t	Student-t	Student-t	

Table 3.11: Equity Market Analysis under APT-GARCH models: Hang Seng Index

	Pre-Crisis Period: Hang Seng					Post-Crisis Period: Hang Seng				
	GARCH	GARCH.HL	AGARCH	AGARCH.HL	Average	GARCH	GARCH.HL	AGARCH	AGARCH.HL	Average
Beta	0.7458 (13.3606)***	0.7452 (13.3560)***	0.7579 (13.4265)***	0.7558 (13.8139)***	0.7512	0.8454 (10.7339)***	0.8399 (10.6721)***	0.8534 (11.1701)***	0.8556 (11.1816)***	0.8486
HKD	-2.3136 (-1.8110)*	-2.3057 (-1.8011)*	-1.8540 (-1.4618)	-1.6589 (-1.2874)	2.0331	-1.8904 (-1.0538)	-2.1245 (-1.1372)	-1.8606 (-0.9169)	-1.8510 (-0.9016)	Impotent
DXY	-0.0479 (-0.4726)	-0.0485 (-0.4777)	-0.0757 (-0.7565)	-0.0953 (-1.0579)	Impotent	0.1202 (0.6915)	0.1370 (0.7956)	0.0724 (0.4169)	0.0653 (0.3752)	Impotent
GOLD	0.0221 (0.4795)	0.0222 (0.4802)	0.0012 (0.0231)	-0.0014 (-0.0299)	Impotent	0.1108 (1.4922)	0.1218 (1.6827)*	0.0773 (1.0603)	0.0857 (1.1631)	Impotent
CRB	-0.0097 (-0.1304)	-0.0092 (-0.1239)	-0.0003 (-0.0040)	0.0058 (0.0735)	Impotent	-0.0252 (-0.2076)	-0.0450 (-0.3747)	-0.0700 (-0.6580)	-0.1146 (-1.0702)	Impotent
VIX	-0.0122 (-0.3713)	-0.0121 (-0.3698)	-0.0155 (-0.4754)	-0.0150 (-0.4741)	Impotent	0.0550 (0.8709)	0.0634 (1.0230)	0.0808 (1.4625)	0.0856 (1.5217)	Impotent
HL		-0.0091 (-0.1119)		-0.0457 (-0.6030)	Impotent		-0.0714 (-0.7979)		-0.0499 (-0.6595)	Impotent
Adj. R²	0.3368	0.3352	0.3371	0.3353	0.3361	0.5921	0.5911	0.5932	0.5925	0.5922
ARCH	0.0471 (3.6337)***	0.0474 (3.5978)**			Impotent	0.0352 (2.2573)*	0.0327 (1.8405)*			Impotent
GARCH	0.9529 (73.5290)***	0.9527 (72.5431)***		0.9528	0.0473	0.9648 (61.9184)***	0.9673 (54.4842)***			0.9661
LEVERAGE			-0.0431 (-1.5289)	-0.0553 (-2.0699)**	Impotent			-0.2229 (-2.0393)**	-0.2165 (-1.9660)**	-0.2197
Log likelihood	934.37	934.58	944.86	945.705		505.46	506.17	504.45	504.62	
Distribution	Student-t	Student-t	Student-t	Student-t		Student-t	Student-t	Student-t	Student-t	

Table 3.12: Equity Market Analysis under APT-GARCH models: ASX All Ordinaries Index

	Pre-Crisis Period: Hang Seng					Post-Crisis Period: Hang Seng				
	GARCH	GARCH.HL	AGARCH	AGARCH.HL	Average	GARCH	GARCH.HL	AGARCH	AGARCH.HL	Average
Beta	0.4738 (18.0674)***	0.4582 (16.5179)***	0.4714 (17.8264)***	0.4552 (16.4603)***	0.4647	0.8534 (14.7750)***	0.7947 (14.3598)***	0.8526 (14.7575)***	0.7811 (14.2913)***	0.8205
AUD	-0.0354 (-0.7352)	-0.0351 (-0.7140)	-0.0342 (-0.7196)	-0.0337 (-0.6934)	Impotent	-0.1350 (-1.8503)*	-0.0929 (-1.2391)	-0.1347 (-1.8499)*	-0.0875 (-1.1989)	-0.1349
DXY	0.2089 (4.0032)***	0.1891 (3.8083)***	0.2134 (4.0506)***	0.1970 (3.9068)***	0.2021	0.3528 (3.5540)***	0.3527 (3.7272)***	0.3533 (3.5386)***	0.3539 (3.6971)***	0.3532
GOLD	0.1300 (4.9110)***	0.1302 (4.9083)***	0.1311 (4.9699)***	0.1321 (4.9879)***	0.1309	0.0420 (1.0465)	0.0679 (1.5009)	0.0417 (1.0242)	0.0682 (1.4984)	Impotent
CRB	-0.0160 (0.6672)	-0.0112 (-0.2973)	-0.0133 (-0.3548)	-0.0082 (-0.2172)	Impotent	0.0499 (0.7261)	0.0228 (0.3307)	0.0493 (0.7158)	0.0161 (0.2289)	Impotent
VIX	0.0114 (0.4631)	0.0088 (0.5630)	0.0106 (0.6778)	0.0081 (0.5180)	Impotent	0.0356 (1.0597)	0.0525 (1.5557)	0.0360 (1.0721)	0.0573 (1.7793)*	0.0573
HL		-0.2120 (-3.5867)***		-0.2142 (-3.4536)***	-0.2131		-2422 (-3.8059)***		-0.2698 (-4.0276)***	-0.2560
Adj. R²	0.4272	0.4439	0.4266	0.4432	0.4352	0.6995	0.7086	0.6996	0.7082	0.7040
ARCH	0.0291 (1.1720)	0.0214 (1.0181)	0.0164 (0.3593)	0.0120 (0.3617)	Impotent	0.0870 (1.9541)*	0.1112 (2.1337)**	0.0797 (1.3681)	0.0626 (1.3012)	0.0991
GARCH	0.9498 (22.7291)***	0.9614 (27.3753)***	0.9450 (19.8200)***	0.9560 (23.4779)***	0.9531	0.8895 (18.1755)***	0.8664 (16.2998)***	0.8933 (18.4209)***	0.8911 (18.9454)***	0.8851
LEVERAGE			0.0230 (0.4391)	0.0241 (0.5526)	Impotent			0.0087 (0.1018)	0.0896 (0.9261)	Impotent
Log likelihood	1199.70	1203.90	1199.79	1204.05		612.67	618.61	612.68	619.16	
Distribution	Student-t	Student-t	Student-t	Student-t		Student-t	Student-t	Student-t	S Student-t	

Table 3.13: Currency Market Analysis under APT-GARCH models: Australian Dollar (AUD)

	Pre-Crisis Period: AUD					Post-Crisis Period: AUD				
	GARCH	GARCH.HL	AGARCH	AGARCH.HL	Average	GARCH	GARCH.HL	AGARCH	AGARCH.HL	Average
DXY	-0.7086 (-16.1708) ***	-0.7104 (-15.8947) ***	-0.6722 (-16.9276) ***	-0.6720 (-17.3382) ***	-0.6908	-0.4482 (-6.1480) ***	-0.4495 (-5.9542) ***	-0.4075 (-5.6300) ***	-0.4137 (-5.4820) ***	-0.4297
MSCI	0.1566 (5.8428)***	0.1562 (5.8285) ***	0.1587 (5.8427) ***	0.1622 (6.2278) ***	0.1584	0.4217 (18.9831) ***	0.4210 (16.7632) ***	0.3983 (16.9193) ***	0.3979 (14.6239) ***	0.4097
CRB	0.1367 (3.7545) ***	0.1379 (3.7757) ***	0.1436 (3.9804) ***	0.1400 (4.0765) ***	0.1396	0.2127 (4.7610) ***	0.2115 (4.6724) ***	0.2124 (4.6750) ***	0.2095 (4.4959) ***	0.2115
VIX	-0.0358 (-2.2643) **	-0.0358 (-2.2608) **	-0.0406 (-2.5159) **	-0.0359 (-2.2300) **	-0.0370	-0.0362 (-1.3939)	-0.0356 (-1.3655)	-0.0326 (-1.0664)	-0.0309 (-1.0118)	Impotent
HL		-0.0261 (-0.6481)		-0.0462 (-1.1015)	Impotent		-0.0064 (-0.1592)		-0.0188 (-0.4218)	Impotent
Adj. R^2	0.4164	0.4163	0.4184	0.4197	0.4177	0.7532	0.7521	0.7523	0.7513	0.7522
ARCH	0.0185 (1.1335)	0.0228 (1.2776)			Impotent	0.1371 (2.5516) ***	0.1388 (2.4371) **	0.0249 (0.4415)	0.0337 (0.5834)	0.1380
GARCH	0.9675 (38.3688) ***	0.9615 (34.1272) ***			0.9645	0.6705 (6.7252) ***	0.6688 (6.3884) ***	0.7503 (8.1662) ***	0.7361 (7.4011) ***	0.7064
LEVERAGE			-0.0326 (-2.1846) **	-0.0335 (-2.3291) **	-0.0331			0.1234 (1.3119)	0.1274 (1.1638)	Impotent
Log likelihood	1198.972	1199.111	1202.302	1203.498		672.7331	672.7454	672.8748	672.9653	
Distribution	Student-t	Student-t	Student-t	Student-t		Student-t	Student-t	Student-t	Student-t	

Table 3.14: Currency Market Analysis under APT-GARCH models: Brazilian Real (BRL)

	Pre-Crisis Period: BRL					Post-Crisis Period: BRL				
	GARCH	GARCH.HL	AGARCH	AGARCH.HL	Average	GARCH	GARCH.HL	AGARCH	AGARCH.HL	Average
DXY	0.0671 (1.4248)	0.0620 (1.3111)	0.0608 (1.1983)	0.0537 (1.0905)	Impotent	0.2618 (3.0231) ***	0.2615 (2.9956) ***	0.2412 (2.8287) ***	0.2406 (2.8045) ***	0.2513
MSCI	-0.3286 (-10.6854)***	-0.3242 (10.1804) ***	-0.3187 (-8.6072) ***	-0.3175 (-8.7538) ***	-0.3223	-0.3484 (-10.3303) ***	-0.3484 (-9.9588) ***	-0.3312 (-9.9489) ***	-0.3267 (-9.7055) ***	-0.3387
CRB	-0.0975 (-3.0142) **	-0.1038 (-3.2358) ***	-0.0960 (-2.5367) **	-0.0939 (-2.4727) ***	-0.0978	-0.2578 (-3.7661) ***	-0.2582 (-3.7667) ***	-0.2437 (-3.4404) ***	-0.2344 (-3.2249) ***	-0.2485
VIX	0.0178 (1.4322)	0.0191 (1.5343)	0.0143 (0.9333)	0.0150 (0.9528)	Impotent	0.0600 (1.4443)	0.0602 (1.4513)	0.0471 (1.0815)	0.0388 (0.8842)	Impotent
HL		0.0721 (1.6436)*		0.0571 (1.0872)	Impotent		-0.0029 (-0.0590)		0.0436 (0.7992)	Impotent
Adj. R²	0.1210	0.1292	0.1199	0.1270	0.1243	0.6395	0.6376	0.6316	0.6315	0.6351
ARCH	0.1155 (6.4300) ***	0.1151 (6.3850) ***			0.1153	0.1820 (2.4703) **	0.1827 (2.4237) **	0.2974 (2.2819) **	0.3149 (2.3149) **	0.2442
GARCH	0.8845 (49.2223) ***	0.8849 (49.1082) ***			0.8847	0.6815 (6.5364) ***	0.6806 (6.4743) ***	0.6277 (4.9136) ***	0.6330 (4.7793) ***	0.6557
LEVERAGE			0.0355 (0.7825)	0.0412 (0.8988)	Impotent			-0.2639 (-1.7326) *	-0.2927 (-1.8768) *	-0.2783
Log likelihood	1051.517	1052.215	1056.467	1056.927		626.6410	626.6423	628.8003	629.0638	
Distribution	Student-t	Student-t	Student-t	Student-t		GED	GED	GED	GED	

Table 3.15: Currency Market Analysis under APT-GARCH models: Canadian Dollar (CAD)

	Pre-Crisis Period: CAD					Post-Crisis Period: CAD				
	GARCH	GARCH.HL	AGARCH	AGARCH.HL	Average	GARCH	GARCH.HL	AGARCH	AGARCH.HL	Average
DXY	0.2846 (10.7231)***	0.2865 (10.8926)***	0.2974 (11.5824)***	0.2967 (11.5970)***	0.2913	0.1978 (2.9386)***	0.1952 (2.9071)***	0.1817 (2.9562)***	0.2092 (3.3499)***	0.1960
MSCI	-0.0914 (-4.4456)***	-0.0905 (-4.3754)***	-0.0921 (-4.3055)***	-0.0911 (-4.2595)***	-0.0913	-0.2748 (-10.5544)***	-0.2749 (-10.3673)***	-0.2913 (-11.4529)***	-0.2842 (-11.23)***	-0.2813
CRB	-0.0883 (-3.4514)***	-0.0866 (-3.4248)***	-0.0859 (-3.2971)***	-0.0848 (-3.2795)***	-0.0864	-0.1745 (-4.1400)***	-0.1731 (-4.0602)***	-0.1298 (-3.0847)***	-0.1300 (-3.0915)***	-0.1619
VIX	0.0027 (0.2650)	0.0029 (0.2851)	0.0011 (0.1027)	0.0015 (0.1481)	Impotent	0.0134 (0.5268)	0.0122 (0.4706)	-0.0050 (-0.2040)	-0.0045 (-0.1811)	Impotent
HL		-0.0646 (-1.3759)		-0.0520 (-1.0852)	Impotent		0.0134 (0.2822)		-0.0662 (-1.2522)	Impotent
Adj. R²	0.2736	0.2724	0.2748	0.2737	0.2736	0.6474	0.6454	0.6411	0.6381	0.6430
ARCH	0.0969 (2.2423)**	0.1039 (2.3409)**	0.1703 (2.3110)**	0.1612 (2.2868)**	0.1331	0.0947 (2.3052)**	0.0932 (2.2492)**			0.0940
GARCH	0.7462 (5.2982)***	0.7228 (5.0549)***	0.6381 (6.4075)***	0.6439 (3.6110)***	0.6878	0.8823 (21.0399)***	0.8853 (20.9392)***			0.8838
LEVERAGE			-0.1279 (-1.6000)*	-0.1146 (-1.3937)	Impotent			-0.1445 (-2.1335)**	-0.1833 (-2.5772)**	-0.1639
Log likelihood	1312.143	1312.947	1313.447	1313.981		698.9180	698.9530	702.0894	702.7577	
Distribution	GED	GED	GED	GED		GED	GED	GED	GED	

Is the World Heading towards Crisis-Induced Irrational Exuberance?

Table 3.16: Currency Market Analysis under APT-GARCH models: Swiss Franc (CHF)

	Pre-Crisis Period: CHF					Post-Crisis Period: CHF				
	GARCH	GARCH.HL	AGARCH	AGARCH.HL	Average	GARCH	GARCH.HL	AGARCH	AGARCH.HL	Average
DXY	1.1207 (57.6650) ***	1.2338 (55.7965) ***	1.2035 (57.1333) ***	1.2043 (56.9849) ***	1.1906	1.0924 (23.0242) ***	1.0948 (23.2381) ***	1.0975 (22.4574) ***	1.0983 (24.0164) ***	1.0958
MSCI	0.0809 (7.2093) ***	0.0812 (6.7131) ***	0.0738 (6.3232) ***	0.0740 (6.3568) ***	0.0775	0.1049 (5.3800) ***	0.1070 (5.5306) ***	0.1088 (5.6403) ***	0.1081 (5.6403) ***	0.1072
CRB	0.0033 (0.2206)	0.0034 (0.2328)	0.0016 (0.1107)	0.0018 (0.1223)	Impotent	0.0216 (0.6550)	0.0166 (0.5137)	0.0177 (0.5219)	0.0177 (0.5219)	Impotent
VIX	0.0012 (0.2128)	0.0026 (0.3919)	0.0043 (0.7462)	0.0042 (0.7103)	Impotent	-0.0353 (-1.8401) *	-0.0299 (-1.5914)	-0.0418 (-2.0834) **	-0.0418 (-2.0351) **	-0.0372
HL		0.0114 (0.6087)		0.0071 (0.3789)	Impotent		-0.0550 (-1.4568)		-0.0898 (-2.4215) **	Impotent
Adj. R^2	0.7025	0.6980	0.7071	0.7061	0.7034	0.5749	0.5762	0.5735	0.5743	0.5747
ARCH	-0.0021 (-7.3118) ***	0.0089 (3.5902) ***				0.2705 (2.2652) **	0.2539 (2.3043) **			0.2622
GARCH	1.0021 (3543.97) ***	0.9911 (400.6386)			Impotent	0.6750 (6.4331) ***	0.6907 (7.1848) ***			Impotent
LEVERAGE			0.0290 (0.2896)	0.0370 (0.3559)	Impotent			-0.1798 (-2.1757) **	-0.2132 (-2.4914) **	-0.1965
Log likelihood	1475.682	1480.542	1489.956	1490.016		728.5514	729.5139	734.7977	734.4325	
Distribution	Student-t	Student-t	Student-t	Student-t		Student-t	Student-t	Student-t	Student-t	

Table 3.17: Currency Market Analysis under APT-GARCH models: Euro (EUR)

	Pre-Crisis Period: EUR					Post-Crisis Period: EUR				
	GARCH	GARCH.HL	AGARCH	AGARCH.HL	Average	GARCH	GARCH.HL	AGARCH	AGARCH.HL	Average
DXY	-1.1583 (-101.3371) ***	-1.1551 (-101.7947) ***	-1.1546 (-102.6470) ***	-1.1530 (-102.4194) ***	-1.1553	-1.2098 (-45.9213) ***	-1.2095 (-45.5772) ***	-1.1776 (-44.0742) ***	-1.1753 (-43.7661) ***	-1.1931
MSCI	-0.00823 (-1.6569) *	-0.0079 (-1.5739)	-0.0076 (-1.5235)	-0.0074 (-1.4813)	Impotent	-0.0113 (-1.2790)	-0.0112 (-1.2691)	-0.0093 (-1.0269)	-0.0089 (-0.9930)	Impotent
CRB	0.0021 (0.3726)	0.0022 (0.4157)	0.0019 (0.3491)	0.0020 (0.3806)	Impotent	-0.0268 (-1.4677)	-0.0273 (-1.4976)	-0.0422 (-2.8027) ***	-0.0432 (-2.9123) ***	-0.0427
VIX	-0.0053 (-1.7071) *	-0.0054 (-1.7483) *	-0.0049 (-1.5794)	-0.0050 (-1.6417) *	-0.0052	0.0079 (0.7967)	0.0082 (0.8284)	0.0297 (3.8736) ***	0.0307 (4.5175) ***	0.0302
HL		0.0198 (1.8955) *		0.0148 (1.3175)	Impotent		-0.0076 (-0.3449)		-0.0139 (-0.6213)	Impotent
Adj. R^2	0.8510	0.8511	0.8513	0.8513	0.8512	0.9315	0.9311	0.9293	0.9287	0.9302
ARCH	0.2605 (4.0962) ***	0.2609 (4.3494) ***	0.1722 (2.8584) ***	0.1789 (2.8073) ***	0.2182	0.0309 (0.8820)	0.0318 (0.8651)	0.2259 (1.2835)	0.2204 (1.2314)	Impotent
GARCH	0.6260 (9.5306) ***	0.6681 (12.1689) ***	0.6714 (12.9045) ***	0.6857 (14.0110) ***	0.6628	0.8998 (11.4734) ***	0.8953 (11.0947) ***	0.4477 (1.8443) *	0.4265 (1.7416) *	0.6673
LEVERAGE			0.1895 (1.8296)*	0.1594 (1.4938)	Impotent			0.1040 (0.5387)	0.1544 (0.6553)	Impotent
Log likelihood	2561.528	2562.727	2563.561	2564.262		908.1842	908.2426	908.1737	908.3684	
Distribution	Student t	Student t	Student t	Student t		Student t	Student t	Student t	Student t	

***, ** and * denote statistical significance at the 1, 5 and 10 per cent, respectively. GARCH models have been used in case of symmetric analysis and TGARCH applied to capture any asymmetric effects.

Table 3.18: Currency Market Analysis under APT-GARCH models: British Pound (GBP)

	Pre-Crisis Period: GBP					Post-Crisis Period: GBP				
	GARCH	GARCH.HL	AGARCH	AGARCH.HL	Average	GARCH	GARCH.HL	AGARCH	AGARCH.HL	Average
DXY	-0.7968 (-22.6348) ***	-0.7982 (-22.6302) ***	-0.8043 (-23.7185) ***	-0.8059 (-23.7253) ***	-0.8013	-0.6711 (-10.0055) ***	-0.6668 (-9.9187) ***	-0.6785 (-11.2094) ***	-0.6679 (-10.6827) ***	-0.6711
MSCI	0.0001 (0.0082)	0.0001 (0.0078)	0.0050 (0.2817)	0.0051 (0.2881)	Impotent	0.0338 (1.3405)	0.0339 (1.2936)	0.0579 (2.6975) ***	0.0637 (2.5921) ***	0.0474
CRB	0.0356 (1.4797)	0.0353 (1.4519)	0.0377 (1.5978)	0.0373 (1.5677)	Impotent	-0.0481 (-1.1687)	-0.0536 (-1.3044)	-0.0316 (-0.8403)	-0.0456 (-1.1295)	Impotent
VIX	-0.0160 (-1.5671)	-0.0165 (-1.6190) *	-0.0173 (-1.7105) *	-0.0177 (-1.7696) *	-0.0172	0.0468 (1.9976) **	0.0528 (2.2663) **	0.0133 (0.6316)	0.0260 (1.1133)	0.0498
HL		0.0367 (0.9097)		0.0452 (1.0812)	Impotent		-0.1040 (-2.1916) **		-0.1314 (-5.5495) ***	-0.1177
Adj. R²	0.4965	0.4941	0.4950	0.4920	0.4944	0.4460	0.4604	0.4458	0.4644	0.4542
ARCH	0.0860 (1.6397) *	0.0845 (1.6423) *	0.1603 (1.5098)	0.1692 (1.4617)	0.0853	0.1270 (2.2524) **	0.1205 (2.3432) **			0.1238
GARCH	0.6553 (2.8784) ***	0.6507 (2.8347) ***	0.7132 (3.8095) ***	0.7146 (3.9140) ***	0.6835	0.8204 (10.7996) ***	0.8295 (12.0762) ***			0.8250
LEVERAGE			-0.1665 (-1.4883)	-0.1761 (-1.4635)	Impotent			-0.1994 (-6.7372) ***	-0.1844 (-5.2668) ***	-0.1919
Log likelihood	1339.949	1340.316	1342.258	1342.824		705.5942	707.1327	713.4267	713.4267	
Distribution	Student t	Student t	Student t	Student t		Student t	Student t	Student t	Student t	

***, ** and * denote statistical significance at the 1, 5 and 10 per cent, respectively. Due to negative sign obtained under ARCH term for asymmetric GARCH models in the post-crisis period, EGARCH models have thereby been used. Under EGARCH, there are no such ARCH and GARCH terms, since the coefficient for the log variance in EGARCH has some correspondence with the sum of the ARCH and GARCH terms (See Carol Alexandra, 2008, Practical Econometrics). In that respect, only leverage components have been reported.

Table 3.19: Currency Market Analysis under APT-GARCH models: Indian Rupee (INR)

	Pre-Crisis Period: IND					Post-Crisis Period: IND				
	GARCH	GARCH.HL	AGARCH	AGARCH.HL	Average	GARCH	GARCH.HL	AGARCH	AGARCH.HL	Average
DXY	0.0169 (4.3176) ***	0.0169 (4.2795)***	0.0299 (5.1120) ***	0.0300 (5.0923) ***	0.0234	0.1615 (3.1337) ***	0.1693 (3.2591) ***	0.1595 (3.0802) ***	0.1657 (3.1958) ***	0.1640
MSCI	-0.0077 (-2.6323) ***	-0.0077 (-2.5948)***	-0.0113 (-2.7956) ***	-0.0114 (-2.7673) ***	-0.0095	-0.1472 (-7.2003) ***	-0.1412 (-7.0629) ***	-0.1494 (-7.2912) ***	-0.1430 (-7.1526) ***	-0.1452
CRB	-0.0201 (-3.3701) ***	-0.0201 (-3.3289)***	-0.0139 (-2.1170) **	-0.0138 (-2.0692) **	-0.0170	-0.0132 (-0.3727)	-0.0120 (-0.3378)	-0.0064 (-0.1809)	-0.0024 (-0.0679)	Impotent
VIX	0.0058 (2.5667)**	0.0058 (2.5540)**	0.0044 (1.6360)*	0.0044 (1.6213)*	0.0051	-0.0128 (-0.6984)	-0.0150 (-0.7890)	-0.0113 (-0.6253)	-0.0145 (-0.7930)	Impotent
HL		-0.0020 (-0..0505)		-0.0070 (-0.1605)	Impotent		0.2037 (2.4539) **		0.2451 (2.9297) ***	0.2244
Adj. R²	0.0282	0.0257	0.0392	0.0368	0.0325	0.3188	0.3398	0.3221	0.3457	0.3272
ARCH	0.1372 (7.6882)***	0.1373 (7.6913)***			0.1373	0.1297 (1.8716) *	0.1167 (1.7458) *	0.1493 (1.9149) *	0.1514 (1.8316) *	0.1368
GARCH	0.8628 (48.3299) ***	0.8627 (48.3107) ***			0.8628	0.8171 (9.7262) ***	0.8270 (9.5869) ***	0.8424 (11.2360) ***	0.8760 (12.6238) ***	0.8406
LEVERAGE			-0.1467 (-1.3147)	-0.1477 (-1.3155)	Impotent			-0.1069 (-1.1590)	-0.1363 (-1.5894)	Impotent
Log likelihood	1650.197	1650.198	1665.126	1665.133		742.8461	744.9498	743.4541	746.3441	
Distribution	Student-t	Student-t	Student-t	Student-t		Student-t	Student-t	Student-t	Student-t	

***, ** and * denote statistical significance at the 1, 5 and 10 per cent, respectively. Due to parameter constraint violation under symmetric GARCH in the pre-crisis period, IGARCH has been used and EGARCH employed when estimating the asymmetric GARCH. Under EGARCH, there are no such ARCH and GARCH terms, since the coefficient for the log variance in EGARCH has some correspondence with the sum of the ARCH and GARCH terms in TGARCH. In that respect, only leverage terms have been reported.

Table 3.20: Currency Market Analysis under APT-GARCH models: Japanese Yen (JPY)

	Pre-Crisis Period: JPY					Post-Crisis Period: JPY				
	GARCH	GARCH.HL	AGARCH	AGARCH.HL	Average	GARCH	GARCH.HL	AGARCH	AGARCH.HL	Average
DXY	0.6664 (15.5615)***	0.6775 (15.6876)***	0.6658 (15.4841)***	0.6792 (15.7540)***	0.6722	0.8237 (10.7020)***	0.8107 (11.1087)***	0.8687 (11.2552)***	0.8397 (10.9566)***	0.8357
MSCI	0.0097 (0.4033)	0.0075 (0.3129)	0.0094 (0.3870)	0.0078 (0.3281)	Impotent	0.2783 (10.2084)***	0.2684 (10.4044)***	0.2813 (10.2005)***	0.2634 (9.3979)***	0.2729
CRB	-0.0078 (-0.2319)	-0.0104 (-0.3106)	-0.0084 (-0.2485)	-0.0097 (-0.2867)	Impotent	0.1291 (2.4646)***	0.1047 (2.0969)**	0.1554 (2.8907)***	0.1444 (2.7189)**	0.1334
VIX	-0.0221 (-1.5173)	-0.0219 (-1.5391)	-0.0217 (-1.4948)	-0.0223 (-1.5550)	Impotent	-0.0205 (-0.8011)	-0.0039 (-0.1567)	-0.0275 (-1.0385)	-0.0187 (-0.7031)	Impotent
HL		0.1137 (2.3499)**		0.1191 (2.4341)**	0.1164		-0.1680 (-3.3495)***		-0.1646 (-3.1536)***	-0.1663
Adj. R^2	0.2415	0.2402	0.2417	0.2395	0.2407	0.3407	0.3686	0.3403	0.3710	0.3551
ARCH	0.1214 (2.0343)**	0.1124 (1.8770)*	0.1060 (1.3240)	0.1299 (1.3630)	0.1169	0.0263 (2.0869)**	0.0357 (2.3641)**			0.0310
GARCH	0.7341 (5.6576)***	0.7441 (5.6407)***	0.7243 (5.3680)***	0.7574 (6.0926)***	0.7400	0.9737 (77.3220)***	0.9642 (63.7211)***			0.9690
LEVERAGE			0.0307 (0.3073)	-0.0308 (-0.2957)	Impotent			0.1798 (1.3555)	0.0914 (0.6411)	Impotent
Log likelihood	1203.044	1205.283	1203.107	1205.336		660.5504	664.2277	662.7819	666.7745	
Distribution	Student-t	Student-t	Student-t	Student-t		Student-t	Student-t	Student-t	Student-t	

***, ** and * denote statistical significance at the 1, 5 and 10 per cent, respectively. Due to negative sign obtained under GARCH terms in both the symmetric and asymmetric GARCH models in the post-crisis period, IGARCH and EGARCH models have been employed, respectively. Under EGARCH, there are no such ARCH and GARCH terms, since the coefficient for the log variance in EGARCH has some correspondence with the sum of the ARCH and GARCH terms in TGARCH (See Carol Alexandra, 2008, Practical Econometrics). In that respect, only leverage components have been reported.

Table 3.21: Currency Market Analysis under APT-GARCH models: New Zealand Dollar (NZD)

	Pre-Crisis Period: NZD					Post-Crisis Period: NZD				
	GARCH	GARCH.HL	AGARCH	AGARCH.HL	Average	GARCH	GARCH.HL	AGARCH	AGARCH.HL	Average
DXY	-0.6699 (-13.6941) ***	-0.6644 (-13.5620) ***	-0.6721 (-13.5612) ***	-0.6651 (-13.5280) ***	-0.6679	-0.5762 (-6.2122) ***	-0.5763 (6.1079) ***	-0.5967 (-6.1549) ***	-0.5954 (-6.0808) ***	-0.5862
MSCI	0.1434 (4.3668) ***	0.1436 (4.3069) ***	0.1420 (4.4233) ***	0.1427 (4.3674) ***	0.1429	0.3400 (9.0651) ***	0.3399 (8.7659) ***	0.3494 (8.7742) ***	0.3481 (8.5152) ***	0.3444
CRB	0.1744 (3.8890) ***	0.1759 (3.9204) ***	0.1781 (3.9825) ***	0.1793 (4.0151) ***	0.1769	0.1375 (2.1937) *	0.1374 (2.1645) *	0.1443 (2.1002) **	0.1427 (2.0668) **	0.1405
VIX	-0.0449 (-2.4401) **	-0.0452 (-2.4476) **	-0.0465 (-2.4785) **	-0.0465 (-2.4707) **	-0.0458	-0.0421 (-1.1532)	-0.0421 (-1.1511)	-0.0513 (-1.3397)	-0.0503 (-1.3246)	Impotent
HL		-0.0314 (-0.6810)		-0.0309 (-0.6665)	Impotent		-0.0010 (-0.0187)		-0.0246 (-0.5169)	Impotent
Adj. R²	0.3065	0.3065	0.3063	0.3064	0.3064	0.6311	0.6294	0.6315	0.6313	0.6308
ARCH	0.0575 (1.7922) *	0.0623 (1.7373) *	0.1371 (1.6315) *	0.1309 (1.6251) *	0.0970	0.0710 (1.1366)	0.0709 (1.1211)			Impotent
GARCH	0.8693 (10.3330) ***	0.8463 (8.1435) ***	0.7470 (4.0153) ***	0.7484 (4.0159) ***	0.8028	0.7899 (5.5881) ***	0.7900 (5.5821) ***			0.7900
LEVERAGE			-0.0925 (-1.1451)	-0.0861 (-1.1021)	Impotent			0.0061 (0.0559)	-0.0020 (-0.0185)	Impotent
Log likelihood	1124.586	1124.727	1125.091	1125.240		627.2961	627.2967	623.6078	623.7097	
Distribution	Student-t	Student-t	Student-t	Student-t		Student-t	Student-t	Student-t	Student-t	

***, ** and * denote statistical significance at the 1, 5 and 10 per cent, respectively. Due to negative sign obtained under ARCH and GARCH terms for asymmetric TGARCH models in the post-crisis period, EGARCH models have thereby been used. Under EGARCH, there are no such ARCH and GARCH terms, since the coefficient for the log variance in EGARCH has some correspondence with the sum of the ARCH and GARCH terms in TGARCH (See Carol Alexandra, 2008, Practical Econometrics). In that respect, only leverage components have been reported.

Table 3.22: Currency Market Analysis under APT-GARCH models: Russian Rouble (RUB)

	Pre-Crisis Period: RUB					Post-Crisis Period: RUB				
	GARCH	GARCH.HL	AGARCH	AGARCH.HL	Average	GARCH	GARCH.HL	AGARCH	AGARCH.HL	Average
DXY	0.1213 (7.6470)***	0.1259 (7.9575)***	0.1000 (6.3270)***	0.1098 (6.7956)***	0.1143	0.5486 (23.3610)***	0.5490 (22.6740)***	0.5591 (17.2852)***	0.5607 (16.9909)***	0.5544
MSCI	-0.0190 (-1.9459)*	-0.0190 (-1.9578)*	-0.0145 (-1.5411)	-0.0156 (-1.6117)*	-0.0170	-0.0534 (-5.8160)***	-0.0535 (-5.7386)***	-0.0715 (-5.6052)***	-0.0791 (-5.9561)***	-0.0644
CRB	-0.0082 (-0.6723)	-0.0077 (-0.6404)	-0.0047 (-0.3886)	-0.0040 (-0.3300)	Impotent	-0.0104 (-0.7758)	-0.0126 (-0.9115)	0.0067 (0.3383)	-0.0012 (-0.0575)	Impotent
VIX	-0.0014 (-0.2909)	-0.0013 (-0.2513)	-0.0011 (-0.2304)	-0.0014 (-0.2739)	Impotent	-0.0273 (-2.9825)***	-0.0312 (-3.2812)***	-0.0380 (-3.0847)***	-0.0406 (-3.1413)***	-0.0343
HL		-0.2167 (-3.1982)***		-0.2258 (-3.2786)***	-0.2213		0.0733 (1.9755)*		0.0574 (1.1341)	Impotent
Adj. R^2	0.1080	0.1173	0.1023	0.1152	0.1107	0.3696	0.3822	0.3714	0.3806	0.3760
ARCH	0.1383 (2.2227)**	0.1271 (2.1703)**	0.0805 (1.3898)	0.0742 (1.3404)	0.1327	0.1830 (7.4176)***	0.1799 (7.2103)***			0.1815
GARCH	0.7227 (9.3877)***	0.7272 (9.5724)***	0.7517 (12.4628)***	0.7452 (11.3590)***	0.7367	0.8170 (33.1092)***	0.8201 (32.8665)***			0.8186
LEVERAGE			0.2118 (1.9674)**	0.2142 (1.8564)*	0.2130			0.0202 (0.1482)	0.0498 (0.3791)	Impotent
Log likelihood	1573.415	1576.591	1575.123	1578.398		741.6344	742.2555	752.3031	752.2536	
Distribution	Student-t	Student-t	Student-t	Student-t	Student-t	Student-t	Student-t	Student-t	Student-t	Student-t

***, ** and * denote statistical significance at the 1, 5 and 10 per cent, respectively. In the post-crisis periods, the sum of ARCH and GARCH terms exceeded one so that recourse has been made towards IGARCH for symmetric GARCH analysis and EGARCH for asymmetric GARCH analysis. Under EGARCH, there are no such ARCH and GARCH terms, since the coefficient for the log variance in EGARCH has some correspondence with the sum of the ARCH and GARCH terms in TGARCH (See Carol Alexandra, 2008, Practical Econometrics). In that respect, only leverage components have been reported.

Table 3.23: Currency Market Analysis under APT-GARCH models: South African Rand (ZAR)

	Pre-Crisis Period: ZAR					Post-Crisis Period: ZAR				
	GARCH	GARCH.HL	AGARCH	AGARCH.HL	Average	GARCH	GARCH.HL	AGARCH	AGARCH.HL	Average
DXY	0.6107 (9.4648) ***	0.5655 (9.0323) ***	0.6423 (9.8495) ***	0.5652 (9.0304) ***	0.5959	0.3400 (3.1423) ***	0.3390 (3.1246) ***	0.3400 (3.1418) ***	0.3385 (3.1724) ***	0.3394
MSCI	-0.1330 (-3.4215) ***	-0.1411 (-3.8773) ***	-0.1288 (-3.1135) ***	-0.1415 (-3.9115) ***	-0.1361	-0.4816 (-10.3814) ***	-0.4791 (-10.5308) ***	-0.4807 (-10.2724) ***	-0.4649 (-10.1923) ***	-0.4766
CRB	-0.1003 (-1.7548) *	-0.1024 (-1.7881) *	-0.1262 (-2.2039) **	-0.1061 (-1.8400) *	-0.1088	-0.1205 (-1.6076) *	-0.1175 (-1.5669)	-0.1203 (-1.5975)	-0.1140 (-1.5156)	Impotent
VIX	0.0197 (0.8468)	0.0196 (0.8912)	0.0254 (1.0346)	0.0219 (0.9884)	Impotent	0.0226 (0.5642)	0.0173 (0.4323)	0.0224 (0.5545)	0.0129 (0.3199)	Impotent
HL		0.1627 (3.3863) ***		0.1810 (3.6823) ***	0.1719		0.0771 (1.6615) *		0.0860 (1.7606) *	0.0816
Adj. R^2	0.1400	0.1681	0.1402	0.1691	0.1544	0.5544	0.5565	0.5545	0.5576	0.5558
ARCH	0.1489 (2.7286) ***	0.1043 (2.8920) ***	0.3101 (2.5458) **	0.1203 (3.0607) ***	0.1709	0.0923 (1.6555) *	0.0932 (1.7097) *	0.0932 (1.5030)	0.1074 (1.6240) *	0.0976
GARCH	0.7670 (10.5930) ***	0.8698 (21.0128) ***	0.5388 (4.3828) ***	0.8839 (19.0863) ***	0.7649	0.8637 (12.8598) ***	0.8678 (13.4054) ***	0.8647 (11.9009) ***	0.8853 (13.9945) ***	0.8704
LEVERAGE			-0.2681 (-2.0090) **	-0.0501 (-0.9770)	Impotent			-0.0041 (-0.0418)	-0.0559 (-0.5811)	Impotent
Log likelihood	981.2064	984.3691	982.8170	984.9567		593.4969	594.5268	593.4977	594.6559	
Distribution	Student-t	Student-t	Student-t	Student-t	Student-t	Student-t	Student-t	Student-t	Student-t	Student-t

***, ** and * denote statistical significance at the 1, 5 and 10 per cent, respectively. GARCH and TGARCH models have been used to capture symmetric and asymmetric effects, respectively.

Table 3.24: Commodity Market Analysis under APT-GARCH models: Coffee

	Pre-Crisis Period: Coffee					Post-Crisis Period: Coffee				
	GARCH	GARCH.HL	AGARCH	AGARCH.HL	Average	GARCH	GARCH.HL	AGARCH	AGARCH.HL	Average
Beta	0.8658 (8.3420)***	0.8419 (7.0680)***	0.7679 (6.2835)***	0.7679 (6.1367)***	0.8108	0.9421 (7.3330)***	0.9418 (7.2553)***	0.9858 (7.3053)***	0.9987 (7.4864)***	0.9671
MSCI	0.2960 (3.2499)***	0.2908 (2.9966)***	0.2049 (2.2017)**	0.2002 (2.1654)**	0.2480	0.0111 (0.1509)	0.0298 (0.3793)	-0.0125 (-0.1497)	-0.0059 (-0.0688)	Impotent
VIX	-0.1856 (-3.6266)***	-0.1864 (-3.5345)***	-0.2064 (-4.1344)***	-0.2014 (-4.0081)***	-0.1950	-0.2064 (-2.8853)***	-0.2012 (-2.9234)***	-0.2392 (-3.3069)***	-0.2520 (-3.5730)***	-0.2247
DXY	-0.0278 (-0.1947)	-0.0635 (-0.4469)	0.0043 (0.0284)	0.0137 (0.0919)	Impotent	0.0669 (0.4997)	0.1219 (0.9259)	-0.0215 (-0.1089)	0.0034 (0.0172)	Impotent
HL		0.0268 (0.4500)		-0.0780 (-1.1724)	Impotent		0.0792 (1.1946)		0.0871 (1.3387)	Impotent
Adj. R²	0.0949	0.0934	0.1008	0.0970	0.0965	0.3302	0.3293	0.3316	0.3323	0.3309
ARCH	-0.0233 (-59.2904)***	-0.0263 (-299.8972)***			-0.0248	-0.0296 (-3.9851)	-0.0268 (-12.0730)***			-0.0282
GARCH	1.0233 (2607.759)***	1.0263 (11687.36)***			1.0248	1.0296 (138.51)***	1.0268 (463.04)***			1.0282
LEVERAGE			0.2028 (2.4037)***	0.2028 (2.4037)**	0.2028			0.0526 (0.5746)	0.0213 (0.2291)	Impotent
Log likelihood	722.07	726.69	719.42	719.42		462.16	462.43	458.90	459.70	
Distribution	Student-t	Student-t	Student-t	Student-t		Student-t	Student-t	Student-t	Student-t	

***, ** and * denote statistical significance at the 1, 5 and 10 per cent, respectively. Due to violation of GARCH parameters, IGARCH has been used under symmetric GARCH and EGARCH for asymmetric GARCH. Under EGARCH, there are no such ARCH and GARCH terms, since the coefficient for the log variance in EGARCH has some correspondence with the sum of the ARCH and GARCH terms in TGARCH (See Carol Alexandra, 2008, Practical Econometrics). In that respect, only leverage components have been reported.

Table 3.25: Commodity Market Analysis under APT-GARCH models: Corn

	Pre-Crisis Period: CORN					Post-Crisis Period: CORN				
	GARCH	GARCH.HL	AGARCH	AGARCH.HL	Average	GARCH	GARCH.HL	AGARCH	AGARCH.HL	Average
Beta	0.5528 (7.4388)***	0.5397 (7.4549)***	0.5185 (6.2780)***	0.5190 (6.3018)***	0.5325	1.2727 (9.9766)***	1.2866 (10.1893)***	1.2286 (7.8118)***	1.2430 (7.8334)***	1.2577
MSCI	0.0361 (0.7454)	0.0340 (0.7164)	0.0164 (0.2668)	0.0206 (0.3415)	Impotent	-0.1532 (-1.8759)*	-0.1483 (-1.8346)**	-0.0927 (-0.9336)	-0.0894 (0.9035)	-0.1508
VIX	-0.1438 (-4.8960)***	-0.1389 (-5.0056)***	-0.1447 (-4.4023)***	-0.1419 (-4.4286)***	-0.1423	-0.2857 (-3.6811)***	-0.2928 (-3.7621)***	-0.3094 (-3.5306)***	-0.3144 (-3.4521)***	-0.3006
DXY	-0.1873 (-1.8567)*	-0.1927 (-1.9944)**	-0.2133 (-1.8340)*	-0.2177 (-1.9376)*	-0.2028	-0.4040 (-2.0179)**	-0.3954 (-1.9448)*	-0.4320 (1.7106)*	-0.4229 (-1.6691)*	-0.4136
HL		-0.1355 (-2.5020)**		-0.1287 (-1.9882)**	-0.1321		0.0688 (1.1068)		0.0637 (0.9396)	Impotent
Adj. R²	0.1268	0.1212	0.1297	0.1191	0.1242	0.4140	0.4145	0.4123	0.4127	0.4134
ARCH	0.1033 (5.4779)***	0.1150 (5.7694)***			0.1092	0.0305 (1.4866)	0.0338 (1.5263)			Impotent
GARCH	0.8967 (47.5583)***	0.8850 (44.4024)***			0.8909	0.9695 (47.1928)***	0.9661 (43.5634)***			0.9678
LEVERAGE			0.1602 (2.9491)***	0.1494 (2.6514)***	0.1548			-0.1397 (-1.4208)	-0.1279 (-1.2667)	Impotent
Log likelihood	824.4862	825.9924	836.9888	838.4218		420.9569	421.3289	425.6866	426.0225	
Distribution	Student-t	Student-t	Student-t	Student-t		Student-t	Student-t	Student-t	Student-t	

***, ** and * denote statistical significance at the 1, 5 and 10 per cent, respectively. Due to violation of GARCH parameters, IGARCH has been used under symmetric GARCH and EGARCH for asymmetric GARCH. Under EGARCH, there are no such ARCH and GARCH terms, since the coefficient for the log variance in EGARCH has some correspondence with the sum of the ARCH and GARCH terms in TGARCH (See Carol Alexandra, 2008, Practical Econometrics). In that respect, only leverage terms have been reported.

Table 3.26: Commodity Market Analysis under APT-GARCH models: Sugar

	Pre-Crisis Period: SUGAR					Post-Crisis Period: SUGAR				
	GARCH	GARCH.HL	AGARCH	AGARCH.HL	Average	GARCH	GARCH.HL	AGARCH	AGARCH.HL	Average
Beta	1.0853 (6.3480)***	1.0856 (6.3488)***	1.0940 (6.4945)***	1.0937 (6.4924)***	1.0897	1.8369 (7.4694)***	1.8370 (7.4880)***	1.8392 (7.4849)***	1.8391 (7.4944)***	1.8381
MSCI	0.0734 (0.7877)	0.0736 (0.7838)	0.0661 (0.7376)	0.0660 (0.7344)	Impotent	-0.2181 (-1.8281)*	-0.2161 (-1.7420)*	-0.2190 (-1.8358)*	-0.2178 (-1.7836)*	-0.2178
OIL	-0.2309 (-2.9525)***	-0.2311 (-2.9484)***	-0.2375 (-2.9947)***	-0.2372 (-2.9839)***	-0.2342	-0.2221 (-2.2000)**	-0.2218 (-2.1990)**	-0.2254 (-2.2545)**	-0.2249 (-2.2448)**	-0.2236
VIX	-0.0278 (-0.4653)	-0.0273 (-0.4560)	-0.0221 (-0.3540)	-0.0225 (-0.3618)	Impotent	-0.2536 (-2.4254)**	-0.2546 (-2.4276)**	-0.2488 (-2.3175)**	-0.2498 (-2.3053)**	-0.2517
DXY	0.0648 (0.3232)	0.0643 (0.3189)	0.0790 (0.3955)	0.0794 (0.3970)	Impotent	0.3988 (1.3175)	0.4006 (1.3181)	0.3881 (1.2697)	0.3900 (1.2758)	Impotent
HL		-0.0052 (-0.0873)		0.0046 (0.0747)	Impotent		0.0111 (0.1708)		0.0059 (0.0946)	Impotent
Adj. R²	0.1198	0.1173	0.1198	0.1176	0.1186	0.3112	0.3083	0.3110	0.3081	0.3097
ARCH	0.1347 (1.6588)*	0.1357 (1.6643)*	0.2632 (1.8094)*	0.2632 (1.7900)*	0.1992	0.0553 (1.1911)	0.0548 (1.1744)	0.0385 (0.7363)	0.0397 (0.7340)	Impotent
GARCH	0.3450 (0.8996)	0.3418 (0.8929)	0.2019 (0.7040)	0.2025 (0.6981)	Impotent	0.9146 (14.4549)***	0.9148 (14.3322)***	0.9290 (14.2262)***	0.9278 (13.9978)***	0.9216
LEVERAGE			-0.2854 (-1.9128)*	-0.2856 (-1.8940)*	-0.2855			0.0139 (0.3425)	0.0127 (0.2784)	Impotent
Log likelihood	695.0222	695.0247	697.5129	697.5149		368.4226	368.4349	368.4641	368.4673	
Distribution	Student-t	Student-t	Student-t	Student-t		Student-t	Student-t	Student-t	Student-t	

***, ** and * denote statistical significance at the 1, 5 and 10 per cent, respectively. GARCH models and TGARCH models have been used to denote the symmetric and asymmetric effects.

Table 3.27: Commodity Market Analysis under APT-GARCH models: Wheat

	Pre-Crisis Period: WHEAT					Post-Crisis Period: WHEAT				
	GARCH	GARCH.HL	AGARCH	AGARCH.HL	Average	GARCH	GARCH.HL	AGARCH	AGARCH.HL	Average
Beta	0.4456 (4.4054)***	0.4459 (4.3885)***	0.4360 (4.1327)***	0.4354 (4.1229)***	0.4407	1.2075 (6.6188)***	1.2133 (6.5532)***	1.1937 (6.9685)***	1.1966 (6.9875)***	1.2028
MSCI	0.0783 (0.9928)	0.0793 (0.9937)	0.0827 (0.9222)	0.0827 (0.9223)	Impotent	-0.1318 (-1.2130)	-0.1259 (-1.1603)	-0.1155 (-1.0510)	-0.1129 (-1.0196)	Impotent
VIX	-0.1052 (-2.4896)**	-0.1052 (-2.4929)**	-0.1158 (-2.4018)**	-0.1158 (-2.3975)**	-0.1105	-0.3348 (-3.3103)***	-0.3418 (-3.3019)***	-0.3550 (-3.7433)***	-0.3583 (-3.7348)***	-0.3475
DXY	-0.0959 (-0.6588)	-0.0956 (-0.6538)	-0.0725 (-0.4832)	-0.0723 (-0.4804)	Impotent	-0.6429 (-2.5263)**	-0.6383 (-2.4783)**	-0.5268 (-2.0752)*	-0.5250 (-2.0357)**	-0.5833
HL		-0.0124 (-0.1956)		0.0072 (0.1156)	Impotent		0.0485 (0.6608)		0.0287 (0.4027)	Impotent
Adj. R²	0.0456	0.0423	0.0454	0.0432	0.0441	0.3129	0.3112	0.3125	0.3105	0.3118
ARCH	0.0369 (1.8181)*	0.0366 (1.8017)*			-0.0368	0.0601 (1.0520)	0.0615 (0.9979)			Impotent
GARCH	0.9540 (34.3860)***	0.9546 (34.5121)***			-0.9543	0.8645 (5.7463)***	0.8580 (5.2070)***			0.8613
LEVERAGE			0.1437 (1.7813)*	0.1435 (1.7865)*	0.1436			0.1979 (1.8135)*	0.1912 (1.6817)*	0.1946
Log likelihood	770.9525	770.9676	767.8183	767.8234		389.4652	389.6558	390.4443	390.5112	
Distribution	Student-t	Student-t	Student-t	Student-t		Student-t	Student-t	Student-t	Student-t	

***, ** and * denote statistical significance at the 1, 5 and 10 per cent, respectively. Due to violation of GARCH parameters, IGARCH has been used under symmetric GARCH and EGARCH for asymmetric GARCH. Under EGARCH, there are no such ARCH and GARCH terms, since the coefficient for the log variance in EGARCH has some correspondence with the sum of the ARCH and GARCH terms in TGARCH (See Carol Alexandra, 2008, Practical Econometrics). In that respect, only leverage terms have been reported.

Table 3.28: Commodity Market Analysis under APT-GARCH models: Gold

	Pre-Crisis Period: GOLD					Post-Crisis Period: GOLD				
	GARCH	GARCH.HL	AGARCH	AGARCH.HL	Average	GARCH	GARCH.HL	AGARCH	AGARCH.HL	Average
Beta	0.3435 (6.1857)***	0.3369 (6.0741)***	0.3420 (6.2191)***	0.3281 (6.0149)***	0.3376	0.4484 (5.4630)***	0.4311 (5.2273)***	0.4510 (4.6384)***	0.4571 (4.7593)***	0.4469
MSCI	0.0022 (0.0519)	0.0018 (0.0439)	0.0179 (0.4465)	0.0178 (0.4444)	Impotent	-0.2415 (-5.0985)***	-0.2443 (-5.3460)***	-0.2229 (-3.7346)***	-0.2232 (-3.8620)***	-0.2330
VIX	-0.0650 (-2.6996)***	-0.0631 (-2.6222)***	-0.0598 (-2.5800)**	-0.0556 (-2.4294)**	-0.0609	0.0144 (0.3073)	0.0088 (0.1893)	-0.0010 (-0.0180)	-0.0232 (-0.4082)	Impotent
DXY	-0.8138 (-12.4195)***	-0.8150 (-12.3850)***	-0.7735 (-12.0209)***	-0.7710 (-12.0379)***	-0.7933	-0.7379 (-6.5036)***	-0.7906 (-6.9454)***	-0.8091 (-5.6364)***	-0.8476 (-6.1385)***	-0.7963
HL		0.0430 (0.8577)		0.0745 (1.4602)	Impotent		0.1483 (2.9754)***		0.1754 (2.7531)***	0.1619
Adj. R²	0.2902	0.2902	0.2912	0.2908	0.2906	0.3079	0.3194	0.3025	0.3109	0.3102
ARCH	0.1348 (2.5082)**	0.1333 (2.4742)**	0.1864 (2.7150)***	0.2020 (2.7104)***	0.1641	0.1192 (5.7577)***	0.1166 (5.3660)***			0.1179
GARCH	0.8020 (10.8785)***	0.8027 (10.7472)***	0.8485 (15.3155)***	0.8485 (15.1216)***	0.8254	0.8808 (42.5547)***	0.8834 (40.6645)***			0.8821
LEVERAGE			-0.1788 (-2.5146)**	-0.1945 (-2.5731)***	-0.1867			0.1218 (1.6000)*	0.1308 (1.7922)*	0.1263
Log likelihood	1008.187	1008.535	1012.468	1013.515		514.7895	516.7178	521.7359	519.3635	
Distribution	Student-t	Student-t	Student-t	Student-t		Student-t	Student-t	Student-t	Student-t	

Table 3.29: Commodity Market Analysis under APT-GARCH models: Platinum

	Pre-Crisis Period: PLATINUM					Post-Crisis Period: PLATINUM				
	GARCH	GARCH.HL	AGARCH	AGARCH.HL	Average	GARCH	GARCH.HL	AGARCH	AGARCH.HL	Average
Beta	0.3077 (5.3237)***	0.3169 (5.4736)***	0.3555 (5.1646)***	0.3619 (5.2508)***	0.3355	0.5823 (6.7754)***	0.5779 (6.7651)***	0.5792 (5.7733)***	0.5688 (5.6844)***	0.5771
MSCI	0.067485 (1.332839)	0.0755 (1.4867)	0.1021 (1.7524)*	0.1091 (1.8633)*	0.1056	0.1452 (2.5976)***	0.1439 (2.5685)**	0.1797 (2.6462)***	0.1808 (2.6800)***	0.1624
VIX	-0.0431 (-1.6530)*	-0.0428 (-1.6361)*	-0.0614 (-1.9934)**	-0.0634 (-2.0693)**	-0.0527	0.0626 (1.3499)	0.0393 (0.6825)	0.0500 (0.8866)	0.0468 (0.8301)	Impotent
DXY	-0.3654 (-4.3531)***	-0.3574 (-4.2218)***	-0.3256 (-3.2710)***	-0.3200 (-3.2147)***	-0.3421	-0.2993 (-2.4293)**	-0.3086 (-2.5027)**	-0.3130 (-2.2181)**	-0.3244 (-2.2998)**	-0.3113
HL		-0.0367 (-1.0498)		-0.0413 (-0.9895)	Impotent		0.0342 (0.6321)		0.0614 (0.9790)	Impotent
Adj. R²	0.0755	0.0850	0.0772	0.0862	0.0810	0.3711	0.3696	0.3639	0.3620	0.3667
ARCH	0.0648 (4.8355)***	0.0639 (4.8112)***			0.0644	0.1130 (4.3597)***	0.1143 (4.4076)***			0.1137
GARCH	0.9352 (69.8408)***	0.9361 (70.4545)***			0.9357	0.8870 (34.2177)***	0.8857 (34.1443)***			0.8864
LEVERAGE			-0.0095 (-0.2143)	-0.0181 (-0.4077)	Impotent			0.0616 (1.0973)	0.0653 (1.1380)	Impotent
Log likelihood	884.34	884.64	889.65	870.94		490.64	490.77	497.57	498.08	
Distribution	GED	GED	Student-t	Student-t		Student-t	Student-t	Student-t	Student-t	

***, ** and * denote statistical significance at the 1, 5 and 10 per cent, respectively. Due to violation of GARCH parameters, IGARCH has been used under symmetric GARCH and EGARCH for asymmetric GARCH. Under EGARCH, there are no such ARCH and GARCH terms, since the coefficient for the log variance in EGARCH has some correspondence with the sum of the ARCH and GARCH terms in TGARCH (See Carol Alexandra, 2008, Practical Econometrics). In that respect, only leverage terms have been reported.

Table 3.30: Commodity Market Analysis under APT-GARCH models: Silver

	Pre-Crisis Period: SILVER					Post-Crisis Period: SILVER				
	GARCH	GARCH.HL	AGARCH	AGARCH.HL	Average	GARCH	GARCH.HL	AGARCH	AGARCH.HL	Average
Beta	0.5780 (6.0731)***	0.5528 (5.9381)***	0.5835 (6.1146)***	0.5548 (5.9515)***	0.5673	0.8765 (5.6126)***	0.8077 (5.1325)***	0.8676 (4.4831)***	0.7175 (4.1341)***	0.8173
MSCI	0.1467 (2.0390)**	0.1319 (1.8607)*	0.1479 (2.0512)**	0.1324 (1.8667)*	0.1397	-0.0910 (-0.9663)	-0.1019 (-1.0607)	-0.0599 (-0.5277)	-0.0443 (-0.4246)	Impotent
VIX	-0.1022 (-2.4373)**	-0.0959 (-2.3500)**	-0.1027 (-2.4382)**	-0.0959 (-2.3449)**	-0.0992	0.0277 (0.3136)	0.0385 (0.4480)	0.0410 (0.3861)	0.0970 (0.9536)	Impotent
DXY	-0.7161 (-5.9397)***	-0.7275 (-6.2180)***	-0.7180 (-5.9385)***	-0.7278 (-6.2099)***	-0.7224	-1.1412 (-5.2709)***	-1.1874 (-5.5222)***	-1.1217 (-4.4251)***	-1.0441 (-4.1989)***	-1.1236
HL		0.1524 (3.2124)***		0.1522 (3.2023)***	0.1523		0.1465 (2.5451)**		0.1873 (2.8036)***	0.1669
Adj. R²	0.2087	0.2013	0.2090	0.2014	0.2051	0.3919	0.3951	0.3896	0.3887	0.3913
ARCH	0.1728 (1.9973)**	0.1676 (1.9583)*	0.1335 (1.0364)	0.1372 (0.9369)	0.1702	0.0568 (2.6126)***	0.0447 (2.4545)**			0.0508
GARCH	0.0787 (0.3195)	0.0012 (0.0061)	0.1011 (0.3820)	0.0317 (0.1452)	Impotent	0.9432 (43.375)***	0.9553 (52.5032)***			0.9493
LEVERAGE			0.0455 (0.2958)	0.0325 (0.1967)	Impotent			0.1088 (1.7523)*	0.1333 (1.1260)	Impotent
Log likelihood	811.5511	815.6521	811.5726	815.6558		383.4321	385.4376	389.2460	389.1795	
Distribution	Student-t	Student-t	Student-t	Student-t		Student-t	Student-t	Student-t	Student-t	

***, ** and * denote statistical significance at the 1, 5 and 10 per cent, respectively. Due to violation of GARCH parameters, IGARCH has been used under symmetric GARCH. For asymmetric GARCH models, TGARCH has been used in the pre-crisis era while EGARCH has been used in the post-crisis period. Under EGARCH, there are no such ARCH and GARCH terms, since the coefficient for the log variance in EGARCH has some correspondence with the sum of the ARCH and GARCH terms in TGARCH (See Carol Alexandra, 2008, Practical Econometrics). In that respect, only leverage terms have been reported.

References

1. Abel, Andrew B., 1988, Stock prices under time-varying dividend risk: An exact solution in an infinite-horizon general equilibrium model, *Journal of Monetary Economics*, 22(3), 375-393.
2. Acharya, Viral V. and L. H. Pedersen, 2005, Asset pricing with liquidity risk, *Journal of Financial Economics*, 77(2), 375-410.
3. Adrian, T. and F. Franzoni, 2009, Learning about beta: Time-varying factor loadings, expected returns, and the conditional CAPM," *Journal of Empirical Finance*, 16(4), 537-556.
4. Alexander, C., 2008, Market risk analysis, Volume II: Practical Financial Econometrics, Wiley.
5. Andersen, T. G., T. Bollerslev, F. X. Diebold and J. Wu, 2005, A framework for exploring the macroeconomic determinants of systematic risk, *American Economic Review*, 95(2), 398-404.
6. Arisoy, Y. E., 2010, Volatility risk and the value remium: Evidence from the French stock market, *Journal of Banking and Finance*, 34(5), 975-983.
7. Backus, David K. and Allan W. Gregory, 1993, Theoretical relations between risk premiums and conditional variances, *Journal of Business and Economic Statistics*, 11(2), 177-185.
8. Bali, T. G. and R. F. Engle, 2010, The intertemporal capital asset pricing model with dynamic conditional correlations, *Journal of Monetary Economics*, 57(4), 377-390.
9. Banz, R. W., 1981, The relationship between return and market value of common stocks, *Journal of Financial Economics*, 9(1), 3-18.
10. Barinov, A., 2008, Idiosyncratic volatility, growth options, and the cross-section of returns, Working Paper, University of Rochester.
11. Bekaert, G., R. J. Hodrick and X. Zhang, 2009, International Stock Return Comovements, *Journal of Finance*, 64(6), 2591-2626.
12. Black, F., 1972, Capital market equilibrium with restricted borrowing, *Journal of Business*, 45(3), 444-455.
13. Bodnar, G. M., B. Dumas and R. C. Marston, 2003, Cross-border valuation: the international cost of equity capital, NBER Working Paper 10115.
14. Bos, T. and P. Newbold, 1984, An empirical investigation of the possibility of systematic stochastic risk in the market model, *Journal of Business*, 57(1), 35-41.
15. Breeden, D. T., 1979, An intertemporal asset pricing model with stochastic consumption and investment opportunities, *Journal of Financial Economics*, 7(3), 265-296.

16. Bruner, R. F., W. Li, M. Kritzman, S. Myrgren and S. Page, 2008, Market integration in developed and emerging markets: Evidence from the CAPM, *Emerging Markets Review*, 9(2), 89-103.

17. Campbell, J. Y., 1996, Understanding risk and return, *Journal of Political Economy*, 104(2), 298-345.

18. Chen, Cherry C. and Raymond W. So, 2002, Exchange rate variability and the riskiness of US multinational firms: Evidence from the Asian financial turmoil, *Journal of Multinational Financial Management*, 12(4-5), 411-428.

19. De Bondt, Werner F. M., and R. Thaler, 1985, Does the stock market overreact?, *Journal of Finance*, 40(3), 793-805.

20. Durand, R. B., Y. Lan and A. Ng, 2011, Conditional beta: Evidence from Asian emerging markets, *Global Finance Journal*, 22(2), 130-153.

21. Engle, R. F., 1990, Discussion: Stock market volatility and the crash of '87, *Review of Financial Studies*, 3(1), 103-106.

22. Engle, R. F., and V. K. Ng, 1993, Measuring and testing the impact of news on volatility, *Journal of Finance*, 48(5), 1749-1778.

23. Fama, E. F. and K. R. French, 1992, The cross-section of expected stock returns, *Journal of Finance*, 47(2), 427-465.

24. Fama, E. F. and K. R. French, 1993, Common risk factors in the returns on stocks and bonds, *Journal of Financial Economics*, 33(1), 3-56.

25. Fletcher, J., 1997, An examination of the cross-sectional relationship of beta and return: UK evidence, *Journal of Economics and Business*, 49(3), 211-221.

26. Foster, G., C. Olsen, and T. Shevlin, 1984, Earnings releases, anomalies, and the behavior of security prices, *The Accounting Review*, 59(4), 574-603.

27. Gennotte, G. and T. A. Marsh, 1993, Variations in economic uncertainty and risk premiums on capital assets, *European Economic Review*, 37(5), 1021-1041.

28. Ghysels, E., 1998, On stable factor structures in the pricing of risk: Do time-varying betas help or hurt?, *Journal of Finance*, 53(2), 549-573.

29. Graham, J. R. and C. R. Harvey, 2001, The theory and practice of corporate finance: Evidence from the field, *Journal of Financial Economics*, 60(2), 187-243.

30. Groenewold, N. and P. Fraser, 1999, Time-varying estimates of CAPM betas, *Mathematics and Computers in Simulation*, 48(4), 531-539.

31. Hull, J., I. Nelken and A. White, 2004, Merton's model, credit risk and volatility skews, *Journal of Credit Risk*, 1(1), 3-27.

32. Hwang, Y., H. Min, J. A. McDonald, H. Kim and B. Kim, 2010, Using the credit spread as an option-risk factor: Size and value effects in CAPM, *Journal of Banking and Finance*, 34(10), 2995-3009.

33. Iqbal, J. and R. Brooks, 2007, Alternative beta risk estimators and asset pricing tests in emerging markets: The case of Pakistan, *Journal of Multinational Financial Management*, 17(1), 75-93.

34. Isakov, D., 1999, Is beta still alive? Conclusive evidence from the Swiss stock market, *European Journal of Finance*, 5(3), 202-212.

35. Jegadeesh, N. and S. Titman, 1993, Returns to buying winners and selling losers: Implications for stock market efficiency, *Journal of Finance*, 48(1), 65-91.

36. Kim, D., 2006, On the information uncertainty risk and the January effect, *Journal of Business*, 79(4), 2127-2162.

37. Kim, D., 2010, Information uncertainty risk and the seasonality in international stock markets, *Asia-Pacific Journal of Financial Studies*, 39(2), 229-259.

38. Lintner, J., 1965, Security prices, risk, and maximal gains from diversification, *Journal of Finance*, 20(4), 587-615.

39. Lucas, R. E., 1978, Asset prices in an exchange economy, *Econometrica*, 46(6), 1429-1445.

40. Merton, R. C., 1973, An intertemporal capital asset pricing model, *Econometrica*, 41(5), 867-887.

41. Merton, R. C., 1980, On estimating the expected return on the market: An exploratory investigation, *Journal of Financial Economics*, 82(2), 289-314.

42. Mossin, J., 1966, Equilibrium in a capital asset market, *Econometrica*, 34(4), 307-325.

43. Nelson, Daniel B., 1991, Conditional heteroscedasticity in asset returns: A new approach, *Econometrica*, 59(2), 347-370.

44. O'Brien, T. J., 1999, The global CAPM and a firm's cost of capital in different countries, *Journal of Applied Corporate Finance*, 12(2), 73-79.

45. Pastor, L. and R. F. Stambaugh, 2003, Liquidity risk and expected stock returns, *Journal of Political Economy* 111(3), 642-685.

46. Pettengill, G. N., S. Sundaram and I. Mathur, 1995, The conditional relation between beta and returns, *The Journal of Financial and Quantitative Analysis*, 30(01), 101-116.

47. Post, T. and Pim van Vliet, 2006, Downside risk and asset pricing, *Journal of Banking and Finance*, 30(3), 823-849.

48. Reinganum, M. R., 1981, A new empirical perspective on the CAPM, *Journal of Financial and Quantitative Analysis*, 16(4), 439-462.

49. Reserve Bank of Australia, Financial Stability Report 2011.
50. Ross, S. A., 1976, The arbitrage theory of capital asset pricing, *Journal of Economic Theory*, 13(3), 341-360.
51. Rubinstein, M., 1976, The valuation of uncertain income streams and the pricing of options, *Bell Journal of Economics*, 7(2), 407-25.
52. Sharpe, W. F., 1964, Capital asset prices: A theory of market equilibrium under conditions of risk, *Journal of Finance*, 19(3), 425-442.
53. Shiller, R. J., Irrational Exuberance, 2nd Edition, Princeton University Press, 2005.
54. Theriou, N.G., V. P. Aggelidis, D. I. Maditinos and Ž. Ševic, 2010, Testing the relation between beta and returns in Athens stock exchange, *Managerial Finance*, 36, 1043-1056.
55. Welch, I., 2008, The consensus estimate for the equity premium by academic financial economists in December 2007, Working Paper, Brown University.
56. Yao, T., T. Yu, T. Zhang and S. Chen, 2011, Asset growth and stock returns, *Pacific-Basin Finance Journal*, 19(1), 115-139.

CHAPTER FOUR

DETERMINANTS OF BANKS' PROFITABILITY FOR OECD COUNTRIES UNDER THE US SUBPRIME CRISIS: IN QUEST FOR GLOBAL FINANCIAL STABILITY POLICIES

This chapter examines how banks' specific and macroeconomic factors influenced their profitability before and after the crisis. The study is innovative, since it is based on the employment of new metrics such as interest expense to income ratio, staff costs, fees and commissions' payable to receivable ratio, interbank deposits, customers' deposits and investments in securities. Results show that capital and funding costs constitute the most important factors in influencing banks' profitability. Evidence is also found as to investments in securities positively impacting upon profitability. The PIGS dummy demonstrates that Portugal, Italy, Greece and Spain were all subject to problems even before the crisis. At the macroeconomic-wide level, the study shows that exports and GDP growth deters NPLs, while unemployment and inflation give NPLs a push.

4.0 Introduction

Many studies have been conducted in order to gauge on the factors that impact bank profitability. As stressed by Golin (2001), sufficient earnings constitute the essential ingredient for maintaining banks' solvency. Above all, studies pertaining to determinants of bank profitability are presently being reinvigorated in light of the crisis. Such a state of affairs enables policy-makers to gain insights about any crisis-induced change in drivers for profitability. Equipped with such knowledge, policy-makers are then better placed in terms of their risk management endeavour to consolidate financial stability. The latest research on banks' profitability which integrates the crisis effect is that of Dietrich and Wanzenried (2011); unfortunately though, their findings cannot be generalised for global policies implementation since their paper is limited to Switzerland's banking system.

The current study explores the forces that affect the Organisation for Economic Cooperation and Development (OECD) banks' profitability based on country-wise aggregate bank data. It can be argued that the use of country-wise aggregate data obscures firm-specific forces which dominate both industry and country forces—some banks have pretty much collapsed while others have been muddling through. However, this paper clings to a country-wise aggregate bank data assessment to probe into country risks financial stability at the global level. For instance, if a country has two large banks which are doing pretty well and 19 small banks which are posting losses, on an aggregate basis, the country is deemed to be performing well, due to the fact that it is imbued with low financial stability risks. Another major contribution of the paper pertains to the use of some unique metrics such as staff costs and investments in securities.

The present study builds on the work of García-Herrero et al. (2009) and Dietrich and Wanzenried (2011) to probe into determinants of banks' profitability for OECD countries, before and after the crisis. To capture the effects of the crisis, a pooled estimation technique is applied. Moreover, recourse is made towards the Generalised Methods of Moments (GMM) approach which has proved effective in many studies, since it is best able to account for the persistence of bank profits. The paper differs from earlier studies on several fronts. First, the sample consists of a large number of countries, including some which have key roles in the global financial system, like the US and Europe. Second, recourse is made towards aggregate data on all commercial banks for each country so that analysis is holistic in assessing banks' financial stability at the international level. Third, the study is richer in terms of the use of new metrics for gauging on banks' profitability, including the use of fees and commissions and investments in securities. Last but not least, non-performing loans are also incorporated and modelled, in view of having fully-fledged analysis of credit risk management policies to be envisaged in light of the US crisis.

Results show that the determinants of banks' profitability are sensitive to the type of dependent variable employed, with a pronounced explanatory power noted in the case of Net Interest Margin. In addition, findings suggest that the capital of banks exerts the highest economic impact on their profitability with their impacts being considerably more pronounced in the post-crisis era. In addition, there exists crystal clear evidence of persistence in banks' profitability, validating the use of GMM econometric techniques. The PIGS dummy variable used is found to lag behind a negative impact on performance prior to the onset of the crisis, meaning that Portugal, Italy, Greece and Spain did face significant stress in their banking system well before the crisis. Most importantly, at the macroeconomic-wide level, the study shows that exports and GDP growth undermine the level of NPLs, while unemployment and inflation stimulate higher NPLs.

The chapter is structured as follows: Section 4.1 deals with the theoretical/empirical literature on determinants of bank profitability; Section 4.2 focuses on the data, econometric models and variables; Section 4.3 presents the empirical results; and Section 4.4 concludes.

4.1 Theoretical background

The literature on bank profitability has attracted considerable interest from both academicians and practitioners. Essentially, the empirical literature on bank profitability can be split into two major parts; country-specific focus like that of Berger (1995), Neely and Wheelock (1997), Ben Naceur and Goaied (2008) and Garcia-Herrero et al. (2009), or assessing a sample of countries[1] like the studies performed by Molyneux and Thorton (1992), Demirgüç-Kunt and Huizinga (1999), Staikouras and Wood (2003) and Pasiouras and Kosmidou (2007). In spite of the fact that differences prevail both between and within these two different approaches, some commonality in results does exist, for example clinging to the same metrics for profitability assessment. As far as the determinants that are used to model bank profitability are concerned, the mainstream bank profitability studies usually adopt a two-pronged approach: bank-specific determinants and macro-specific factors.

Another strand of the literature on bank profitability focuses on the shift away from traditional intermediation activities towards other sources of income, labelled as non-interest income and comprising of commission and fee income and trading income. These non-interest income transactions also include transaction services like cash management, safekeeping services, investment banking activities and securities brokerage. Indeed, changes in regulation and technology have scaled up competition so as to stimulate banks to diversify their activities base[2] to ensure profits stabilisation (see Saunders and Walter, 1994). Additionally,

---

[1] Despite using a sample of countries, these studies consider only firm-specific data.
[2] Albertazzi and Gambacorta (2009) capture diversification by using the ratio of non-interest income over gross income. Expansion of off-balance-sheet items has also been a way for banks to scale up profits under credit securitisation and credit derivatives.

Lepetit et al. (2008) state that high competition on conventional intermediation activities in Europe has encouraged banks to drift more towards non-interest activities. DeYoung and Roland (2001) further point out that income emanating from lending activities is stable, while that coming from non-interest income may be subject to larger fluctuations on the back of higher costs on borrowers to switch under loans relative to service facilities, operational leverage in which a rise in non-interest income needs additional bank staff, and financial leverage whereby non-interest income activities do not impose capital requirements on banks. Stiroh (2004) argues that the high correlation between interest income growth and non-interest growth manifests itself by virtue of the cross-selling of distinct products to the same customers.

The literature on bank profitability also focuses on financial stability issues. Demirgüç-Kunt and Detragiache (1999) point out that bank profitability constitutes an important predictor of financial crises. Consequently, financial stability motives have also urged new research which links bank profitability to the business cycles based on a macro-prudential assessment. Such analysis befits the Financial Sector Adjustment Programme established in 1999 by the International Monetary Fund and the World Bank. Under macro-prudential assessment, the aim is geared towards eliminating fragile structures of the financial system rather than anticipating any shock that induces a crisis. Downswings of the business cycles unleash worsening impacts on loan portfolios, which in turn trigger credit losses as to undermine bank profitability levels. Above all, such a fall in bank profitability may intensify the downswing of the business cycles via bank lending channels to the private sector. Van den Heuvel (2002) points out that a fall in bank profitability generates direct repercussions on real economic activities like consumption and investments via the banks' capital channel. In essence, low bank profitability undermines equity so that based on external equity financing being costly, banks are compelled to scale down lending. Moreover, Albertazzi and Gambacorta (2009) find that banks' profits are procyclically related to economic cycles.

Without profits, no bank can survive. The empirical literature has used different metrics to capture bank profitability. The most widely used metric for profitability assessment rests on net profits to total assets and net interest margin. Some studies resort towards net profits to total equity (Dietrich and Wanzenried (2011). Studies usually assess a set of bank's attributes on their profitability. In that respect, size is widely used whenever modelling bank profitability. The underlying rationale is that larger banks have larger scope to avail of economies of scale and hence significant costs reduction possibilities, as evidenced by Goddard et al. (2004). Beyond that, larger banks are able to harness maximum benefits while reducing risk via wider loan portfolio diversification and significant cross-selling opportunities for their products. Furthermore, it is widely acclaimed, chiefly following the crisis, that the best performing banks are generally those which have strong capital cushioning mechanisms or a robust equity base (see Demirgüç-Kunt and Huizinga (1999), Goddard et al. (2004) and Garcia-Herrero et al. (2009)). The justifying mechanism works via a higher capital base acting as a deterrent to any bankruptcy potential so that funding costs are reduced for the banks.

Risk is considered as the most vital element affecting bank profitability. The old adage in finance "There ain't no such thing as a free lunch" clearly bears testimony to the fact that without risk, there are no profits. The most widely used measurement for risk in the literature pertains to loans to total assets ratio, as loans constitute the core business activities of any operating bank. The empirical evidence is however mixed. Abreu and Mendes (2001) find a positive effect of loans on bank profits in the case of France, Germany, Portugal and Spain, while Staikouras and Wood (2003) find negative evidence of loans on bank profitability in the case of 13 European Union banking markets.

Operational efficiency has also been given much significance in the literature as measured by the cost-to-income ratio. Indeed, if a bank is generating more income from its assets relative to its costs, then this definitely adds up to its profitability level, so that a negative relationship is anticipated to subsist between cost-to-income ratio and profitability. Dietrich and Wanzenried (2011) confirm such a negative relationship.

Studies have also factored in external forces or macroeconomic determinants of bank profitability. For instance, taxation in the financial system does constitute an important factor for assessing bank profitability. In the same vein, GDP growth and inflation have been widely used in most studies. GDP growth is expected to positively influence the level of profits since it captures the evolution of the business cycles. Hassan and Bashir (2003) and Pasiouras and Kosmidou (2007), among others, find positive evidence between GDP and bank profitability. However, Demirgüç-Kuntand Huizinga (1999) and Carbo Valverde and Rodriguez (2007) confirm a negative relationship between economic growth and bank profitability, attributable to reduced risk premiums of banks during upswings of the business cycles. As far as inflation is concerned, Perry (1992) states that only unanticipated inflation reduces banks' profits while anticipated inflation enhances bank profitability on the back of quicker interest rates adjustments.

The next section deals with the data and model specification, along with the various metrics employed.

4.2 Data, Econometric Models and Variables

4.2.1 Data

Celebrating its 50th anniversary in 2011 with 34 member countries in its group, the Organisation for Economic Cooperation and Development (OECD) principally aims to stimulate policies that enhance the economic and social well-being of people around the globe. The distinctive feature of OECD is that it consists of very advanced economies like the US and European countries but also emerging economies like Mexico and Turkey. An assessment of banks' profitability for OECD countries will be synonymous to an indirect assessment of the worldwide state of financial stability from the banks' perspective.

Table 4.1: List of Countries

AUSTRIA	GERMANY	MEXICO	SPAIN
BELGIUM	GREECE	NETHERLANDS	SWEDEN
CHILE	HUNGARY	NORWAY	SWITZERLAND
DENMARK	IRELAND	POLAND	TURKEY
FINLAND	ITALY	PORTUGAL	UK
FRANCE	LUXEMBOURG	SLOVAKIA	US

Data for this study has been gathered from the OECD banking statistics database 2000-2009 with aggregate banks' specific factors captured via information from the balance sheet and income statements. Other data like Non-Performing Loans, Unemployment, Inflation, GDP growth and Exports have been collected from the World Bank database. I explicitly ignore five countries from the sample of 29 countries, as their data is irregular in the OECD statistics. For instance, Korea has been removed as its data is utterly an outlier in the sample, chiefly when it comes to analysing the size effect post converting in Euro.[3] The final sample, as depicted in Table 4.1, consists of 24 countries' aggregate data on banking statistics spanning the period 2000 to 2009. In view of

---

[3] When computing size, all countries were leveled by converting all assets into euro-denominated values using exchange rate data from GOCURRENCY.com.

analysing the effect of the crisis on banks' profitability, the sample has been split into two parts; the pre-crisis era from 2000 to 2006 and post-crisis period from 2007 onwards, based on a pooled estimation approach. The variables and their respective definitions are shown in Table 4.2.

4.2.2 Econometric Models

4.2.2.1 Pooled Estimation

The study resorts to pooled data estimation under country-year observations to gauge the effects of the crisis on banks' profitability. The model is run twice, once for the pre-crisis period (from 2000 to 2006) and once for the post-crisis period (2007 to 2008/09). Two metrics for bank profitability are employed in the study, namely net profits over total assets (NPBT) and net interest income over total assets (NIM).

NPBT sends signals about the ability of the bank to generate income out of the total assets employed. In essence, it depicts the extent to which assets are being effectively and efficiently managed as to result in higher profits.

Net interest margin metric has been widely used in many studies because it directly embeds the main activities of banks, which are based on charging higher interest on loans relative to those on their deposits; this is technically labelled as the interest rate spread. The concept of NIM is best explained by Ho and Saunders (1981), who consider banks as dealers that demand positive interest rate spread based on uncertainty which emanates from asynchronous deposit supplies and loan demands. Consequently, banks charge a cost based on a bid-ask price; bid price reflects the price paid on deposits, while ask price pertains to the price received on loans. The econometric model is specified as follows.

$$PRO_{it} = \alpha + \sum_{i=1}^{6} \lambda_i X_{it} + \sum_{j=1}^{14} \delta_j Z_{jt} + \beta\, PIGS_{it} + \varepsilon_{it}$$

$$(1)$$

Equation (1) constitutes a pooled regression analysis to remove any crisis-induced differences in terms of the different forces that influence banks' profitability. PRO represents the profitability variable, which is captured by NIM and NPBT respectively.

Table 4.2: Definition of variables

Macroeconomic Variables	
Unemployment	Unemployment rate
GDP growth	Yearly GDP growth
Inflation rate	Yearly change in CPI
Stock Market Capitalisation	Stock Market Capitalisation/GDP
Exports	Exports of goods and services/ GDP
Effective Tax Rate	Total Tax/Pre-Tax Profit
Country-Banks-Specific Factors	
Profitability	Net interest income/Total Assets
	Net profit before tax/Total Assets
Operational efficiency	Interest expenses/Interest Income
	Fees and commissions payable/ Fees and commissions receivable
	Staff costs/Gross Income
NPA	Bank nonperforming loans/Total loans
PIGS dummy	1 if Portugal, Italy, Greece and Spain; 0 otherwise
Capital strength (Equity)	Total equity/Total assets
Loan/Asset specialisation ratio	Loans/Total assets
	Cash and balance with Central Bank/Total assets
	Securities/Total assets
Deposits/Liabilities specialisation ratio	Interbank deposits/Total assets
	Customer deposits/Total assets
	Bonds/Total assets
Size	Natural Log of Total Assets
Retained earnings	Retained Profits/Total assets
Funding costs	Interest expenses/Total deposits

X vector encapsulates the vector of all macroeconomic variables like unemployment, GDP, CPI, market capitalisation, exports and effective tax rates. Z vector factors in all the country-banks-specific elements such as staff costs, capital, size and funding costs, among others. PIGS represents a dummy variable which is one in the case of Portugal, Italy, Greece and Spain. The error term ε_{it} is well-behaved and white noise. Table 4.2 provides detailed information relating to the six macroeconomic variables, 14 banks-specific forces and the dummy variable.

4.2.2.2 Panel Data Estimation

The drawback of pooled regression analysis is that it utterly ignores the dynamics of the variables so that panel data regression is considered for the same model specification under equation (1). The GMM Arellano and Bover (1995) econometric approach is used to account for profit persistence which is well documented in the form of market power in previous studies such as Mueller (1977) and Berger et al. (2000). The persistence parameter, denoted by φ, under GMM reflects a dynamic model. φ close to zero reflects a competitive banking structure while a parameter value close to one signifies a less competitive one. The underlying rationale for using the dynamic panel model is due to Baltagi and Kao (2000), who point out that a least squares estimation approach generates biased and inconsistent estimates so that dynamic panel is better suited to reducing such a problem.

The GMM approach is imbued with many blessings. GMM estimator generates consistent estimation of the parameters. Most importantly, GMM enables an interesting tweak in the model in the case of endogeneity issues, for example, causality running not only from equity to profitability but vice versa (bi-directional causality effects). Indeed, banks that are more lucrative can scale up their equity by retaining profits. In the same vein, more profitable banks are able to provide for higher staff costs so that both equity and staff costs are incorporated as instrument variables in the GMM model. Finally, GMM estimator controls for unobserved heterogeneity. A second panel model is run with NPLs as the dependent model following the strand of literature that directly considers NPLs as a bad output into the production process (see Berg et al. (1992)). All macroeconomic variables and loans are considered in the NPLs panel model. The next section deals with each independent variable and their expected impact on banks' profitability.

4.2.3 Variables

Independent Variables: Banks' Specific forces at Country Level

a. Equity

A body of literature exists with respect to bank capital and its risk level. Recently, Jokipii and Milne (2011) argued that the relationship between bank capital and risk also depends on the time period—short-run or long-run—under consideration. Technically speaking, the higher the capital level, the lower the risk level perceived and hence the less costly the external finance required by the bank, so that this triggers enhanced profitability level. Aggarwal and Jacques (2001) and Rime (2001) find a positive relationship between capital and risk because banks that have increased their capital levels also tend to scale up their risks accordingly. According to capital buffer theory by Milne and Whalley (2001), banks will tend to maintain capital level above the minimum required level due to both explicit and implicit costs[4] of capital falling below the required minimum level. Berger (1995) and Goddard et al. (2004) also find a positive relationship between equity and profitability.

However, a negative relationship can also subsist. By having higher capital, this means reduced risk in terms of undermined lending possibilities and accordingly reduced risk premiums charged by the banks. Shrieves and Dahl (1992) find evidence of a negative relationship between capital and risk, attributable to banks exploiting the deposit insurance subsidy.

b. Operational efficiency

Cost-to-income ratio has been widely used as a yardstick to assess efficiency. Athanasoglou et al. (2008) and Dietrich and Wanzenried (2011) confirm the presence of a negative relationship between cost-to-income ratio and profitability in line with the fact that the less efficient a bank, the lower its profitability level should be. Instead of using the cost-to-income ratio in line with previous empirical studies, the current study resorts to a more detailed assessment of operational efficiency by using interest expense-income ratio (interest operations), staff costs over total assets and fees and commissions payable-receivable ratio (trading operations).

---

[4] Explicit costs pertain to penalties imposed by the regulatory authority, while implicit costs refer to regulatory interference.

Dietrich and Wanzenried (2011) do not explicitly model the non-interest income—like fees and commissions received—in their model. The current study uses fees and commissions, which represent an important part of the banking business. Ironically, it is expected that with the onset of the crisis, most banks would cling to fees and commissions as their underpinning force to ensure stable profits, since profit margins emanating from fees and commissions are usually higher relative to those from interest operations.[5]

Staff costs have been considered in the model because they usually constitute the lion's share of most banks' operating expenses. Agoraki (2010) points out a positive relationship between operating expenses and the net interest margin of commercial banks. The underlying rationale is based on the fact that banks simply transfer their operating costs to customers. However, Claeys and Vander Vennet (2008) argue that operational efficiency may lower transaction costs to customers to thereby scale down net interest margins so that a negative relationship may also occur between NIM and staff costs.

c. Non-Performing Loans

Ioannidis et al. (2010) state that bad asset quality may trigger downward pressures on bank profitability by scaling down interest income and increasing provisioning costs. Traditional bank risk measure is usually captured by Non-Performing Loans (NPLs). A higher level of NPLs is expected to erode the profitability of banks by straining hard on the banks' loanable resources. Moreover, the negative impact may also be caused by an increase in monitoring costs, as suggested by Berger and DeYoung (1997). In addition, Hoshi and Kashyap (2010) confirm that NPLs have been at the centre of the Japanese banking crisis. However, Chen (2011) does not find any evidence of NPLs affecting the share price performance of Japanese banks.

d. Loans, Cash, Securities, Deposits (Interbank Deposits, Customer Deposits), Bonds

The balance sheet structure of any bank bears significant effects on its profitability level. Higher loans generate higher scope for profits as they constitute the crude form of profit generation for banks. Angbazo (1997), Abreu and Mendes (2003) and, Maudos and Fernández de Guevara (2004), all corroborate a positive relationship between credit risk and net interest

---

[5] This is expected to be accentuated by the fact that most advanced economies are caught in the liquidity trap.

margin. The positive relationship also occurs on the back of higher risk premiums charged by banks which are subject to larger provisions levels based on higher credit risk taken.

Apart from loans which provide income to the banks, recourse is made towards cash held with central banks to generate a holistic assessment of the forces that drive profitability of banks. For instance, apparently, the greater the level of cash held with central banks, the lesser the scope for giving out more loans; this then squeezes on the banks' returns. However, assessing the other side of the coin, more cash held with central banks is synonymous with an enhanced liquidity management at the expense of higher profits. The empirical evidence is mixed with a positive impact found by Abreu and Mendes (2001) and a negative effect in the case of Staikouras and Wood (2003).

Investments in securities, which pertain to income emanating from trading activities, are expected to provide a boost to bank performance. Previous studies have overlooked such a variable. The objective is to shed light on the risk-return trade-offs embodied in the distinct activities of banks. These investments are expected to diversify the revenue base of the banks, such as in the form of non-interest activities as pointed out by Lepetit et al. (2008), and thereby help to stabilise banks' profitability.

In the same vein, higher deposits imply cheaper and stable funding to the banks relative to borrowed funds, so that an upward pressure is exerted on profits. Interestingly, the current study employs a decomposed assessment for deposits, namely interbank deposits[6] and deposits made by customers. Alternatively stated, both retail and wholesale fundings have been incorporated to derive greater results. Huang and Ratnovski (2009) advance a model to show that wholesale financiers can have incentives to withdraw funding based on noisy signals of bank asset quality, which result in the failure of solvent banks. Finally, bonds issued have also been given due consideration. A negative impact is expected to manifest in the case that the costs under bonds issued exceed the benefits in terms of higher level of loanable resources.

e. Size

Size is measured as the natural logarithm of total assets and is anticipated to generate a positive effect on profitability via the economies of scale

---

[6] Interbank deposits from liability side have been considered and those from asset side ignored in the model since they are highly correlated, as shown in correlation coefficients Table 3 in the appendix section. Such high correlation coefficient may be indicative of natural hedging policies clung to by most banks whenever they deal with the interbank markets.

channel and larger scope for diversification medium, as evidenced by the findings of Goddard et al. (2004). Moreover, Boyd and Runkle (1993) point out that the resulting economies of scale will reduce the costs of gathering and processing information. However, should considerable agency costs prevail, then a negative effect may also occur through diseconomies of scale as per the findings of Stiroh and Rumble (2006) and Pasiouras and Kosmidou (2007). In that respect, the size variable is squared to capture for any non-linearity effects.

f. Funding costs
No bank can operate without deposits. However, deposits entail costs. The variable funding costs constitute the proxy to label the unit price of fund. Dietrich and Wanzenried (2011) find evidence that funding costs entail a negative effect on profitability. A positive impact may potentially manifest in the case of cheaper funding costs due to lower perceived risk of the banks.

g. Retained earnings
The study resorts to retained earnings following the current stressful situations whereby banks have no choice but to look at their retained earnings as the best metric for future growth. The main advantage of retained earnings as per the Pecking Order Hypothesis is that although it is applied for non-financials it has the same underlying rationale, in that it represents the banks' own source of funds, which is undeniably less costly than external financing.

Independent Variables: Macroeconomic forces at Country Level

a. Effective tax rate
To be consistent with prior empirical studies, recourse is made towards the effective tax rate, defined as taxes paid divided by before-tax profits, to capture the effect of tax on profitability. A higher effective tax rate is anticipated to result in a downward pressure on profitability of banks. Albertazzi and Gambacorta (2009) consider corporate income taxation to see how Anglo-Saxon countries differ from European countries in terms of return on equity. Their findings show small impacts of taxation on return on equity of banks, due to the fact that banks can transfer a large part of their tax burden to outsiders such as borrowers and depositors.

b. GDP growth, Export,[7] Unemployment and Market Capitalisation

GDP growth is expected to enshrine the profitability of banks because higher GDP growth is synonymous with upswings in the business cycles, which generate positive momentum to lending. Alternatively stated, an enhancement in economic conditions scales up the demand for loans by households, which in turn strengthens the banks' profitability levels. Hassan and Bashir (2003), Kosmidou (2008) and Pasiouras and Kosmidou (2007), all find a positive correlation between economic growth and financial performance. In addition, Albertazzi and Gambacorta (2009) find evidence of GDP growth rate positively influencing banks' return on equity. However, Demirgüç-Kuntand Huizinga (1999), Demirgüç-Kunt et al. (2004) and Carbo Valverde and Rodriguez (2007) end up with a negative relationship between economic growth and banks' profitability. This can be explained by improved economic activities that result in reduced loan delinquencies so that banks are willing to revise down their risk premiums.

Apart from GDP growth, the current study also uses exports and unemployment rate as other proxies to capture the state of the business cycles. Abreu and Mendes (2001) find a negative effect of unemployment on the performance of banks. Exports have been included to gauge on the extent to which exports enshrine the financial intermediation activities of banks in the form of a vibrant banking system that also benefits from higher inflows of foreign currencies.

Market capitalisation is also taken on board. Albertazzi and Gambacorta (2009) state that high stock market capitalisation ratio is synonymous with a robustly competing financial market relative to the banking sector so that a negative relationship manifests. However, Boyd and Smith (1999) find a positive relationship based on debt and equity markets behaving as complements rather than substitutes. Moreover, Ben Naceur (2003) states that as the stock market enlarges, this generates more information and eases the tasks of banks in identifying and monitoring customers so that higher market capitalisation should elicit higher banks' profitability.

c. Inflation rate

Inflation also affects the bottom line of any bank, depending on whether inflation expectations are well anchored. Empirical evidence is mixed in the case of inflation. Demirgüç-Kunt and Huizinga (1999) and Drakos (2002) find a positive relationship between banks' profitability and inflation, while Abreu and Mendes (2003), Agoraki (2010) and, Martínez

---

[7] Imports have been found to be highly correlated with exports so that only the latter has been retained during the estimation.

and Mody (2004) find a negative relationship. In the case that the inflation is fully anticipated, then this leads to quicker interest rates adjustments for the banks with higher profits being reaped. On the other hand, as Perry (1992) points out, under unanticipated inflation, banks tend to be sluggish in their interest rate adjustments so that banks' costs rise faster than revenues as to undermine profitability.

d. PIGS Dummy

A PIGS dummy is used to capture the performance of Portugal, Italy, Greece and Spain in view of gauging how these highly vulnerable European countries fare up during the crisis episode. The analysis is considered to be chiefly vital in terms of deriving enriching results for policy implications.

4.3 Results

As per the correlation coefficients shown in Table 4.3 in the appendix section, the interbank deposits from the assets side is highly correlated to that from the liabilities side so that only interbank deposits have been retained for the analysis. Preliminary data investigation reveals that size to its square is not statistically significant so that the study clings to size itself in all the models used. All results reported under pooled estimation approach are based on robust estimations, with Variance Inflation Factors confirming the absence of any multicollinearity problems. Results are reported under both NPBT and NIM.

4.3.1 Results under Pooled Estimation Approach

Table 4.4 depicts the results for the pooled estimation approach. For the post-crisis analysis, only variables which are statistically significant based on a stepwise regression analysis have been retained for the final regression. Equity is found to be the only explanatory variable that affects NPBT while interest expenses/interest income, equity, securities, customer deposits and interest expenses/deposits affect NIM. The explanatory power is relatively higher under NIM compared to NPBT and that holds independent of the period under focus. As expected, the positive sign under equity is consistent with the fact that higher equity does act as a buffer against unpleasant future shocks so that the higher the equity level, the higher the level of profits achieved; this is in line with previous studies such as Demirgüç-Kunt and Huizinga (1999), Goddard et al. (2004) and Pasiouras and Kosmidou (2007). For equity, the effects are particularly higher in the post-crisis period for NPBT, with a significant upward move noted from 9.6 % to 24%. Such a finding bodes well with the fact that the US subprime crisis has underscored the need for banks to have ample equity in order to absorb any feasible losses and to thereby not jeopardize the lending channel of banks. This result also explains the rationale as to why governments in the most advanced countries were ready to buy toxic assets in view of enhancing the equity states of the banks and thereby mitigate the level of systemic risk that loomed large on the international financial system. Similar positive evidence is noted for equity on NIM in spite of a lower magnitude effect compared to NPBT, mainly under the post-crisis episode.

Under NIM, the funding costs variable avails of the highest economic effect in the post-crisis era, most plausibly attributable to cheaper deposits which followed the slash cut in interest rates under stronger accommodative monetary policy stance. Such a finding is also compatible with the lower effect of -5% of interest expenses/interest income on NIM compared to its pre-crisis impact of -7%. Overall findings suggest that equity and funding costs variable have been particularly helpful in boosting the bottom line of banks during the crisis period. Such a finding, though intuitive, is however in contrast to that of Dietrich and Wanzenried (2011) who confirm a negative equity sign before the crisis but no effect post the crisis. This signifies that broader country assessments can differ relative to within country assessment or country specific investigation, ironically providing added incentives to use aggregate country-wise banks' data when gauging on policies at a global financial stability level.

Strong evidence is also found as to investments in securities leaving a positive impact on banks' profits under NIM with the same magnitude effects noted irrespective of the period under scrutiny. This result signifies that it is a good strategy for banks to diversify their conventional financial intermediation activities towards non-interest income activities like investments in securities. No studies have ever factored in investments in securities and the positive finding adds luster as to its use whenever modeling banks' profitability.

The PIGS dummy variable is statistically significant but only in the pre-crisis era, confirming that these four countries were already facing problems in terms of undermined banks' profitability. This could also be caused by the lack of diversified activities base found by Albertazzi and Gambacorta (2009) for Italy, Spain and Portugal. The impotency of the dummy after the crisis could reflect stricter conditions (such as austerity measures) being imposed on these countries in view of consolidating the goals established under the European Monetary Union.

Table 4.4: Pooled Estimation Results

Independent Variable	Pre Crisis		Post Crisis	
	Dependent Variable			
	NPBT	**NIM**	**NPBT**	**NIM**
EXP	0.000002	0.000032		
	0.16	2.17**		
UNEM	0.000109	-0.000273		
	0.81	-2.19**		
MKTCAP	-0.000001	0.000017		
	-0.12	2.17**		
GDPGRO	0.00081	-0.00043		
	3.63*	-1.76***		
NPL	-0.00044	0.00060		
	-2.6*	3.78*		
INFLA	-0.00048	0.00011		
	-2.2**	0.71		
EFFTAX	0.00020	-0.00002		
	2.09**	-0.41		
SIZE	-0.00021	0.00004		
	-0.51	0.1		
INTEXPINTINC	-0.00127	-0.07498		-0.05312
	-0.14	-8.34*		-10.85*
STAFF	-0.00586	-0.03113		
	-0.65	-2.9*		
PIGS	-0.00236	-0.00216		
	-2.01**	-3.01*		
EQUITY	0.09681	0.08161	0.27990	0.09797
	3.19*	3.82*	7.66*	2.83*
LOANS	-0.00895	0.01109		
	-1.32	2.75*		
CASH	0.02647	0.02493		
	1.12	1.76***		
SEC	0.00419	0.02388		0.02699
	0.53	2.95*		4.21*
INTBANK	-0.02066	0.01339		
	-2.14*	1.87***		
CUSTDEP	0.00155	0.02115		0.01913
	0.27	4.15*		4.96*
RETAINED	-0.00067	-0.00040		
	-0.45	-0.56		
INTEXDEP	-0.00286	0.21856		0.29620
	-0.09	5.61*		12.93*
FEESCOM	-0.01300	0.00376		
	-1.54	0.82		

Table 4.4: Pooled Estimation Results (Continued)

BONDS	0.00599	0.01317		
	0.47	1.22		
CONSTANT	0.01634	0.02691	-0.00937	0.01626
	1.88***	3.24*	-3.48*	3.06*
Obs	168	168	59	59
F(21, 146)	44.32	97.92		
F(1, 57)			58.62	
F(5, 53)				273.84
Prob > F	0	0	0	0
R-squared	0.7552	0.9532	0.5876	0.9602
Root MSE	0.00382	0.00297	0.00617	0.00281

*, **, *** denote statistical significance at the one, five and ten per cent level, respectively. T-values are reported below the regression coefficient values. Only statistically significant variables have been retained for the post-crisis investigation based on a stepwise regression analysis. Under macroeconomic variables, EXP, UNEM, MKTCAP, GDPGRO, INFLA and EFFTAX stand for exports, unemployment, market capitalisation, GDP growth, inflation and effective tax rate. Under banks-specific factors, NPLs, SIZE, INTEXPINTINC, STAFF, EQUITY, LOANS, CASH, SEC, INTBANK, CUSTDEP, RETAINED, INTEXDEP, FEESCOM and BONDS respectively represent non-performing loans, size, interest expenses/interest income, staff costs, equity, loans, cash and balance with central bank, securities, interbank deposits, customer deposits, retained profits, interest expenses/total deposits, fees and commissions payable to receivable ratio and bonds. PIGS variable constitutes a dummy variable to capture for country effects relating to Portugal, Italy, Greece and Spain. See Table 4.2 for a detailed explanation on all the variables used.

Interestingly, the loans variable does not appear to be really providing strong income growth, chiefly for NPBT irrespective of the period under scrutiny. However, García-Herrero et al. (2009) do find a higher effect of loans (measured as loan growth) though the statistical significance manifests at a higher level than the usual 5% significance level. In the case of NIM, despite the fact that loans exert a positive effect on profitability, the effect is nevertheless exceptionally low with an impact hovering around 1.1% before the crisis and no effect post the crisis, implying that the crisis is already thwarting the ability of loans to have an enshrining effect on profits. Such a low economic impact has also been found by Dietrich and Wanzenried (2011) and Olson and Zoubi (2011), and it can feasibly be explained by highly competitive banking structures in most OECD countries. This is later confirmed through the value of persistence parameter in the panel data analysis section.

Under NIM, staff costs hinder on profitability levels but only before the crisis; this could be symptomatic of banks already downsizing their staff post the crisis in view of ensuring survival. In fact, post the onset of the crisis, many international banks have attempted to curtail staff costs in view of ensuring adequate profits. Previous studies, such as that of Pasiouras and Kosmidou (2007), have resorted to the cost-to-income ratio and have also found a negative relationship. However, a more disaggregated analysis in terms of staff costs is considered to be more conducive towards revealing the true effect of staff costs on banks' profitability. Cash and interbank deposits have enhancing effects on banks' performance under NIM in the pre-crisis period, although not following the crisis. Such a finding is interesting as it clearly shows that liquidity states of banks were much better before the crisis although not afterwards, due to frozen interbank markets and liquidity shortages. In a parallel manner, Pasiouras and Kosmidou (2007) also end up with a positive impact of their liquidity metric but only for domestic banks.

Although some of the macroeconomic forces exhibit the a priori expected signs, they are not economically significant in the pre-crisis period and not statistically significant in the post-crisis era. Albertazzi and Gambacorta (2009) find a positive impact of stock market capitalisation on net interest income. However, the current finding could be due to a broader focus based on aggregate banks' data in lieu of individual banks' data. This could also signify that at a country level, equity and debt markets do not exert major substitutions or complements effects, with both markets susceptible to undergoing the same momentum unleashed by each country's level of financial development.

The positive effect of equity and negative impact of interbank deposits under NPBT are both consistent with the fact that internally available funds via equity have no external premium being charged, and thereby enshrine the returns of the banks relative to interbank market financing, even before the onset of the crisis. However, interbank market triggers a positive impact in the case of NIM, plainly showing that the profitability metric used significantly matters.

4.3.2 Results under Panel Estimation Approach-NPBT and NIM

Results for the panel data estimation based on GMM are shown in Table 4.5. Results without accounting for endogeneity effects are shown in the first and third column, while results incorporating endogeneity issues are depicted in the second and fourth column. The Wald test systematically confirms a high explanatory power in the case of NIM relative to NPBT which is in parallel evidenced by the larger number of statistically significant variables under NIM relative to NPBT. Profits persistence is confirmed by the lagged variables with 16% to 18% for NIM and 34% to 35% for NPBT.

These persistence effects have also been confirmed by Dietrich and Wanzenried (2011) with similar values obtained. Under NIM as the dependent variable, interest expenses/interest income causes a negative effect of 5% to 6%. These findings clearly point out high competitive forces that characterise most of the OECD countries. Despite the fact that the macroeconomic variables are statistically significant in some cases, they are all still imbued with low economic impact. The positive impact for equity is also corroborated under the panel approach mainly for NPBT similar to findings under the pooled estimation approach. In fact, equity unleashes the highest economic impact under NPBT, emerging as the second strongest driver for profitability after the persistence parameter.

Like the previous results under pooled estimation approach, loans are found to be impotent. As previously mentioned, Dietrich and Wanzenried (2011) do find similar results in terms of low economic significance. These findings suggest that OECD countries are imbued with a highly competitive banking structure, as also substantiated by the persistence coefficients. Such competitive banking structures imply undermined abilities of the banks to consolidate on their capital via accumulation of profits. Such a state of affairs is also confirmed from the asset side of the balance sheet with none of the following components like loans, cash or securities impacting on the profitability of banks. The most plausible explanation lies in the use of aggregate banks' data. However, this could also convey the signal that when looking through the lens of aggregate data, things become clearer in terms of global financial stability; excessive competition could be impinging on the ability of banks to secure strong profits to build up capital and thereby scaling up the resiliency of their respective financial systems. Ironically, the existence of oligopolistic banking structures that permeate developing countries and which trigger robust profits for the few larger banks, implies that the latter are best able to consolidate financial stability relative to banks that are found in developed countries.

Table 4.5: Panel Results: NIM & NPBT

Independent variable	Dependent Variable			
	NIM		*NPBT*	
Endogeneity	No	NIM, EQUITY, STAFF	No	NIM, EQUITY, STAFF
L1.	0.16054	0.18427	0.34403	0.35397
	2.18**	3.38*	3.72*	3.82*
EXP	-0.00008	-0.00009	-0.00022	-0.00024
	-1.54	-1.75***	-2.3**	-2.53**
UNEM	0.00023	0.00027	0.00086	0.00075
	1.15	1.36	2.42**	2.15**
MKTCAP	0.00001	0.00001	0.00007	0.00007
	0.81	1.08	4.9*	5.26*
GDPGRO	0.00005	-0.00001	0.00021	0.00014
	0.52	-0.15	1.27	0.86
NPL	0.00001	-0.00003	-0.00099	-0.00095
	0.04	-0.2	-3.29*	-3.14*
INFLA	-0.00034	-0.00045	0.00055	0.00057
	-2.03**	-3.16*	2.1**	2.19**
EFFTAX	0.00003	0.00005	0.00004	0.00005
	0.26	0.4	0.18	0.22
SIZE	-0.00390	-0.00463	0.00240	0.00162
	-2.89*	-3.43*	0.94	0.65
INTEXPINTINC	-0.05909	-0.06218	-0.01228	-0.01270
	-9.41*	-9.9*	-1.1	-1.13
STAFF	-0.10120	-0.10320	0.01379	0.01653
	-6.67*	-6.71*	0.5	0.6
EQUITY	0.04806	0.04303	0.17685	0.18575
	1.68***	1.52	3.36*	3.61*
LOANS	0.00004	0.00595	-0.00824	-0.00583
	0.01	0.86	-0.64	-0.48
CASH	0.00739	0.01216	-0.00020	0.00109
	0.76	1.25	-0.01	0.06
SEC	0.00317	0.00421	-0.00574	-0.00648
	0.42	0.55	-0.41	-0.47
INTBANK	0.02407	0.02892	-0.00907	-0.00307
	3.03*	3.79*	-0.63	-0.21
CUSTDEP	0.03442	0.03193	-0.01725	-0.01846
	4.21*	3.86*	-1.17	-1.27
RETAINED	0.00021	0.00031	-0.00035	-0.00033
	1.16	1.73***	-1.1	-1.03
INTEXDEP	0.14556	0.16011	0.01633	0.02355
	5.89*	6.51*	0.37	0.54
FEESCOM	0.04877	0.04890	-0.05140	-0.05357
	6.75*	8.14*	-6.03*	-6.3*

Table 4.5: Panel Results: NIM & NPBT (Continued)

BONDS	0.00121	-0.00355	0.02330	0.01726
	0.13	-0.38	1.35	1.02
CONSTANT	0.08026	0.08950	-0.00933	0.00084
	3.77*	4.18*	-0.24	0.02
Obs	179	179	179	179
Number of groups	24	24	24	24
Min Obs per group	7	7	7	7
Avg Obs per group	7.4583	7.4583	7.4583	7.4583
Max Obs per group	8	8	8	8
Wald chi2(21)	1533.05	1460.98	591.49	594.98
Number of instruments	29	32	30	32
Prob > 0	0	0	0	0

*, **, *** denote statistical significance at the one, five and ten per cent level, respectively. T-values are reported below the regression coefficient values. Only statistically significant variables have been retained for the post-crisis investigation based on a stepwise regression analysis. Under macroeconomic variables, EXP, UNEM, MKTCAP, GDPGRO, INFLA and EFFTAX stand for exports, unemployment, market capitalisation, GDP growth, inflation and effective tax rate. Under banks-specific factors, NPLs, SIZE, INTEXPINTINC, STAFF, EQUITY, LOANS, CASH, SEC, INTBANK, CUSTDEP, RETAINED, INTEXDEP, FEESCOM and BONDS respectively represent non-performing loans, size, interest expenses/interest income, staff costs, equity, loans, cash and balance with central bank, securities, interbank deposits, customer deposits, retained profits, interest expenses/total deposits, fees and commissions payable to receivable ratio and bonds. See Table 4.2 for a detailed explanation on all the variables used.

From the liabilities' perspective, there is again positive evidence in terms of interbank deposits and customer deposits affecting NIM with an average effect of 3%. This provides further indications of the liquidity aspects of the banks in optimising on their returns. As expected, staff costs cause a downward force on profitability under NIM only, and independent of whether endogeneity is being accounted for or not. More specifically, staff costs entail the highest negative impact of 10% on NIM. Such a finding corroborates the efforts by banks to adopt efficiency in their staff expenses management as it directly bears knock-on effects on their bottom line, let alone the downsizing effects adopted by most international banks in view of reducing their costs.

In a parallel manner, size does not seem to influence banks' performance; though size is statistically significant, it has poor economic significance in the case of NIM. Funding costs constitute the most vital variable in unleashing the highest economic impact of 14% to 16% on NIM, with Fees and Commissions variable posting a positive effect of about 5%.

Overall, panel findings further endorse the cross-sectional results, in addition to the fact that funding costs, equity and staff costs play preponderant roles in supporting the bottom line of the banks. Findings also point out that the choice of the profitability metric matters so that proper distinction should be established. In the current study, staff costs and funding costs work pretty well under NIM while equity works best under NPBT.

4.3.3 Results under Panel Estimation Approach-NPLs

Results confirm a dynamic nature of NPLs whereby its' lagged value generates a positive effect of 36% on NPLs, indicative of rather strong trailing effects endowed under NPLs. GDP growth, unemployment and inflation constitute the main variables that influence the level of NPLs. It transpires that GDP and exports, respectively, entail a 25% and 9% fall in NPLs. Basically, higher GDP growth is synonymous with upswings in the business cycles or growing momentum in the economy; higher economic activities therefore incite higher confidence as to reduce dangers of bankruptcy and unemployment, both of which feed into less NPLs. Such a finding has also been confirmed by García-Herrero et al. (2009). In a parallel manner, rising exports generate higher export incomes to corporate, which enable them to pay for any contracted loans. Second round-effects are also noted since corporates also employ people who are then remunerated and consequently able to pay for loans such as personal loans or housing loans.

High unemployment generates insolvencies for borrowers which eventually translate into higher NPLs, with an effect hovering around 24%. This explains as to why focus should be laid on safeguarding employment during the crisis times to shun any repayment problem that would endanger the whole gamut of the financial system. Alternatively stated, such a finding is of paramount significance as it directly illustrates the real need for government to secure employment during stressful times to obviate rising NPLs that would make banks become weaker and weaker and eventually undermine the financial system. In essence, banks too have responsibility of adjusting the tenor of their loans in view of giving ample manoeuvre to borrowers in terms of an aligned repayment capacity as per the prevailing economic conditions, chiefly when remunerations have already been revised downwards on the back of sluggish world demand.

Table 4.6: Panel Results: NPLs

Independent Variable	Dependent Variable
Endogeneity	NPL
NPL	
L1.	0.36830
	4.15*
EXP	-0.09471
	-2.59*
UNEM	0.24109
	1.65***
MKTCAP	0.00946
	1.74***
GDPGRO	-0.35668
	-5.62*
INFLA	0.20678
	3.55*
EFFTAX	-0.02407
	-0.25
LOANS	-1.32536
	-0.28
CONSTANT	4.73938
	1.44
Obs	179
Number of groups	24
Min Obs per group	7
Avg Obs per group	7.46
Max Obs per group	8
Wald chi2(8)	235.85
Number of instruments	17
Prob > 0	0

*, **, *** denote statistical significance at the one, five and ten per cent level, respectively. T-values are reported below the regression coefficient values. EXP, UNEM, MKTCAP, GDPGRO, INFLA, EFFTAX and LOANS stand for exports, unemployment, market capitalisation, GDP growth, inflation, effective tax rate and loans. See Table 4.2 for a detailed explanation on all the variables used.

Inflation is also found to cause a positive effect of 20% on NPLs, meaning that higher inflation could be generating higher uncertainties as to adversely affect incomes of the borrowers, which eventually filters down into higher non-performing assets. However, the negative effect of GDP predominates over that of inflation, showing the need to focus more on growth aspects in lieu of price stability concerns. Furthermore, higher loans do not, per se, trigger higher NPLs.

4.4 Conclusions

This study differs from all previous empirical studies pertaining to determinants of banks' profitability. First, recourse is made towards unique aggregate banks' financial statements data for OECD countries, which is specifically suited to gauging the effects at a global level. Second, the study is comprehensive since it caters for the effects of the financial crisis under the pooled estimation approach. Third, the study is innovative as it resorts to a detailed version of the cost-to-income ratio. Similarly, the study factors more specific elements of both the assets and liabilities side of the banks' financial statements, including interbank deposits, investments in securities and cash held with central banks. Fees and commissions have also been considered. Fourth, the study also models the level of Non-Performing Loans.

Overall, the findings of the study point out that equity, funding costs and staff costs do have a significant say in the bottom line of the banks. The positive effect of equity clearly endorses the policy undertaken by most governments in increasing the healthy state of equity of banks by buying bad assets. This further implies that ongoing efforts to further enhance the level of capital strength are well justified. The slash cut in interest rates to contain the crisis did help the banks considerably, as evidenced by the positive impact of funding costs on profitability. The negative effect of staff costs signifies that banks need to further adjust their personnel costs to stimulate profits, though many banks have already undertaken radical strategies like outright downsizing. Finally, the effect of the PIGS dummy for the pre-crisis period signifies that Portugal, Italy, Greece and Spain were already subject to problems before the crisis. Such a finding signifies a rather too quick entry into the European Monetary Union system without rigorous adherence to all preset criteria, as later unveiled in the form of window dressing/cooking the books.

Investments in securities and interbank deposits seem occasionally to entail positive effects on banks' profitability. This means that banks should further diversify their portfolio into securities to optimise on their returns and that central banks should ensure that the interbank markets are functioning well, since liquidity does affect banks' performance.

The persistence of profits from GMM shows a highly competitive banking structure which is also endorsed by the impotency of the loans variable. Such a finding is of paramount significance since it demonstrates that too much competition may ironically be detrimental for the banking sector. The creation of new rules may therefore be necessary; for instance, standardisation of mark-up pricing philosophy that guarantees a minimum positive impact on profits would be highly welcome. This has the added benefit of not only contributing towards satisfactory/sustainable profits but also eventually towards higher capital, which has been found to be unleashing the highest economic impact on profitability.

Unemployment and inflation incite NPLs while GDP growth constitutes the main factor that undermines NPLs. This implies that government should further spur growth to deter NPLs. Similarly, unemployment should be reduced to the lowest level feasible by avoiding closing down those bruised companies adversely affected by the crisis. In the same vein, inflationary pressures should be properly controlled. However, the negative effect of GDP predominates over that of inflation, providing added vigour for central banks to foster growth in lieu of ensuring price stability. This further necessitates a call for central banks to revise their mandatory role, making it more encompassing by focusing on financial stability first and price stability afterwards. Moreover, the study shows that NPLs entail a higher persistence effect relative to profitability (NIM). Although the study does not distinguish between local and foreign banks, and also ignored the ownership structure due to unavailability of data, nonetheless it does provide important insights with respect to global financial stability policies.

References

1. Abreu, M. and V. Mendes, 2001, Commercial Bank Interest Margins and Profitability: Evidence from Some EU Countries, Paper presented at the Proceedings of the Pan-European Conference Jointly Organised by the IEFS-UK and University of Macedonia Economic and Social Sciences, Thessaloniki, Greece, May 17-20.
2. Abreu, M. and V. Mendes, 2003, Do Macro-Financial variables matter for European bank interest margins and profitability? Financial Management Association International.
3. Aggarwal, R. and K. T. Jacques, 2001, The impact of FDICIA and prompt corrective action on bank capital and risk: Estimates using a

simultaneous equations model, *Journal of Banking and Finance*, 25(6), 1139-1160.

4. Agoraki, Maria-Eleni, 2010, The Determinants of Net Interest Margin during Transition, Department of Accounting and Finance, Athens University of Economics and Business.

5. Albertazzi, U. and L. Gambacorta, 2009, Bank profitability and business cycle, *Journal of Financial Stability*, 5(4), 393-409.

6. Angbazo, L., 1997, Commercial bank net interest margins, default risk, interest-rate risk, and off-balance sheet banking, *Journal of Banking and Finance*, 21(1), 55-87.

7. Arellano, M. and O. Bover, 1995, Another look at the instrumental-variable estimation of error-components models, *Journal of Econometrics*, 68(1), 29-52.

8. Athanasoglou, P., S. Brissimis and M. Delis, 2008, Bank-specific, industry-specific and macroeconomic determinants of bank profitability, *Journal of International Financial Markets, Institutions and Money*, 18(2), 121-136.

9. Baltagi, Badi H. and Chihwa Kao, 2000, Nonstationary Panels, Cointegration in Panels and Dynamic Panels: A Survey, Center for Policy Research Working Papers 16, Center for Policy Research, Maxwell School, Syracuse University.

10. Ben Naceur, S., 2003, The determinants of the Tunisian banking industry profitability: Panel evidence, Paper presented at the Proceedings of the Economic Research Forum (ERF) 10th Annual Conference, Marrakesh–Morocco, December 16-18.

11. Ben Naceur, S. and M. Goaied, 2008, The determinants of commercial bank interest margin and profitability: evidence from Tunisia, *Frontiers in Finance and Economics*, 5(1), 106-130.

12. Berg, S.A., F. R. Forsund and E. S. Jansen, 1992, Malmquist indices of productivity growth during the deregulation of Norwegian banking, 1980-89, *Scandinavian Journal of Economics*, 94, 211-228.

13. Berger, A. N., 1995, The relationship between capital and earnings in banking, *Journal of Money, Credit and Banking*, 27(2), 432-456.

14. Berger, A. N., S.D. Bonime, D. M. Covitz and D. Hancock, 2000, Why are bank profits so persistent? The roles of product market competition, informational opacity, and regional/macroeconomic shocks, *Journal of Banking and Finance*, 24(7), 1203-1235.

15. Berger, A. N. and R. DeYoung, 1997, Problem loans and cost efficiency in commercial banks, *Journal of Banking and Finance*, 21(6), 849-870.

16. Boyd, J. H. and D. Runkle, 1993, Size and performance of banking firms: Testing the predictions of theory, *Journal of Monetary Economics*, 31(1), 47-67.
17. Boyd, J. H. and B. D. Smith, 1999, The Use of Debt and Equity in Optimal Financial Contracts, *Journal of Financial Intermediation*, 8(4), 270-316.
18. Carbo Valverde, S. and F. Rodriguez, 2007, The determinants of bank margins in European banking, *Journal of Banking and Finance*, 31(7), 2043-2063.
19. Chen, S., 2011, Capital ratios and the cross-section of bank stock returns: Evidence from Japan, *Journal of Asian Economics*, 22(2), 99-114.
20. Claeys, S. and R. Vander Vennet, 2008, Determinants of Bank Interest Margins in Central and Eastern Europe: A Comparison with the West, *Economic Systems*, 32(2), 197-216.
21. Demirgüç-Kunt, A. and H. Huizinga, 1999, Determinants of commercial bank interest margins and profitability: some international evidence, *World Bank Economic Review*, 13(2), 379-408.
22. Demirgüç-Kunt, A. and E. Detragiache, 1999, Monitoring banking sector fragility: a multivariate logit approach with an application to the 1996-97 banking crises, Policy Research Working Paper Series 2085, The World Bank.
23. Demirgüç-Kunt, A., L. Laeven and R. Levine, 2004, Regulations, Market Structure, Institutions and the Cost of Financial Intermediation, *Journal of Money, Credit and Banking*, 36(3), 593-622.
24. DeYoung, R. and K. P. Roland, 2001, Product mix and earnings volatility at commercial banks: evidence from a degree of leverage model, *Journal of Financial Intermediation*, 10(1), 54-84.
25. Dietrich, A. and G. Wanzenried, 2011, Determinants of bank profitability before and during the crisis: Evidence from Switzerland, *Journal of International Financial Markets, Institutions and Money*, 21(3), 307-327.
26. Drakos, K., 2002, The Dealership model for interest margins: The case of the Greek banking industry, *Journal of Emerging Finance*, 1(1), 75-98.
27. Ho, T. and A. Saunders, 1981, The determinants of banks interest margins: Theory and empirical evidence, *Journal of Financial and Quantitative Analysis*, 16(4), 581-600.
28. García-Herrero, A., S. Gavilá and D. Santabárbara, 2009, What explains the low profitability of Chinese banks?, *Journal of Banking and Finance*, 33(11), 2080-2092.

29. Goddard, J., P. Molyneux and J. Wilson, 2004, The Profitability of European banks: a Cross-sectional and Dynamic Panel Analysis, The Manchester School, 72(3), 363-381.
30. Golin, J., 2001, The Bank Credit Analysis Handbook: A Guide for Analysts, Bankers and Investors. John Wiley & Sons (Asia) Pre Ltd.
31. Hassan, M. K. and A. H. M. Bashir, 2003, Determinants of Islamic Banking Profitability, Paper presented at the Proceedings of the Economic Research Forum (ERF) 10th Annual Conference, Marrakesh–Morocco, December 16-18.
32. Hoshi T and AK. Kashyap, 2010, Will the U.S. bank recapitalisation succeed? Eight lessons from Japan, *Journal of Financial Economics*, 97(3), 398–417.
33. Huang, R. and L. Ratnovski, 2008, The dark side of bank wholesale funding, Mimeo, *International Monetary Fund*, Washington, DC.
34. Ioannidis, C., F. Pasiouras and C. Zopounidis, 2010, Assessing bank soundness with classification techniques, *Omega*, 38(5), 345-357.
35. Jokipii, T. and A. Milne, 2011, Bank capital buffer and risk adjustment decisions, *Journal of Financial Stability*, 7(3), 165-178.
36. Kosmidou, K., 2008, The determinants of banks' profits in Greece during the period of EU financial integration, *Managerial Finance*, 34(3), 146-159.
37. Lepetit, L., E. Nys, R. Phillipe and A. Tarazi, 2008, Bank Income Structure and Risk: An empirical analysis of European Banks, *Journal of Banking and Finance*, 32(8), 1452-1467.
38. Martínez, M. S. and A. Moody, 2004, How foreign participation and market concentration impact bank spreads: evidence from Latin America, *Journal of Money, Credit and Banking*, 36(3), 511-537.
39. Maudos, J. and J. Fernández de Guevara, 2004, Factors explaining the interest margin in the banking sectors of the European Union, *Journal of Banking and Finance*, 28(9), 2259-2281.
40. Milne, A. and A. E. Whalley, 2001, Time to build and aggregate work-in-progress, *International Journal of Production Economics*, 71(1-3), 165-175.
41. Molyneux, P. and J. Thorton, 1992, Determinants of European Bank Profitability: A Note, *Journal of Banking and Finance*, 16(6), 1173-1178.
42. Mueller, Dennis C., 1977, The effects of conglomerate mergers: A survey of the empirical evidence, *Journal of Banking and Finance*, 1(4), 315-347.

43. Neely, M. C. and D. C. Wheelock, 1997, Why does bank performance vary across states?, Review, Federal Reserve Bank of St. Louis, issue March, 27-40.

44. Olson, D. and T. A. Zoubi, 2011, Efficiency and bank profitability in MENA countries, *Emerging Markets Review*, 12(2), 94-110.

45. OECD Banking Statistics, 2000-2009.

46. Pasiouras, F. and K. Kosmidou, 2007, Factors influencing the profitability of domestic and foreign commercial banks in the European Union, *Research in International Business and Finance*, 21(2), 222-237.

47. Perry, P., 1992, Do banks gain or lose from inflation, *Journal of Retail Banking*, 14(2), 25-40.

48. Rime, B., 2001, Capital requirements and bank behaviour: Empirical evidence for Switzerland, *Journal of Banking and Finance*, 25(4), 789-805.

49. Saunders, A. and I. Walter, I, 1994, Universal banking in the United States. Oxford University Press, New York.

50. Shrieves, R. E. and D. Dahl, 1992, The Relationship Between Risk and Capital in Commercial Banks, *Journal of Banking and Finance*, 16(2), 439-457.

51. Staikouras, Ch. and G. Wood, 2003, The determinants of bank profitability in Europe. In: Paper presented at the Proceedings of the European Applied Business Research Conference, Venice, Italy, June 9-13.

52. Stiroh, K. J., 2004, Diversification in Banking: Is Noninterest Income the Answer?, *Journal of Money, Credit and Banking*, 36(5), 853-82.

53. Stiroh, K. J. and A. Rumble, 2006, The dark side of diversification: the case of US financial holding companies, *Journal of Banking and Finance*, 30(8), 2131-2161.

54. Van den Heuvel, S. J., 2002, Does bank capital matter for monetary transmission?, Economic Policy Review, Federal Reserve Bank of New York, issue May, 259-265.

Appendix

Table 4.3: Correlation Coefficients

	NPBT	NIM	EXP	IMP	UNEM	MKTCAP	GDPGRO	NPA	INFLA	EFFTAX	SIZE	SIZE2	INTEXPINTINC
NPBT	1												
NIM	0.2179	1											
EXP	-0.152	-0.3492	1										
IMP	-0.1292	-0.3012	0.9721	1									
UNEM	0.1865	0.3192	-0.1846	-0.0841	1								
MKTCAP	-0.0032	-0.3457	0.155	0.0678	-0.3469	1							
GDPGRO	0.3709	0.0561	0.189	0.2067	0.0986	0.1328	1						
NPA	-0.1608	0.5558	-0.2532	-0.1865	0.6122	-0.3817	-0.0864	1					
INFLA	-0.2697	0.644	-0.0903	-0.0712	0.1318	-0.2463	0.0875	0.5008	1				
EFFTAX	0.0722	0.0242	0.0019	0.0159	-0.0211	0.0079	0.0273	0.0042	-0.0012	1			
SIZE	-0.3028	-0.456	-0.1683	-0.2185	-0.3385	0.378	-0.2714	-0.2366	-0.2714	-0.0945	1		
SIZE2	-0.296	-0.4383	-0.1781	-0.2238	-0.3148	0.3708	-0.2672	-0.2246	-0.2657	-0.1005	0.9982	1	
INTEXPINTINC	-0.4119	-0.4922	0.4941	0.4472	-0.3549	0.1637	0.0233	-0.1641	0.0532	-0.0329	0.2236	0.2016	1
STAFF	0.2438	0.1273	-0.416	-0.3946	0.1291	0.0949	-0.0275	0.0433	-0.2412	0.0135	-0.0121	-0.005	-0.7645
PIGS	-0.0499	-0.0107	-0.325	-0.2347	0.1783	-0.1486	-0.0839	0.1146	-0.0627	0.0905	0.0696	0.0587	-0.244
EQUITY	0.4822	0.6657	-0.4385	-0.3727	0.3205	-0.2538	0.0543	0.2796	0.2547	0.0443	-0.4199	-0.408	-0.5595
LOANS	0.242	0.1509	-0.3804	-0.4052	-0.1058	-0.0884	-0.0397	-0.2217	-0.2184	-0.0008	-0.1391	-0.1303	-0.4453
CASH	0.2898	0.4172	0.0683	0.172	0.287	-0.387	0.1802	0.1692	0.1372	0.0167	-0.5788	-0.5522	-0.3179
INTBANKASET	-0.3288	-0.5637	0.54	0.5048	-0.0664	0.3125	0.0223	-0.1087	-0.1536	-0.0328	0.1737	0.153	0.5963
SEC	0.0509	0.2811	0.153	0.2065	0.1433	-0.0879	0.1501	0.2668	0.3245	-0.0179	-0.0442	-0.0435	0.1823
INTBANK	-0.3619	-0.6132	0.6045	0.5773	-0.2458	0.2044	0.0248	-0.2586	-0.1167	-0.0586	0.2064	0.1822	0.7351
CUSTDEP	0.2775	0.6574	-0.2519	-0.1428	0.4836	-0.2374	0.1915	0.4136	0.3325	0.0214	-0.4351	-0.4083	-0.5048
RETAINED	-0.0647	0.0752	-0.0791	-0.0607	0.062	-0.0728	0.0895	0.0856	0.0426	-0.1596	-0.0311	-0.0187	-0.0923
INTEXDEP	-0.2156	0.5555	0.0092	-0.0044	-0.0698	-0.2105	0.0486	0.4062	0.7447	0.0108	-0.2075	-0.2118	0.3524
FEESCOM	-0.5828	0.0312	0.3176	0.3185	-0.0454	-0.1778	-0.1346	0.1827	0.4355	-0.0073	-0.1697	-0.1816	0.3734
BONDS	-0.3111	-0.6516	0.2276	0.1395	-0.3869	0.0846	-0.1451	-0.3467	-0.3155	-0.0703	0.4154	0.4011	0.4381

Table 4.3: Correlation Coefficient (Continued)

	STAFF	PIGS	EQUITY	LOANS	CASH	INTBANKASET	SEC	INTBANK	CUSTDEP	RETAINED	INTEXDEP	FEESCOM	BONDS
INTEXPINTINC													
STAFF	1												
PIGS	0.2674	1											
EQUITY	0.2456	0.254	1										
LOANS	0.3801	0.1452	0.275	1									
CASH	0.0507	-0.0965	0.3462	0.0423	1								
INTBANKASET	-0.3806	-0.061	-0.4373	-0.66	-0.358	1							
SEC	-0.1799	-0.2602	-0.0357	-0.5723	0.1789	0.0851	1						
INTBANKDEP	-0.4987	-0.0625	-0.5284	-0.5253	-0.3149	0.852	0.1389	1					
CUSTDEP	0.3204	0.0314	0.4933	0.254	0.5282	-0.4645	0.2951	-0.5102	1				
RETAINED	0.1041	-0.0789	-0.0106	-0.0124	0.1699	-0.0711	0.1155	-0.1069	0.1846	1			
INTEXDEP	-0.5074	-0.1658	0.1491	-0.1979	0.0457	-0.13	0.3342	-0.086	0.0844	-0.0184	1		
FEESCOM	-0.439	-0.0725	-0.2799	-0.2642	-0.0421	0.2529	0.0009	0.3297	-0.2062	-0.0652	0.4077	1	
BONDS	-0.2164	-0.0512	-0.5959	0.0289	-0.4224	0.289	-0.3403	0.4487	-0.6983	-0.0532	-0.2415	0.1157	1

CHAPTER FIVE

DOES INTERNATIONAL TRADE INDUCE OR DETER DEBT REPAYMENT CAPACITY OF DEVELOPING COUNTRIES?: LOOKING THROUGH THE LENS OF THE US SUBPRIME CRISIS

This chapter develops a credit risk model that focuses on the repayment capacity of developing countries in the world, with specific focus given to international trade. The research is not only innovative but also timely in terms of policy implications, chiefly following the adverse effects of the US subprime crisis on the debt levels of countries in the world. Should international trade be wealth-promoting for developing countries, then, there will be added incentives for them to foster trade. Otherwise, this will imply that international trade merely constitutes resource misallocations with poor sustainable policies in the long-term. A pooled estimation approach is employed to disentangle the adverse effects of the world's worst crisis on the repayment capacity of the developing countries. Results show that international trade has been particularly influential on the debt repayment capacity of developing countries during the pre-crisis period. However, post the crisis, no such effects prevail. Such a finding adds significant momentum to the fact that the crisis may already be curbing growth prospects via the trade channel for the developing countries, with potential rekindling effects on protectionism. Above all, the impotency of international trade metrics, coupled with a pronounced negative effect of external debt on repayment capacity during the crisis period, amount to strong evidence of a crisis-induced external debt overhang.

5.0 Introduction

It is little wonder that many studies have been conducted in the field of international trade, by virtue of the benefits that it confers in terms of efficiency in the use of resources under the law of comparative advantage and higher standard of living. However, for developing countries, international trade is of paramount significance, not only in meeting their resource requirements but also in enabling them to generate resources that would enable them to have a sustainable repayment capacity. Indeed, compared to domestic debt whereby the repayment can be extracted from internal resources, for external debt, a country needs to have ample foreign income inflows to ensure a sound external debt repayment capacity. When developing countries import to meet their consumption and production requirements, they also need to export to generate income, which eventually assists them to be solvent for any contracted external loans. Hence, external debts are sustainable for developing countries as long as they possess a sound exporting arm. Unfortunately, no study has been envisaged that links international trade to the debt repayment capacity of developing countries in the world. The current study is highly warranted mainly after the US subprime crisis engendered detrimental effects on many developing countries.

To the author's best knowledge, this paper presents the very first systematic analysis of the effects of international trade on the foreign debt servicing capacity of developing countries in the world, and derives several very important policy implications. The research undertaken also fills the void by examining the impact of distinct forces on the repayment capacity of developing countries in the world using a large data set that spans over 20 years for 42 countries.

Results show that there is a pressing need for developing countries to improve on the quality of their labour force and move further towards higher value-added trade, in particular trade in services, which has been found to be greatly increasingly post the onset of the subprime crisis. Besides, there is strong evidence that the benefits of FDI manifest with lags and that the negative impact of external debt on repayment capacity has been particularly pronounced post the crisis. In addition, the impotency of credit from banking sector reflects a rather subdued interaction between the private and public sectors among the developing countries. The non-positive effect of import cover signifies that it does not constitute a widely used metric for country risk evaluation whenever external lenders grant loans to developing countries. Moreover, while the trade channel exerts no effect on repayment capacity, external debt generates a significantly higher negative impact on repayment capacity, depicting the existence of a potentially crisis-induced external debt overhang. In essence, governments from developing countries should be cautious about the use of external financing as there is a deficiency in the inflows of foreign currencies.

The remainder of this chapter is structured as follows: Section 5.1 discusses the theoretical foundation and importance of the study on debt servicing capacity; Section 5.2 describes the econometric model, data and metrics used as the independent forces; Section 5.3 presents the empirical results and discusses the findings; and finally, Section 5.4 concludes with vital policy implications and suggestions for future research.

5.1 Literature Review

With the recent crisis, the external debt state for many countries has obtained unparallel attention since it helps to assist higher economic growth. Researchers like Claessens (1990), Cassimon and Vaessen (2007) and Ferrarini (2008) have provided evidence that external borrowings can help towards achieving higher economic growth when the borrowing is being used productively and at a sustainable level. However, assessing the other side of the coin, large external debt entails important costs like the curtailing of financial resources for local development needs. When a country contracts external debt, the resources that are dispensed for servicing of the external debt could have been ploughed back in the economy to promote higher growth. Such a phenomenon has been coined as debt overhang, and it manifests whenever there is a higher external debt burden relative to the country's repayment capacity. Under such a circumstance, there is substantial deterrence on local investments and economic growth (Pattillo et al. (2002). Two main channels are usually cited for the operation of the debt overhang: an illiquidity effect and an incentive effect. The former occurs when limited resources have to be split among consumption, investment and external transfers to effect out the debt servicing, while the latter manifests in the case that anticipations of future tax burdens deter current private investments.

As per the International Monetary Fund (IMF, 2000) definition, a plethora of indicators are used to gauge on whether a country's external debt is sustainable; these include debt to GDP ratio, foreign debt to exports ratio, share of foreign debt to total debt and short-term debt to total debt, among others. Manasse and Roubini (2009) point out three types of risks associated with debt, namely the solvency risk, the illiquidity risk and finally the currency risk. According to them, solvency risk manifests when external debt lies in excess of 49.7% of GDP. Liquidity risk occurs when short-term debt exceeds 130% of reserves while currency risk occurs in case of fixed exchange rates.

Probing deeper, the IMF (2000) states another set of indicators for debt, such as external debt service to exports ratio and the government debt service to current fiscal revenue ratio. These ratios are angled towards the short-term liquidity requirements of a country and are particularly useful as early warning signs for any country risk evaluation. Moreover, the IMF (2000) points out that current account balance can be utilised as a metric to gauge on the extent of external debt sustainability. The underlying rationale is that if a country is subject to burgeoning current account deficits and there is issuance of debt to finance the same deficits but without any concrete growth manifesting, then this constitutes an issue of concern in terms of illiquidity problems and heightened external vulnerability.

Consequently, it becomes important to focus on international trade and debt servicing capacity as an important predictor for external debt management. However, to date, no study has been entertained in that perspective. Indeed, most of the empirical studies on debt have focused on the interactions between economic growth and debt without giving due consideration as to how international trade influences the external debt repayment capacity of developing countries. Indeed, as countries take more and more external debt, international trade entails important benefits. First, international trade generates an inflow of income in foreign currencies which can be used for repayments of external debt. An added benefit is that if the income inflows are denominated in the same currency as that of the imports, this would be synonymous to natural hedging. Second, international trade enables developing countries to resource themselves when they are deficient in terms of input requirements used for processing of output for exports. It is with this view in mind that this research paper has been undertaken to both shed light on the linkage that prevails between a developing country's debt servicing capacity and its international trade, as well as assess the effect of the crisis on such a link. The next section probes into the econometric model.

5.2 Econometric Model and Data

$$DSCR_i = \alpha_0 + \beta_1 LABOURPART_i + \beta_2 TRADESER_i + \beta_3 FDI_i + \beta_4 EXTERDEBT_i + \beta_5 RES_i$$
$$+ \beta_6 CREDIT_i + \beta_7 INV_i + \beta_8 IMPCOV_i + \beta_9 IT_i + \varepsilon_i$$

$$(1)$$

Where:

DSCR: Debt Service Coverage Ratio
LABOURPART: Labour Participation
TRADESER: Trade in Services
FDI: Foreign Direct Investment
EXTERDEBT: External Debt
RES: Reserves
CREDIT: Credit from Banking Sector
INV: Investment
IMPCOV: Import Cover
IT: International Trade

Each variable used in equation (1) is defined in Table 5.1 in the appendix section with all data collected from the World Bank database for the period spanning 1990 to 2009. The model type used is pooled data regression analysis where all country-year observations have been assembled together. To prevent any heteroscedasticity problems, robust estimators have been employed. Above all, post estimating the model, Variance Inflation Factors have been used to ensure that multicollinearity does not constitute an issue of concern. In a parallel manner, a pre-estimation multicollinearity diagnostic test has been implemented via correlation coefficients and none of them exhibited significant values. Prior to undertaking the regression analysis, each variable has been individually plotted to remove any potential outlier problems. In that respect, two countries have been overlooked for the analysis, namely, Botswana and Egypt[1]. The final list of countries used for the analysis is shown in Table 5.2 in the appendix section. Stepwise regression analysis has been used to sieve out the financial regression model to be applied[2].

Labour constitutes an important source of development for many developing countries in the world. It is anticipated that labour participation will entail a positive impact on DSCR via its stimulating effects on output. Indeed, compared to developed countries whereby the tertiary or services sector tends to predominate over the primary and secondary sectors in terms of growth enhancement mechanism, for developing countries, growth is tilted towards the manufacturing/agriculture sectors, in which labour constitutes an important component. Many studies have focused on the impact of labour participation on unemployment (Österholm (2010), Emerson (2011)). Österholm (2010) finds evidence of a long-run

---

[1] Both countries exhibited significantly higher DSCRs.
[2] Two additional variables have been used beforehand, namely savings and remittances, but none of the results were significant and thereby subsequently ignored.

relationship that prevails between labour participation and unemployment, which questions the unemployment invariance hypothesis, whereby long-run unemployment rate is independent of the labour force. In essence, the higher the level of labour participation, the lower the unemployment level and hence the smaller the level of lost production or output. Higher domestic activities unleashed by higher labour participation are expected to unleash a positive impact on the external debt servicing capacity of developing countries because more wealth is created. Above all, a higher level of domestic activities is synonymous with higher ability of the government to raise revenues for its existing budget deficits from local economic units, so that this undermines the need for any current external borrowings. In a parallel manner, lower unemployment levels signifies fewer strains being exerted on the government purse in terms of any potential expenditure on the unemployed, so that this indirectly consolidates the external debt repayment capacity. Based on the above arguments, labour participation is expected to create a positive effect on DSCR.

As per the IMF definition, international trade in services is defined as service transactions between the residents and non-residents of an economy. According to the World Trade Organisation (2008), trade in services constitutes the fastest growing component of international trade since early 1990s, with average yearly growth rates close to 10%. As Hill (1977) argues, the distinctive feature of services is that there is the simultaneous production and consumption at the same point in time and feasibly in the same location. In contrast to trade in goods, trading in services confers the benefit of having a more stable activity level, which induces greater confidence and hence higher inflows of income to developing countries. Another benefit of trade in services is that it entails higher value-added effects relative to goods. Indeed, as a country moves towards a sophisticated financial system, there is a sequential drift towards the services sector. Trade in services is expected to generate a positive effect on DSCR.

FDI constitutes an important part of capital flows to developing countries. FDI[3] is expected to boost the host country's repayment capacity via enhancement effects on its economic growth potential. It is widely acknowledged that FDI stimulates exports by promoting the transfer of technology (Findlay, 1978), encouraging local firms to have higher

---

[3] Any foreign investment can be split either into FDI or portfolio investments. FDI technically represents capital investments like acquisitions of companies or new construction projects, while portfolio investments take after investments towards securities (bonds or stocks).

efficiency like the foreign firms (Markusen and Venables (1999)), enabling access to large foreign markets, and generating a more knowledgeable workforce (Kobrin, 2005) via positive spillover effects. Another channel via which FDI can be repayment-enhancing is through its reduced need for external debts. Indeed, in the event that foreign private companies invest in public project of developing countries, this would undeniably undermine the need for higher external debts so that an improved DSCR would clearly manifest. However, assessing the other side of the coin, FDI can also be damaging in terms of scaling down savings and investments, gnawing at the potential of local firms to move towards a mature exporting firm and affecting the local market with no pronounced effects on exports. For instance, Bornschier and Chase-Dunn (1985) point out the possibility that FDI can distort the use of productive forces as they encourage the formation of monopolies, which breed inefficiencies. Pigato (2000) argues that such distortion is particularly important for Africa, which tends to be intensive in natural sectors and hence likely to have many barriers to entry. While Balasubramanyam, Mohammed and David (1996), in a study of 46 countries from 1970 to 1985, find positive evidence of FDI on growth chiefly when the workforce is educated and export-promotion policies are encouraged, Hermes and Lensink (2003), in a study of 67 developing countries for the period 1970 to 1995, report that FDI has a significant negative effect on the host country. The empirical evidence for FDI is thereby mixed.

External debt should trigger a downward pressure on DSCR since the higher the level of external debt, the higher the corresponding repayments would be. Any government is faced with the daunting task of financing its budget deficits via borrowings, which can take the form of either domestic borrowing or foreign (external borrowings). However, the advent in using external debt is that it imposes a commitment for local government to ensure that there is prudent use of the external loan proceeds towards real growth-oriented projects (Daseking and Joshi (2005). In addition, Jayaraman and Lau (2009) stress that borrowed funds should be channelled into growth-oriented investment. This has the added benefit in terms of ensuring a reputed and credible image for the eyes of the major international lenders, who will therefore be more willing to lend and at finer rates.

According to Rodrik (2006), the cost of holding reserves stands around one per cent of GDP for developing countries. Technically speaking, developing countries cling to reserves accumulation as a safety measure or safety valve against feasible risk of an external debt crisis, with the so-called buffer stock models developed in the 1960s and 1970s (e.g., Heller,

1966; Kenen and Yudin, 1965; Kelly, 1970; Frenkel and Jovanovic, 1981). A negative relationship is expected to hold between reserves and DSCR. The underlying rationale is that reserves influence the level of external debt in that higher reserves induce developing countries to take more external debt since they already know that they avail of ample margin cover in terms of payments. However, a positive relationship can also manifest in the case that reserves work more on the cost side of external borrowings relative to the quantity side.

A higher level of credit from the banking sector induces higher output and employment with higher possibility of tax revenues for the government; this therefore squeezes the need for any external debt borrowings. Thereafter, such a reduced level of external debt translates into a lower level of debt repayments, which ultimately feed into a stronger repayment capacity. However, credit from the banking sector can generate a negative effect on DSCR in the case that higher credit generates higher public sector borrowing requirements based on strong synergies and interaction between the private and the public sectors of the economy. In that specific case, higher credit would trigger a dwindling repayment capacity effect.

Constituting an important ingredient of aggregate demand, investment in a country requires significant use of resources so that it is most likely that external borrowings will be needed to cater for any deficiency in the amount of funds needed for investment, chiefly when local savings happen to be deficient. Subsequently, the higher the level of investments, the more likely that government will need to contract external loans so that a negative relationship is expected to subsist between investments and DSCR. However, such negative impact will prevail mainly in the short-run. In the long-run, higher investment will enable developing countries to have a higher generation of internal wealth so that there is lesser reliance on external borrowings. However, such a state of affairs will manifest only when developing countries adopt robust structural programmes in view of consolidating growth.

A more direct way to gauge on a country's external debt solvency state is to focus on the ability of the country's reserves to its imports ratio, labelled as the import cover.[4] However, the empirical evidence for import cover is practically non-existent. Import cover is expected to cause a positive impact on DSCR because the higher the level of import cover for a country, the stronger the country's resilience to any shock, and hence the

---

[4] A widely used rule is that reserves should make good for at least three months' of imports.

more likely that the cost charged for any external borrowings will be low. Such a variable could be deemed analogous to the margin cover metric used in the banking sector.

The most vital metric or variable which lies at the foundation for our analysis pertains to the international trade variable. Based on the fact that exports may entail a different effect compared to imports, three different metrics for international trade have been considered in the current study; in particular, imports, exports and the level of openness. A priori, exports are expected to contribute positively to DSCR as they induce higher income inflows in terms of foreign currencies. Indeed, external debt denominated in foreign currencies has to be serviced by inflows of foreign currencies. Consequently, a country which is subject to a strong exporting arm will most likely avail of a strong external debt solvency state. As far as imports are concerned, a negative relationship is expected to prevail since higher imports would be symptomatic of lower net inflows. However, since the DSCR is computed using gross inflows, a positive sign may manifest should imports signify resourcing of more foreign raw materials to locally produce more goods for exports, which in turn transmit higher gross income inflows. Finally, based on the very fact that most developing countries are net importers in the world, it is anticipated that the effect of imports would be more acute than that for exports.

5.3 Results

Results of the regressions are shown in Table 5.3. Labour Participation is found to unleash a positive impact on DSCR with an average effect of 5.45% on DSCR. The positive effect bodes well with the fact that labour constitutes a vital ingredient for growth in many developing countries. However, this finding should be viewed with some caution since the impact is statistically significant only for the overall period; for the pre- and post-crisis periods, labour participation has no direct bearing on the repayment capacity of developing countries. Such a finding directly questions the quality of the active labour force found in developing countries.

The effect of trade in services is significantly more pronounced than any of the other independent variables considered in the model, emphatically showing its significance as a repayment inducing mechanism with one per cent change in trade in services entailing around 13-14 per cent and 29-30 per cent in the overall/pre- and post-crisis periods, respectively. Above all, the size of its effect is found to be chiefly higher in the post-crisis period. Such a finding suggests that trade in services constitutes an important ingredient in promoting external debts repayments after the onset of the subprime crisis.

Consistent with our a priori expectations, FDI triggers a positive impact on DSCR for the overall and the pre-crisis periods. However, the impact is statistically insignificant irrespective of the model and period under consideration, meaning that FDI for developing countries does not really enhance their debt repayment capacity. The impotency of FDI on DSCR concurs with empirical evidence pointing out that FDI is not really growth-enhancing for host countries. In fact, Ndikumana and Verick (2008) find a restricted impact of FDI in Africa by virtue of poor synergies that prevail between local investment and FDI. Interestingly, Dupasquier and Osakwe (2005) state that compared to Africa, which receives FDI primarily in primary sectors, most Asian FDIs are channelled into the secondary sector, which induces a diversified export base of the economy. For the current study, the impotency of FDI on DSCR can be attributed to three main causes. First, the effect may not be contemporaneous but rather lagged, as it takes time for the flows to generate positive knock-on effects on the economy. Second, it could be that FDI tends to be tilted towards specific sectors so that, as a whole macroeconomic-wide analysis, no major positive effects are witnessed. Finally, this could reflect the point advanced by Ndikumana and Verick (2008) whereby domestic investments are done in the usual ways without trying to avail of the latest foreign technology and expertise that are embedded in the FDI.

The higher the loan amount borrowed, the higher the repayments would be. In the same vein, the larger the level of external debt for a specific country, the higher the associated repayments of principals and interests would be, so that this is susceptible to trigger an undermined repayment capacity. The results are significant for all periods but with the magnitude being exceptionally high in the crisis era, moving up from around -4.6% in the pre-crisis period to -26% in the post-crisis period under the openness metric. The underlying rationale is that though the level of average external debts and average maturity periods may be the same and so the corresponding repayment amounts, the crisis has nevertheless led towards undermined income flows to developing countries as to thereby strain hard on their DSCRs.

The negative sign for credit is congruous with the fact that, the higher the level of domestic credit, the higher the level of external borrowings made by the government, so that the higher the repayments amount will be, and hence the lower the DSCR. However, credit is significant at the ten per cent level only for the overall period; it is statistically insignificant for both the pre- and post-crisis periods, and does not really affect DSCR.

Such a finding shows that credit from the banking sector of developing countries does not really affect the level of their external borrowings; this is by virtue of poor synergies between the private and public sectors, since domestic credit tends to be skewed towards the private sector.

In line with our expectation, investment sparks off a negative effect but only for the overall and pre-crisis periods. The negative effect means that the higher the investment level, the higher the level of external borrowings and subsequent corresponding repayments, all of which would be symptomatic with a fall in the DSCR. Under the pre-crisis period, the negative impact revolves in the range of -7% to -9%, which signifies that any investment undertaken by developing countries imposes around one tenth of yearly external debt repayments.

Import Cover entails a negative impact on DSCR, ranging from -3% to -4.8% in the pre-crisis period and significantly higher values ranging from -10% to -14.5% in the post-crisis period. The negative sign contradicts the stated hypothesis whereby higher import cover acts as an enshrining mechanism—the higher the import cover, the lower the risk level perceived by external lenders so that a lower cost may be imposed. Delving deeper, such a finding can possibly depict a positive "quantity debt channel" whereby high import cover elicits high levels of external debt as to drive down DSCR.

For the overall period of analysis, openness is found to have a positive impact on DSCR, meaning that the more open a developing country, the more likely that it benefits from an enshrined repayment capacity for its external debts. Alternatively stated, this can simply imply that the more open a developing country, the higher the level of inflows in terms of exports income and income earned from residents' investments elsewhere. However, it transpires that the openness variable is statistically significant at the one per cent level in the pre-crisis period relative to the post-crisis era, whereby it is not only statistically insignificant but it also has a negative sign. Such a finding sends clear signals that during the financial crisis, the more open a developing country is, the more likely that trade will not be enhancing its repayment capacity. To evaluate the proper impact of exports and imports separately on DSCR, the metric for international trade is first captured via exports and then through imports.

In the case of exports, again a positive statistically significant sign is noted for the pre-crisis era, while for the post-crisis period, the sign is not only statistically insignificant but also negative. Hence, similar conclusions can be drawn to those of the openness variable, in that, post the manifestation of the US crisis, exports are not really helping developing countries to enhance their debt servicing capacity. The underlying rationale is that with bruised economies emanating from the developed world, exports have generally fallen so that there are no income inflows.

As far as imports are concerned, their positive impact tends to be higher than that of exports. The positive sign for imports clearly shows that developing countries require imports of raw materials to enable them to produce more exports; these then eventually translate into higher income inflows. The positive sign appears by virtue of DSCR being computed based on gross basis without any deductions made for outflows (distinctive feature of DSCR at a macroeconomic wide analysis). The negative sign witnessed in the post-crisis period can be attributed to the very fact that higher imports could not directly translate into higher income inflows due to slowdown in demand from advanced economies.

Table 5.3: Factors Impacting on DSCR

Variables	Overall Period			Pre-Crisis			Post-Crisis		
	OPEN	EXPORT	IMPORT	OPEN	EXPORT	IMPORT	OPEN	EXPORT	IMPORT
LABORPART	5.4026	5.4513	5.5565	2.7606	2.8074	3.0192	11.9681	10.7161	13.1786
	2.25**	2.27**	2.33**	1.29	1.32	1.41	1.03	0.92	1.11
TRADESER	13.7463	14.6789	13.6856	13.4097	14.7895	13.1373	30.8815	29.0901	32.7785
	4.86*	5.2*	4.83*	5.03*	5.56*	4.87*	1.76***	1.65***	1.85***
FDI	4.0086	5.8435	1.2297	1.3525	3.7978	-2.3194	-0.2641	-0.9861	7.3978
	0.57	0.83	0.17	0.25	0.68	-0.40	-0.01	-0.03	0.19
EXTERDEBT	-5.9867	-5.9914	-6.0261	-4.5568	-4.5732	-4.6215	-26.2353	-27.1691	-25.8022
	-7*	-7.01*	-7.04*	-5.65*	-5.69*	-5.68*	-4.07*	-4.36*	-3.86*
RES	8.1765	11.0507	7.7151	0.9082	5.4687	-0.5476	20.7872	14.7113	26.1344
	1.68***	2.72*	1.3400	0.19	1.32	-0.09	1.38	1.16	1.39
CREDIT	-2.1915	-2.2453	-2.0753	-1.5822	-1.6875	-1.3784	-4.6485	-4.9215	-4.2963
	-1.76***	-1.79***	-1.7***	-1.29	-1.37	-1.16	-1.41	-1.49	-1.27
INV	-6.0995	-5.2275	-6.6497	-8.4533	-7.2017	-9.2891	-9.2534	-10.4055	-7.4522
	-1.69***	-1.4000	-1.77***	-2.42**	-2.11**	-2.53**	-0.72	-0.82	-0.56
IMPCOV	-5.1738	-6.1414	-4.8845	-3.3414	-4.8131	-2.7368	-12.1066	-10.0050	-14.5759
	-3.52*	-5.26*	-2.73*	-2.43**	-4.37*	-1.59	-2.31**	-2.37**	-2.03**

Does International Trade Induce or Deter Debt Repayment Capacity?

OPEN	3.1260	4.4008	6.3676	4.6065	6.4420	9.7411	-4.0900	-3.2492	-13.1302
	2.29**	2.18**	1.99**	3.53*	3.25*	3.12*	-0.76	-0.44	-0.94
CONSTANT	6.7859	7.1361	6.6444	6.7627	7.3178	6.4474	17.6082	17.5136	17.9673
	3.55*	3.78*	3.4*	4.05*	4.44*	3.79*	1.82***	1.79***	1.87***
$F(9, 830)$	40.03	39.65	39.31	45.87	45.32	43.6	5.18	4.8	4.85
Prob > F	0.0000	0.0000	0.0000	0.0000	0.0000	0.0000	0.0000	0.0000	0.0000
R-squared	0.3193	0.3185	0.3173	0.3505	0.3480	0.3463	0.3415	0.3384	0.3453
Observations	840	840	840	756	756	756	84	84	84

*, ** and *** denote statistical significance at the 1%, 5% and 10% level, respectively.

5.4 Conclusions

Credit risk manifests not only at household level and firm level but also at country level, in the form of external debt solvency state. In that respect, the repayment of loans is directly linked to the general macroeconomic state of a country. With globalisation, there tends to be greater comovements among distinct countries' macroeconomic cycles, especially following the US subprime crisis, so that debt servicing will be affected similarly for virtually all countries in the world, particularly for those emanating from the developing world. This research attempts to shed light on how international trade affects the debt servicing capacity of developing countries pre and post the subprime crisis. The research is both innovative and timely.

The fact that labour participation does not affect DSCR in both the pre- and post-crisis periods signifies that developing countries could be having a labour participation, which is still deficient in terms of expertise, productivity and efficiency. In that respect, government should further consolidate their investments on human capital and stimulate access to internet and educational resources to unrelentingly leverage the quality of their active labour force. Another plausible cause of the impotency for labour participation pertains to the value-added they have at the end of the day. In essence, it could simply mean that despite having strong labour participation, the value created is still too low as to accommodate for the higher levels of external debt repayments. This generates the added incentive for developing countries to optimise more on their trade in services channels.

Trade in services is found to be a vital element in inducing repayment capacity of developing countries mainly after the crisis. Such a finding is of paramount significance as it shows that the main element that will enable developing countries to have stronger repayment capacity pertains to the level of trade they have in their services. This signifies that, as part of the proactive risk management strategies for government found in developing countries, it is imperative to adhere towards service-oriented sectors like Business Processing Outsourcing, Telecommunications, and Technology, among others, all of which are likely to be resilient to the crisis. Hence, as part of sound financial stability measures taken by developing countries, it is vital that they adhere towards policies that would consolidate their services sector. In that respect, it would be considerate for governments of developing countries to adopt stimulating measures like lowering taxes and increasing subsidies to further develop their services sector component as part of the adjustment policies to further boost their resilience.

The impotency of FDI on DSCR adds substance to the fact that FDI tends to be more sector-specific so that no economy-wide benefits are susceptible to manifest. Furthermore, this also shows that FDI does not assist in reducing the level of external debt intake of the developing countries because FDI tends to be more private-based and mostly made by venture capitalists towards private sector investments. In a parallel manner, this could also reflect very poor synergies between FDI and the local companies in terms of human capital, knowledge and technology transfers. However, such impotency of FDI can plausibly be due to the prevalence of lagged effects in lieu of instantaneous impacts. Should that be the case, then, there is an urgent need for policy-makers to ponder over the potential effects of the crisis on the DSCR of developing countries in the world. Indeed, in that case as the causality is expected to be lagged, this could simply signify that with the financially bruised financial systems of developed countries, there will be a fall in FDI, so that detrimental knock-on effects loom large on the economic horizons.

External debt is found to spark off downward pressures on DSCR of the developing countries, with a conspicuously pronounced effect noted in the post-crisis period. This finding entails vital implications. On one hand, this could signify that, due to unhealthy economic conditions of the developed countries, there is a general fall in the demand for products from the developing countries so that this automatically squeezes on the level of income flows to the developing countries. On the other hand, the fact that developing countries are also adjusting their economies and need funds means that they are compelled to borrow more to withstand the adverse effects of the worst financial crisis on their economies. Based on the fact that the crisis has weakened the repayment capacity of developing countries, international institutions like the IMF and the World Bank should try to be more lenient in their lending conditions to developing countries. For instance, they can lengthen the maturities of the external debt issued by them as part of a sound external debt management strategy.

The impotency of reserves signifies that developing countries which are endowed with higher reserves do not envisage taking higher external debt. The no-effect situations in both the pre- and post-crisis periods can reflect the fact that reserves tend to be more as a stock component while DSCR is more like a dynamic or flow metric of assessment.

No evidence is found as to credit from banking sector influencing the level of DSCR for developing countries. The most plausible explanation is that there still prevail low levels of public-private partnerships because credit from the banking sector tends to be tilted towards the private sector, while external debt tends to be skewed towards the public sector.

The finding that investment does not affect DSCR during the post-crisis period can reflect the following state of affairs. Based on an anticipated sluggish foreign demand, many developing countries may have reduced their investment levels to shun off any undue pressures on the future repayment capacity. Or, more realistically, this can simply reflect the low level of available funds from developed countries to give away as loans to developing countries as their economies soak up the funds under the fiscal stimulus packages and quantitative easing measures.

The non-positive sign noted for import cover shows that external lenders do not incorporate it as an important metric for cost assessment. A plausible explanation can emanate from the fact that external lenders like the IMF are more concerned about project viability with its ensuing social benefits in lieu of import cover.

Independent of the metric used for international trade, it clearly transpires that post the crisis, international trade is not contributing much in easing the debt repayment profile of developing countries. Ironically, compared to the pre-crisis period, the signs have turned negative for each of the metrics of international trade considered. Such a finding is of paramount significance as it demonstrates that the US subprime crisis has severely undermined economic activities throughout the world, which may generate severe retaliations and a potential rekindling of protectionist measures. However, according to the World Trade Organization, protectionist measures covered just 0.2 per cent of world trade between May and October 2010, down from 0.8 per cent between October 2008 and October 2009. By contrast, during the Great Depression of the 1930s, the crisis led to systematic increases in tariffs for years. Ironically, the current crisis is said to be worse than that of the Great Depression and yet, the protectionism level is still low due to important forces established, including floating exchange rate systems which give freedom to internal policy management, concrete measures taken by the G-20, bailouts of important institutions and automatic stabilizers that promote macroeconomic stability. Dadush et al. (2011) also point out that protectionism has been well contained during the crisis on the back of solid national, regional and multinational trade architecture. Nonetheless, should things turn sour again, for example, if another financial meltdown occurred on the back of the debt crisis, bouts of protectionism would undeniably manifest as bruised economies try their utmost to safeguard employment. The US economy was downgraded for the first time in 70 years to AA+ (excellent) from AAA (outstanding) by Standard and Poor's on the 5th of August 2011, clearly showing that the intensified level of debt crisis in European countries had already gnawed at the level of economic activities.

The last but not the least policy implication from this study is that the crisis may induce some form of debt overhang for developing countries in the case that the crisis generates a higher external debt burden relative to the country's repayment capacity, meaning that there is substantial deterrence on local investments and economic growth. The pronounced effect of external debt and the impotency of international trade metrics further endorse the existence of such external debt overhang.

As with any study, the current research also contains some deficiencies or shortcomings. First, it would be more interesting to entertain a panel data analysis but since DSCR has not been found to be stationary, it is not feasible to implement such an analysis. Nonetheless, such a concern is somewhat disparaged because under a panel data approach, it would not have been feasible to disentangle the effects of the crisis based only on 3 years of post-crisis data. Second, due to data limitations, some other variables—such as terms of trade and cost of external debt—have been overlooked; these would undeniably be interesting to analyse, chiefly under country risk evaluation. In the same vein, it was not feasible to have more microeconomic information about the external debt, such as their average maturity structure. Nonetheless, the current study is highly innovative and vital for policy-makers based on gauging the effects of the crisis on the external debt repayment capacity of developing countries.

References

1. Balasubramanyam, V. N., M. Salisu, and D. Sapsford, 1996, Foreign Direct Investment and Growth in EP and IS countries, *Economic Journal, Royal Economic Society*, 106(434), 92-105.

2. Bornschier, V. and C. Chase-Dunn, 1985, Transnational Corporations and Underdevelopment, New York: Praeger.

3. Cassimon, D. and J. Vaessen, 2007, Theory, Practice and Potential of Debt for Development Swaps in the Asian and Pacific Region, *Economic Systems* 31(1), 12-34.

4. Claessens, S., 1990, The Debt Laffer Curve: Some Estimates, *World Development*, 18(12), 1671-1677.

5. Dadush, U., S. Ali and R. Odell, 2011, "Is Protectionism Dying?", *The Carnegie Papers, 3-5*, Washington, DC: Carnegie Endowment for International Peace.

6. Daseking, C. and B. Joshi, 2005, Debt and New Financing in Low-income Countries: Looking Back, Thinking Ahead, Washington, D.C.: International Monetary Fund.

7. Dupasquier, C. and P. N. Osakwe, 2005, FDI in Africa: Performance, Challenges, and Responsibilities, *Journal of Asian Economies*, 17(2), 241-260.

8. Emerson, J., 2011, Unemployment and labor force participation in the United States, *Economics Letters*, 111(3), 203-206.

9. Ferrarini, B., 2008, Proposal for a Contingency Debt Sustainability Framework, *World Development*, 36(12), 2547-2565.

10. Findlay, R., 1978, Relative Backwardness, Direct Foreign Investment and the Transfer of Technology: A Simple Dynamic Model, *Quarterly Journal of Economics*, 92(1), 1-16.

11. Frenkel, J. A. and B. Jovanovic, 1981, Optimal International Reserves: A Stochastic Framework, *Economic Journal*, 91(362), 507-514.

12. Heller, R., 1966, Optimal International Reserves, *Economic Journal*, 76(302), 296-311.

13. Hermes, N. and R. Lensink, 2003, Foreign Direct Investment, Financial Development and Economic Growth, *Journal of Development Studies*, 40(1), 142-163.

14. Hill, T. P., 1977, On goods and services, *The Review of Income and Wealth*, 23(4), 315-338.

15. IMF, 2000, Debt- and reserve-related indicators of external vulnerability. <http://www.imf.org/external/np/pdr/debtres/debtres.pdf>.

16. Jayaraman, T. K. and E. Lau, 2009, Does external debt lead to economic growth in Pacific island countries, *Journal of Policy Modelling*, 31(2), 272-288.

17. Kelly, M., 1970, Demand for International Reserves, *American Economic Review*, 60(4), 655-667.

18. Kenen, P. and E. Yudin, 1965, The Demand for International Reserves, *Review of Economics and Statistics*, 47(3), 242-250.

19. Kobrin, S., 2005, The Determinants of Liberalization of FDI Policy in Developing Countries: 1991–2001, *Transnational Corporations*, 14(1), 67-103.

20. Manasse, P. and N. Roubini, 2009, "Rules of thumb" for Sovereign Debt Crises, *Journal of International Economics*, 78(2), 192-205.

21. Markusen, J. and A. J. Venables, 1999, Foreign Direct Investment as a Catalyst for Industrial Development, *European Economic Review*, 43(2), 335-338.

22. Ndikumana, L. and S. Verick, 2008, The Linkages between FDI and Domestic Investment: Unravelling the Developmental Impact of Foreign Direct Investment in Sub-Saharan Africa, *Development Policy Review*, 26(6), 713-726.

23. Österholm, P., 2010, Unemployment and Labour-Force Participation in Sweden, *Economics Letters*, 106(3), 205-208.

24. Pattillo, C., H. Poirson, and L. Ricci, 2002, External Debt and Growth, *IMF Working Paper* 02/69, Washington, D. C., International Monetary Fund.

25. Pigato, M., 2000, Foreign Direct Investment in Africa: Old Tales and New Evidence, World Bank, Washington, D.C.

26. Rodrik, D., 2006, The social cost of foreign exchange reserves, *International Economic Journal, Korean International Economic Association*, 20(3), 253-266.

Appendix

Table 5.1: Definition of Variables	
Variable	**Definition**
DSCR	Exports of goods, services and income/sum of principal repayments and interest actually paid in foreign currency, goods, or services on long-term debt, interest paid on short-term debt, and repayments (repurchases and charges) to the IMF
LABOURPART	Economically active population/Total Population
TRADESER	Sum of service exports and imports divided by the value of GDP
FDI	Foreign Direct Investment/GDP
EXTERDEBT	Total External debt stocks/GDP
RES	Total reserves/GDP
CREDIT	Domestic Credit provided by Banking Sector/GDP
INV	Gross capital formation/GDP
IMPCOV	Reserves/Imports

Table 5.2: List of Countries

Argentina	Honduras	Panama
Belize	Indonesia	Peru
Bolivia	India	Philippines
Brazil	Jordan	PapuaGuinea
CoteIvoire	Kenya	Paraguay
Cameroon	StLucia	Rwanda
Colombia	SriLanka	Sudan
Costarica	Morocco	Senegal
Dominican	Madagascar	Elsalvador
Ecuador	Mexico	Thailand
Fiji	Mauritius	Tunisia
Gabon	Malaysia	Turkey
Ghana	Niger	StVincent
Guatemala	Pakistan	Venezuela

CHAPTER SIX

DEBT MANAGEMENT STRATEGIES

With the onset of the crisis, much stress has been laid on issues related to debt sustainability. During recessionary periods, it is common to find increasing public debts and declining private debts. Two main forces influence the debt level of a country, namely government revenues and expenditures. A government is solvent when the present value of its future primary surplus is equal to the current values of government debt. At the base of sound debt risk management, the ultimate aim is geared towards scaling down any mismatch between financial assets and financial liabilities; this usually manifests in the form of natural hedging whereby the liabilities are structured to match the assets.

Following the crisis, many countries have undergone difficulties in foreign currency borrowings for the following reasons. First, there is a dearth of foreign currencies receipts due to a fall in exports caused by sluggish world demand. Second, there are pressures on existing foreign reserves chiefly for those countries which attempt to maintain the same imports level despite having declining exports. Third, stressful conditions also prevail in international markets which have increased the costs of foreign borrowing.

Governments are subject to revenues and expenditures and natural hedging will manifest as a direct function of the components of these revenues and expenditures. In the case that the major component of revenues and expenditures is denominated in foreign currency, this provides incentives to have recourse towards external debt. In the same vein, should a large portion of revenues and expenditures be subject to interest rate changes, this unleashes incentives to use floating rate instruments. Finally, should a large component of revenues and expenditures be denominated in local currency, this generates inclination towards domestic debt.

Compared to developed countries, developing countries are subject to certain specific problems with respect to their debt management. The following policies are suggested to enhance their debt management structures. Ironically, the crisis may be deemed as the proper time for developing countries to leverage their debt management structures in order to align them to those that prevail in developed countries before the onset of the crisis.

1. The costs of raising debt tend to be high in developing countries due to inefficiencies that permeate the debt markets so that the development of the local bond markets would significantly assist in curtailing costs. For instance, by stimulating a more diverse investor base, this helps in reducing the borrowing costs. A diversified investor base signifies a mixture of institutions that have diverse asset-liability management, such as banks, insurance companies, pension funds and corporate.

2. The debt characteristic of developing countries tends to exhibit a bunched redemption profile which is tilted towards short-term maturity. This thereby results in rollover risk, which directly emanates from the excess liquidity of commercial banks that prefer short-term maturities aligned to their asset-liability structure. Consequently, there is the pressing need to develop the investor base to further consolidate demand and thereby evenly spread out the redemption profile to mitigate risk. Proper market intelligence is prerequisite to ensure that issuances are successful and funding for government is secured in a timely manner.

3. Among all the ingredients required in order to ensure an effective debt management system, communication is vital. In essence, sound and consistent communication should be promoted among all the stakeholders to prevent any loss of confidence in the instruments. Beyond that, effective communication assists in scaling up the level of credibility as to reduce the costs of raising debt.

4. To enhance the pricing of bonds, it is imperative to generate zero-coupon yields, say by using the Nelson-Siegel model. However, lack of regular issues adversely buffets the debt management system in developing countries, thereby distorting the yield curve. Yield curves are vital in determining the markets' future expectations of interest rates and inflation, in addition to the fact that private bond issuers, prima facie, base themselves on government yield curve to determine their own yields (bond prices adjusted for their own risk premiums). For developing countries that are subject to increased demand mainly for their short-term maturities of debt instruments, the short-end part of the yield curve is well-anchored and realistic in terms of monetary policy stance. However, in the case of the upper segment of the yield curve, it is unrealistic because it is based on irregular long-term issues. It can be argued that longer term demand for government instruments is likely to be low by virtue of a predominating banking sector that

clings to shorter debt maturities. Nonetheless, this segment of the debt market can be developed by inciting corporates, individuals and foreigners to enter into the longer term maturities. Tax incentives can be used as a policy tool to boost such demand.

5. Developing countries tend to be endowed with underdeveloped secondary markets with the debt being particularly illiquid. This means that primary issues stay good only when deemed as held-to-maturity investments in lieu of available-for-sale investments. To increase the convertibility of government instruments from held-to-maturity states to available-for-sale modes, the secondary markets should be given a major boost, both in terms of depth and breadth.

6. There is the need to have proactive debt risk management strategies to mitigate risks. There is also the need to have integrated risk management in a properly defined debt management framework that clearly spells out all the strategies, whether short-term or long-term. Indeed, risk management should be deemed to be an inherent feature of the debt management task. For instance, if government borrowing is heavily tilted in a given currency, it is considered apt that government lending is also denominated in that currency, to induce matching between cash inflows and outflows. In the same vein, in the case that a government-backed institution is expected to fail, this should be directly captured as an increase in contingent liabilities and should thereby be considered as part of total debt.

7. Despite the fact that there is no universal practice with respect to the code of practice relating to debt management, the widely accepted debt management metric rests on the debt-to-GDP ratio. The international norm with respect to the debt-to-GDP ratio is based on 60%.

8. Contingent liabilities and guarantees should be included in total public debt. Indeed, these off-balance sheet items constitute latent debt. Contingent liabilities tend to be high for developing countries on the back of high debt levels and also due to many government-backed institutions, poor debt management structures, a dearth of players to enlarge the economic base and higher trade balance risk. It is vital to note that contingent liabilities remain hidden deficit in the form of off-balance items until a triggering event converts the off-balance item to being an on-balance item. However, being a latent risk, it is considerate to incorporate it whenever calculating the total level of public debt.

9. Debt managers need to have sound knowledge of all aspects related to debt management. Lack of knowledge about derivatives use which can be used to hedge residual risk (risk that remains after natural hedging

has done its part) needs to be surmounted. Similarly, mastery of the distinct borrowing channels should also be important to gauge on the liquidity implications of borrowings. For instance, when a central bank issues instruments to borrow in the local currency, this generates a fall in liquidity in the monetary circuit. On the other hand, if there is issuance to borrow in foreign currency, this does not affect liquidity in the system. Similarly, proper knowledge of the economy is vital, such as the months in which tax payments are made to the government. Finally, proper forecasting and modelling mechanisms should also be developed.

10. A sound coordinated fiscal policy is of vital significance with respect to proper debt management. High public debts are symptomatic with fears of mounting taxes by investors and hence this poses feasible risks to higher economic growth. Governments can resort to inflation-indexed instruments like inflation-indexed bonds or floating rate government securities in the case of mounting inflation. The advantage of using these instruments is that they impose a real commitment on the government and related authorities to have low inflation, since higher inflation signifies higher costs of financing. Despite the very fact that inflation scales down the value of public debt, high inflation creates distortions into the economic system in the form of uncertainty as to gnaw at economic growth prospects. Consequently, high inflationary pressures should be avoided.

11. Sluggish discipline processes are widely noted in many developing countries. New domestic debt is mainly raised to finance maturing domestic debt in order to ward off liquidity distortions in the monetary circuit. Similarly, new foreign debt is issued predominantly to finance maturing foreign debt. It would be better if debt management processes were leveraged as to become more dynamic and proactive.

12. The concept of debt sustainability is enhanced in the case that debt raised is used principally to finance capital expenditures in lieu of consumer goods. Subsequently, the way that funds raised from debt are used is vital to gauge on its sustainability. I suggest that the end use of funds should also be monitored and recorded in the debt management system to directly gauge on the quality of debt raised—whether for consumption or capital purposes. Besides, developing countries should be wary not to develop excessive external debt as this may transfer into difficulties in financing imports, which may then unleash undermined economic growth chiefly when imports of raw materials are rechanneled as exports of goods.

13. Sound debt management systems should be established. Good corporate governance structures and proper recording systems should also be implemented. CS-DRMS and DMFAS constitute the two most widely used debt recording systems. It is also imperative to have a sound debt management system that can generate timely reports for prompt risk management like reports on currency composition, interest rate composition and instrument-type composition. In the same vein, it is preponderant to have sophisticated integrated tools in the debt management system like stress testing, forecasting and out-of-sample analysis. Above all, it is important to have a sound macroeconomic modelling to have an effective debt management system because the debt level of a country is inherently linked to its macroeconomic state of affairs.

14. Debt management function should be freed from any monetary policy involvement by not placing the debt management unit in a central bank. Only two countries in the world have violated such a principle. There is also a political risk that can lead towards poor debt management decisions.

15. For countries subject to high levels of external debt, this signifies mounting vulnerability of the economy to external shocks. It is also vital to note that external debt is particularly sensitive to current account shocks. Above all, in the case that a country is subject to a large proportion of foreign currency debt, this implies that even a small shock can engender a currency crisis. Hence, proper thresholds should be set up as to the maximum level of external debt that can be accommodated. Moreover, the foreign debt management strategy of any country is inherently linked to that country's level of reserves. The lower the foreign debt levels, the lower the pressures being exerted on foreign reserves and hence the stronger the position of the country in obviating crises. Above all, countries which avail of balance of payments surpluses tend to position themselves in better economic conditions as accumulating foreign reserves assist them in bearing any unforeseen shocks.

16. Most countries long for depreciating currencies in view of enhancing their exports and this holds mainly for economies that hinge heavily on exports to boost growth. However, currency appreciation is particularly positive for countries subject to high external debts level as it helps to implicitly reduce the costs burden. Similarly, rising inflation assists in reducing the costs of domestic debt. However, both currency appreciation and inflationary pressures should manifest naturally. They

must not be artificially generated as to scale down the costs of total debt.

17. To have both well-functioning and liquid bond markets, it is essential to have primary dealers (appointed markets players, usually banks to market government securities). These primary dealers confer many benefits, such as encouraging an efficient price discovery system in both primary and secondary markets, enhancing liquidity, scaling down government costs of borrowing in the long-term and also increasing the number of participants.

The crisis may herald positive news for developing countries in terms of presenting the ripe time for them to improve on their debt management structures. All the above policies help to ensure credibility in the debt management system so that there is sound rollover of debt. Credibility also assists in lengthening the debt maturity, which is particularly vital for developing countries. The reason is that developing countries tend to be imbued with shallow debt markets with tilted preference towards short-term instruments. Finally, credibility induces proper coordination between monetary and fiscal policies.

CHAPTER SEVEN

MITIGATING THE WORLD'S TRIDENT CRISES-BURGEONING DEBT, AGEING POPULATION AND CLIMATE CHANGE: IN QUEST FOR SUSTAINABLE POLICIES[1]

The US crisis has brought the international financial system to the edge of a breakdown with recessionary periods looming large on the economic horizon. However, two other crises are simultaneously affecting planet earth, namely the detrimental effects of climate change coupled with an ageing population. This innovative research attempts to find solutions to curb the effects of the three crises. Overall, the paper finds that man can come out of this labyrinth of intertwined ordeals by fostering an utterly new approach to policies. Long-term approaches to decision-making, network optimisation, social banks, radical changes in the work environment, limits to speculation in derivatives, policy-oriented research, a shift from Egonomics to Economics, checks on growth of the artificial economy and a re-engineering of bank loans approvals via the inclusion of sustainability reports, will all create a better state of living. Above all, this paper shows that the equilibrium concept used by economists is flawed and needs to be revisited to factor in the metaphysical world, since true equilibrium manifests when the material world is balanced with the metaphysical world.

7.0 Introduction

The US crisis, which began in the form of a financial crisis, eventually turned into an economic crisis and thereafter into a debt crisis, left the world in veritable turmoil on a number of different fronts. In 2012, policy-makers expressed concerns that the year was going to be tough. However,

---

[1] There may be some overlapping components in this chapter with respect to the second chapter since this chapter has been written separately from the second chapter.

no one has yet designed a truly holistic approach in interpreting the message behind the crisis. Was it God-made or man-made? Why? What are the concrete solutions to be adopted? Alternatively, is the crisis something already planned by the Almighty in line with Malthus' (1978) principle of equilibrium? This paper attempts to find solutions to address the crises that currently buffet humanity, namely the debt crisis, climate change and an ageing population.

The high exposure to toxic assets linked to the US crisis devastated many countries, with Greece witnessing substantial cuts in government expenditures and rising unemployment. Finance has been blamed as the ultimate cause of the financial crisis on the back of a consistently rising artificial economy, significantly ahead of the real economy. Such a negative catalyst has been nurtured by absence of one of the major underpinnings of financial theory, namely perfect information flow. In essence, Akerlof (1970) points out two forms of information asymmetry: adverse selection and moral hazard. However, it is an irony to note that, despite significant advancements accomplished in the area of technology and financial   liberalisation worldwide, both versions of information asymmetry permeated the financial institutions in advanced economies. Indeed, in spite of wielding credit information bureaus about customer historical credit background, banks still committed adverse selection. In a parallel manner, moral hazard manifested since customers failed to respect the ethical and moral issues in question.

The crisis also generated significant effects on the debt sustainability issues of developed countries in the world, with strong negative bequests to newborns, already becoming borrowers right from the conception stage in the womb. This also entails vital intergenerational conflicts in terms of higher working hours on the working population and lower future pensions. Ongoing vicious circles of higher risk premiums have been associated with burgeoning debt levels. Ironically, massive injections of funds into the economy, directed towards de-leveraging of private sector debt, merely leverage public debt.

Another crisis, namely climate change, is also affecting humankind. In fact, as per the Inter-governmental Panel on Climate Change report (2007), there is a unanimous agreement among leading climate change scientists that human activities have played a preponderant role in the global warming process. Without concrete and concerted efforts from various economies, man is highly susceptible to face disastrous consequences, such as the wiping out of small islands due to rises in sea levels. In the same vein, severe droughts, hurricanes and cyclones are likely to manifest with stronger intensity, despite a fall in their respective frequency of occurrence.

Figure 7.1: World Buffeted by Trident Crises

As if two crises were not sufficient, another crisis has already engulfed humankind in terms of dwindling birth and death rates. Indeed, many countries, in particular the advanced economies, are subject to an ageing population which will engender significance readjustments to the whole economic process, starting from production to demand management policies. The most pronounced effects of an ageing population comprise of reduced savings, rising demand for healthcare and strains on the government purse. In essence, ageing populations are expected to add oil to the existent fire and aggravate the adverse effects of the financial crisis. Figure 7.1 depicts the trident crises.

The above challenges do not seem to be simultaneously addressed as economists/financial economists cling to economic/financial theories, climate scientists to ecological science and development economists to growth theories. This chapter addresses these challenges by proposing sustainable solutions that would give the world renewed vigour as it carves its path towards the next century. However, to achieve this, there is a need to entirely re-engineer the way things have been done. Because minds are the greatest power in the world by virtue of their sole power to create and destroy, the minds of people have to be reshaped to accommodate for changes, in view of shifting focus towards long-term goals in lieu of myopic objectives, as encapsulated by the words of Keynes (1936): "In the long-run we are all dead." I would adjust his words to instead state, "In the long-run we are all dead, but a positive legacy is perpetually left behind to strengthen inter-generational bonds."

The rest of this paper is structured as follows: Section 7.1 deals with the causes and consequences of the three crises, along with the chief ironies associated with the financial crisis; Section 7.2 not only addresses the feasible solutions to curb the detrimental effects of the crises but also provides long-term solutions that would significantly reduce any further crisis ahead; and finally Section 7.3 concludes.

7.1 Financial Crisis, Climate Change and Ageing Population

7.1.1 Financial Crisis (Financial Crisis → Economic Crisis → Debt Crisis)

There is widespread consensus among both academicians and practitioners that the crisis has partly been triggered by central banks in developed countries as they clung to an extremely accommodative monetary policy stance coupled with unregulated speculators. The very low interest rates constituted the real bullets used by speculators who created a burgeoning artificial economy, far ahead of the real economy. The underlying rationale is that too low interest rates induced speculators to bet more and more, chiefly when their bonuses were tied to the level of profits made. However, the catalyst of the crisis, just like the Kobe earthquake that jeopardised the strategy deployed by Nick Leeson, emanated from the fall in house prices,[2] which eventually led towards gyrations in terms of significantly undervalued collaterals whereby borrowers defaulted based on net negative equity positions. The situation was rendered chaotic due to massive investments by hedge funds, investment banks and speculators in these risky/toxic subprime mortgage-related assets. This led to second-round/third-round effects in terms of significant falls in fund values and banks becoming undercapitalised with many facing bankruptcy episodes. Ironically, securitisation, initially envisaged to diversify risks, generated strong contagion effects that negatively affected international financial markets.

As the financial crisis affected many sectors, this paved the way towards economic crisis based on harmful real effects that befell consumption and production. Crumbling demand caused lower production and increases in layoffs. To save the economy from catastrophe, the Federal Reserve Bank had no choice but to cling to Quantitative Easing (following impotency of monetary policy) in view of injecting funds into the economy, either directly or indirectly via purchase of bad assets to save major institutions. In that process, the US drastically shifted its capitalist regime to a socialist philosophy on the grounds that the government found it hard to accept failures of systemically important institutions or "too large to fail institutions." This eventually led towards moral hazard effects, with some institutions claiming outright defeat. As government undertook the buying back of toxic assets and injecting funds into the fragile economies, this led to a corresponding rise in government liabilities in terms of burgeoning debt. In that process, the financial system collapse problem was merely transferred into a debt crisis, which currently looms large among mostly advanced economies of the world.

In many countries, there prevails a bank-based financial system. The US banks can partly be held responsible for the cause of the crisis. In essence, they were indirectly financing themselves based on more and more lending geared towards the speculative economy relative to the real economy. Disconnection to the real economy occurred on the back of

---

[2] The fall in house prices was triggered by oil price hikes, which induced households to shift to houses found near their place of work.

house prices moving beyond the income/wages means of the average quality borrower in the economy, leading to a rising "whimsical economy." Such a state of affairs remained healthy as long as everything remained normal, since once one link got disturbed, the whole system collapsed with reverse gear taking in the form of banks harnessing on clients' securities under forced repayments. Debtors contracted these loans with a similar view of making outright gains, since they all possessed the same "animal spirits" anchored in steady housing price increases, so that the proceeds from house sales would far exceed the repayments and accrued interests. Such motivation spurred households who did not have the real means to be solvent to contract mortgage loans and to rely fully on future hikes on house prices in order to make their fortune. In essence, significant dual risks prevailed for both the borrower and the lender. The borrower took funds beyond his means, while the lender provided funds not based on the true income generation capacity of the borrowers, but solely hinging on higher future house prices. Governments did not undertake proper regulation as they considered the invisible hand to best allocate and channel resources in terms of both allocative and productive efficiencies, while banks clung to only one mantra, i.e., 'making more and more money.'

When things got sour, even those banks that were in the financial intermediation business had less money to lend to good enterprises, which had no choice but to curtail employment and output, all of which left behind suppressed consumption and economic activities. Similarly, investments in hedge funds and derivatives linked to mortgage securities were adversely affected, which had the effect of severely damaging the intricate fabrics of the whole gamut of the financial system. Derivatives instruments constitute financial innovation products geared towards containing risks; however, the crisis showed the extent to which these instruments deviated from a down-to-earth focus, since they were also related to fantasy expectations. Moreover, speculative users of the derivatives scaled up the leverage effects of the crisis, pushing forward a growing and diverging artificial economy from the real economy à la the Machiavellian principle and also based on the irrational exuberance philosophy of Shiller (2005). Lack of trust, as stressed by Chorofas (2009), also explained the negative spillover effects. In a nutshell, the crisis showed the extent to which banks camouflaged real risks while providing a glossy picture of their financial statements.

7.1.2 Climate Change

Dubbed as the greatest market failure of all time, climate change effects are unparallel and cut across distinct sectors of the economy. As per the Inter-governmental Panel on Climate Change (2007), there is unequivocal consensus among leading climate scientists that the world is already warming at an increasing pace. The causes of climate change are considered to be more pronounced in the energy and transport sectors, with coal constituting the most carbon-intensive energy source. Despite scepticism expressed about the success of the Kyoto Protocol, which basically failed to forge a strong international bond in Durban in 2011, three main approaches have been adopted to reduce climate change, namely emissions trading, Clean Development Mechanism under the United Nations Framework Convention for Clean Development Mechanism (to compensate developing countries for shifting to low-carbon technologies and development) and Joint Implementation, all of which are directed towards stabilising CO^2 emission at 500 ppm. Most climate change studies consider the CO^2 equivalent for all the different gases so much so that carbon is now internationally defined as the exchange rate for climate change. Deforestation, logging, and soil decay have all stimulated the process of CO^2 emissions which eventually spurred warming as to generate different adverse impacts including aciditation of the oceans, rapid melting of the Greenland ice sheet, land slippage, earthquakes, heat waves, tsunamis, shrinking snows and mountain glaciers, modified patterns of precipitation and rising sea levels.

Most studies on climate change however overlook an important factor that has already mitigated to some extent the adverse effects of global warming. Global warming would have been more catastrophic had there not been vegetation, which basically absorbs around 40% of CO^2 emissions via the photosynthesis process. In the same vein, aerosols have complex effects on climate with a net cooling effect mostly manifesting. However, the problem in gauging true effects of climate change on global temperature has been particularly daunting with respect to the model envisaged. Hurdles in modelling include aerosols being considered as outliers and chaos effects due to very changing nature of the atmosphere and the oceans. Beyond that, there is still disagreement as to the proper social discount rate to apply when gauging on the inter-generational effects of climate change.

7.1.3 Ageing Population

History has shown that demographic changes do play a predominant role in a country's success. Ageing of the population is manifesting at distinct paces and intensities in the world. It is widely accepted that an ageing population exerts direct impacts on economic growth. In European countries and Japan where ageing is particularly taking a larger toll, it is no wonder that efforts have to be mustered to reorient the economic goals. Intuitively speaking, ageing population in developed countries is expected to result in downward pressures on the level of savings based on the conventional life-cycle pattern, with low or even negative savings manifesting post retirement. Conversely, developing countries tend to experience lower savings as a larger segment of their population consists of younger people who consume more and save less. In both cases, lower savings are noted and these are expected to thwart the growth process because savings mobilise capital for investments. This clearly shows that demographic changes do entail important repercussions on the savings-investment nexus, which is a key ingredient for promoting growth.

An ageing population also signifies expanding demand for health services, which will ultimately be subject to rising prices. In many countries, private hospitals are also providing beauty products and surgical operations to reduce the bodily effects of ageing. Overall, the demand for healthcare services is anticipated to undergo a sustained rising trend, propelled by a larger ageing population segment. Consequently, advanced economies experiencing ageing populations are likely to be subject to major strains in public finance, mainly when the government constitutes the major health care provider. Above all, as the crisis affects the economy, governments lose their tax raisings potentials, further thwarting the financing of the public pension system. Indeed, pressures will also be exerted on the pension system, established to provide compensation or financial support for people who are subject to old age, invalidity or premature death.

However, a higher proportion of retirement due to an ageing population can be synonymous with capital bonanza effects with a strong propensity to spur higher growth, as shown by Ehrlich and Lui (1991) and Kalemli-Ozcan et al. (2000). Besides, ageing populations also signify rising trends of bequests, which have been found to enhance capital accumulation, as per Kotlikoff and Summers (1981). Unfortunately, the crisis is expected to reduce the value of bequests based on undermined values of households' assets.

7.1.4 Major ironies triggered by the financial crisis

a. A Blow to Economic Principle: From Capitalism to Socialism and Asymmetric Intervention

The crisis initiated a real blow to policy-makers as it compelled them to adopt unconventional measures to secure and prevent their financial system from complete crash, ultimately engendering a radical shift from free market forces towards a socialist approach. Such a sudden change was considered vital chiefly when monetary policy got entangled in the liquidity trap. Above all, the safety measures undertaken were mainly geared towards systematically larger financial institutions to contain the effects of the crisis. Ironically, medium and smaller firms are usually more linked to the real side of the economy, and they employ a larger chunk of the total labour force-like Small and Medium enterprises. Nonetheless, injections of money into the economies were the only choice left to the authorities to curtail the detrimental impacts of the crisis.

b. Drifting away from the US dollar towards other currencies

Post the crisis, surplus-running countries have tried to identify alternative currencies or substitutes to the US dollar. This has been evidenced by China, which constitutes one of the world's most important holders of US dollar reserves and thereby menaces the long-term value of the US dollar as it reshuffles its currency portfolio towards other currencies. Above all, China has also called for the replacement of the US dollar by SDR, the unit of account used by the IMF for its members; in the meantime, it has already scaled up its reserve holdings in Euro. However, with the Euro debt crisis straining hard on the life of European Monetary Union (in particular the PIGS) and Euro strength, it is less likely that the US dollar will be replaced by the Euro, and the US may still enjoy hegemony of its dollar. Nonetheless, China has already begun to diversify its reserves base by investing in real assets in different countries, with a conspicuous increase in presence noted in African countries.

c. From Yen carry trade to US dollar carry trade

Another interesting facet shown by the crisis pertains to the shift from yen carry trade to the US dollar carry trade following the interest rate cuts made by the Fed and its maintained policy towards low interest rates for an extended period of time. Ironically, such a shift in carry trade can be particularly perilous in the case that it can reverse the whole purpose of Quantitative Easing. Indeed, as investors tilt their portfolios into high-yielding non-US currencies, there are chances that asset price bubbles[3] build up in these currencies, mainly when no major growth is taking shape on the real side of the picture. This could feasibly generate further crises that feed onto the main crisis. In fact, as bruised investors found their portfolio subject to major losses, the US dollar carry trade seems to be particularly suitable in terms of reducing their financial casualties. Another caveat of the carry trade related to their short-term profits nature; it can feasibly crowd out long-term investment projects and thereby thwart growth of the real economy.

d. Derivatives/Securitisation: Financial time bombs rather than risk management instruments
Endowed with voracious needs for strong alphas in the short-term, hedge funds instigated robust investments in derivatives and securitised products/toxic assets to harness high returns, despite the very fact that these instruments acted like financial bombs. As a matter of fact, as hedge funds strived for higher returns without looking at the real side of the economy, they encouraged prices to drift beyond their fundamental values. Such a state of affairs created severe disconnections, chiefly when hedge funds' "magnetic capital" lured more and more money into the illusive wealth creations, which later impacted society, creating recessions, unemployment and poverty. Moreover, the bubbles tend to feed on themselves, by sucking in funds from banks which could otherwise be channelled towards socially optimal uses.

An important element that justifies the existence of real estates and derivatives is that they inherently act as inflation absorbers by absorbing money that would otherwise consume the real economy and generate higher inflation. However, price stability constitutes the role of central banks which therefore need to ensure that the amount of money present in the monetary circuit is aligned to the level of real economic activities.

7.2 Solutions to the Trident Crises

a. Inducing a good mix of Commercial and Social Banks
Despite existing for quite some time, social banking has nonetheless still not yet gained momentum in the sphere of finance. Essentially, a social bank is defined as a financial institution that acts as an intermediary agent in linking surplus and deficit units for the purpose of fighting poverty, spurring social development, and enhancing social cohesion and social

---

[3] This issue is fully addressed in Chapter three.

project developments, all of which activities are geared towards consolidating the standard of living of the society at large. In essence, social banks deviate from mainstream finance by focusing mainly on non-profit motives like commitments to finance projects that lead towards social sustainability, moral values and positive social externalities.

The greatest benefit of social banks is that they are inherently engaged in greening the economies by fostering environmental developments. In that respect, social banks not only remedy the emergence of any speculative-induced crisis, but they also tackle the climate change problem by inducing green finance to promote efficiency and effectiveness in energy use. Another important strategy involves the use of sustainability reports whenever loans are granted to ensure that environmental damages are reduced to the lowest level possible. In the same vein, social banks partly solve the problems related to an ageing population by promoting a more healthy wealth management between the older and younger segment of the population for the betterment of the society as a whole, in lieu of increasing the wealth of only a few players.

Based on the above benefits that social banks confer, it seems plain that such a type of bank directly contributes towards higher financial stability. Consequently, it would be apt if countries worldwide were to adopt a good mixture of commercial and social banks in their financial system.

b. Long-term policies for climate change

The field of climate change constitutes a cross-disciplinary dimension which permeates nearly all subtle fabrics of society. For instance, scarcity of water due to climate change impacts not only on consumption but stretches beyond to the energy sector for hydro power generation. Interestingly, water scarcity is also detrimental to energy production in the case of nuclear power plants because water plays a huge role in furnishing steam and cooling powers. In a parallel manner, the financial crisis has also affected climate change policies by strangling funds that can otherwise be earmarked to deal with both adaptation and mitigation strategies. Ironically, the crisis can be synonymous to a push towards better climate change effects via the following channels:

    a. Reduced activities level leave behind low carbon emissions.

    b. As companies re-engineer their activities, this provides significant scope to revamp the economy and thereby restart afresh with cleaner technologies.

    c. Insurance companies can reduce the adverse effects of the crisis on their business activities by tapping into new products like weather derivatives, sea defense insurance and flood risk insurance, as well as developing or enhancing the development of catastrophe bonds.

Climate change affects the investments of companies as it entails both opportunities and risks. Energy and transport sectors are directly at risk based on their need to decarbonise, while insurance companies face indirect risks via property destruction.[4] For instance, climate change causes property risks which can jeopardise investments made by asset managers. In the same manner, climate change can also increase risks for investment companies which fail to diversify part of their investments towards companies which adopt cleaner technologies and which are cheaper following any new government policy, such as a significant hike in carbon tax. Opportunities relating to climate change can manifest at the lending level in the case that central banks in the world promulgate cleaner technologies by imposing lower risk premiums on green companies, so that the latter can avail of finer rates, lower effective borrowing costs and hence have higher positive returns. In a nutshell, the greatest opportunity from climate change can potentially manifest on the finance side so that to accentuate returns, companies will need to revamp their whole production/investment activities.

To reduce global warming, different strategies have been deployed internationally with adaptation and mitigation policies lying at the forefront of the policy agenda. However, it is vital to note that adaptation cannot replace mitigation, since only the latter has a concrete power to curb the adverse effects of climate change, while the former merely constitutes adjustment mechanisms to scale down the extent of the damage borne. Mitigation policies include the use of clean replacement technologies for fuel, encouraging vegetation which act as carbon sinks, hammering out proper strategies for land use like denser development patterns, seeking alternative forms of transport like cycling and walking, use of energy-efficient cars like electric or hybrid cars, encouraging videoconferencing in lieu of travelling, decarbonising electricity production and stimulating the use of solar power.

Climate change policies need to be related to long-term objectives based on its long-term consequences. They also need to enable countries to have ample time to utterly re-engineer their activities. In that respect, this long-term approach is automatically compatible with the debt crisis, as

---

[4] This has often been coined as climate change acting as a watershed event for insurance companies.

countries can now better accommodate for climate change policies. This also applies in the case of the ageing population problem, which requires long-term planning.

c. Promoting Green Finance

Green finance constitutes an interesting avenue via which both the adverse effects of the climate change crisis and the debt crisis can be reduced. Many countries in the world heavily rely on fuel and coal, and the best way to reduce such reliance is to provide financial incentives to the companies and industries to reduce the intake of polluting energy types. The benefits attached to such reduction would undeniably not only be lower carbon emissions but also lesser financial stability risks. Low risks to financial stability occur because the benefits emanating from green finance take time to manifest, to the effect that this automatically squeezes out the existence of ephemeral profits which are based on "animal spirits"/irrational exuberance. Moreover, the government avails of lower import costs relating to energy imports so that this reduces its debt burden and gives a positive push to the balance of payments position. Finally, as green finance advocates longer term investments perspectives, this systematically ensures a crowding out impact on funds channelled towards the artificial economy.

d. Shift from "Egonomics" to "Economics"

One of the practical ways to deal with the triple crises is to induce "Economics" and not "Egonomics." I coined the term "Egonomics" to reflect the behaviour of economic players like hedge funds, pension funds, investment banks, mortgage dealers, real estate investors, and venture capitalists, which was skewed towards their own economic concerns, which should constitute rational behaviour, but not to the extent as to significantly unleash considerable divergence between the real and the artificial economy. The focus on one's own high alphas categorically endangered the whole gamut of the financial system. In addition, the regulators did not play their proper role as proactive watchdogs. Nonetheless, failure is not fatal and it is the courage to remould the whole international financial system that matters. In that respect, it is vital to have a well-balanced economy with free market forces operating subject to robust and proactive regulatory frameworks. In a parallel manner, people should be made more aware of the climate change crisis, so as to induce more concerted efforts worldwide to preserve the planet. Similarly, developed countries can reduce the adverse effects of an ageing population by creating proper incentives for foreign labour (immigration) so that proper rebalancing manifests at each country's level.

e. Remoulding the academic world: From sophisticated modelling to policy-oriented research

The world is so complex that man always strives to outperform his own species. Indeed, in terms of modelling, man is already well-equipped with proper tools like time series, cross-sectional and panel data econometrics. To my belief, the GARCH modelling of Engle (1982) has been the real development in econometric modelling, due to its strong practical applications. Usually, mathematical papers in the field of finance or economics tend to be imbued with robust mathematical foundations but with only some of them having practical relevance. This tends to be a waste of resources, namely man's psychic energy. However, it can be argued that these mathematical models do have important contributions in moulding thoughts. Indeed, theory is like God while the empirical evidence/practical side of life is like man. However, it is imperative to note that knowledge becomes accomplished[5] when theory meets practice and this definitively explains the rationale for Engle winning the Nobel Prize, since, like other Nobel Prize winners, he succeeded in proving the practical applications of his theory. Currently, considerable efforts are being vested towards maximising efficiency in energy use. In a parallel manner, efficiency should also be struck in the case of psychic or mental energy by inciting more policy-oriented research papers. Above all, new thinking should be further stimulated chiefly in areas of need, such as sustainable finance, economics of water management, transport system, energy management, food security, healthcare and the environment.

f. Looking at man in its holistic dimension (physical and metaphysical): Missing out to feed the souls

The whole world also needs to be re-engineered since man has altogether lost the real meaning of life. Imagine one day you die, without having had time to live life as you wished; what is the use of working hard when many cherished desires remained unfulfilled? Work is deemed as worship and vital to providing man with basic necessities and luxuries so that he can avail of a good quality standard of living, but this has simultaneously led towards the famous 'rat race'. In this process, man has missed out on feeding his soul, and this accounts for the existence of the greedy

---

[5] This can also be explained in the words of Georg Wilhelm Friedrich Hegel (1770-1831): "Theory is the indispensable, but as such not sufficient prerequisite for practice."

speculators, lenders and borrowers. As a matter of fact, any religion focuses on the man-God relationship as pure communication manifesting via the soul medium, and here lies the major disequilibrium that is distorting humankind and will perpetuate until real balancing takes place between material wealth and spiritual wealth. In essence, man has been in quest of material wealth but few have been in quest for spiritual wealth. The best way to present this anomaly is in terms of a basic economic tool,[6] namely via the subtle forces of demand and supply for soul. Demand for soul is to get connected with God, while supply is the number of minutes or hours that man devotes to God. Figure 7.2 shows the case of no proper time given to God to feed the soul, while Figure 7.3 fulfils such a condition to ensure equilibrium.

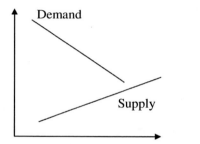

Figure 7.2: No Equilibrium Case   Figure 7.3: Equilibrium Case

I believe that there is a major disconnection in terms of prevailing conditions between secondary level education and the workplace. At secondary level, students are taught how to behave, to practise daily prayers, to respect their elders and to have discipline in life. Ironically however, man is so fragile that such an education process should have continued into tertiary level education, as well as in the workplace. Indeed, in the working environment, bosses, colleagues and employees are all focused towards maximising sales/efforts to ensure high productivity/ profits, to the plain effect that these goals are attained by hook or crook means, symptomatic with unchecked growth. Herein emanates the cause of all crises, even climate change, which has been generated mainly through anthropogenic emissions. To truly reinvent man in its fully-

---

[6] Usually, deep thinking and meditation is the widely acclaimed route for communicating with God.

fledged state, with all of his/her embodiments (both material and soul levels), I personally believe that one working day should be used solely for prayers, physical exercises, getting together and doing social services like an altruistic social helper.

Saturdays and Sundays are merely two out of seven working days so that there is an automatically inherent disequilibrium in the life process. With at least one additional day provided (say Fridays) and used judiciously, this would surely obviate any other potential crisis that would buffet the world and also bring about a more humane approach to growth—whether at the level of finance, climate change or demographic. However, instead of staying at home on Fridays, employees should go to the workplace to do special works like doing group prayers, performing social service tasks to the needy people, doing sports to stay in good health (thereby reducing the healthcare services costs of government), amongst other activities. Similarly, children would avail of special classes on how to behave as good citizens of tomorrow, instilling within them the sense of helping others. If a change in mindset fails to occur—and even if man is able to live in Mars—the same philosophies will create further crises in the future.

g. Hard Core Hurdle in Economics: Shifting from Unit Optimisation to Network Optimisation

Undergraduate courses in economic theories focus on the need to effect optimisation at separate levels for the distinct units of the society, namely households, corporates and banks. Households strive to satisfy their utility function subject to a given budget constraint. Corporates and banks strive to maximise profits subject to costs. Several papers use the same economic underpinning like in Dynamic Stochastic General Equilibrium models. However, the crisis unveiled the main shortcoming of this type of optimisation, in that the focus is laid on only one unit at a time. Consequently, it is not necessary that a bank, which is striving for the highest profits level subject to its costs, will also be maximising the overall wealth or utility of the society, as there are likely to be negative spillover effects in the interaction process. This is why I believe that modelling under optimisation should also factor in these feasible externalities like under a network approach. The latter would capture complex interactions that would subsist among the distinct agents in the economy and would thereby focus on the direct and indirect effects of each agent's actions on GDP. In essence, such a modelling approach would ensure that there subsists stronger compatibility among the distinct units of the society. However, such a notion may appear rather difficult to implement, but it could be that one day the very basic optimisation is completely reworked, as to integrate these feedback effects among distinct units.

Similarly, education still constitutes a difficulty in the area of policy implementation. The underlying rationale is that, by acting as an expert in a specific field, man forgets the other potential implications of his actions. For instance, a financial expert will chiefly aim to maximise the return of his company without having any consideration as to whether higher levels of carbon emissions are being emitted by the company. This explains the need always to have inter-group discussions to address the distinct problems that hit society, especially since any solution taken without having a full-fledged panel of experts is highly susceptible to backfire. After all, man sometimes forgets that the more he knows, the more he does not know, since knowledge constitutes a fathomless sea. Subsequently, it is vital to always have a panel of experts in distinct fields prior to embarking on adaptation of major changes in policies.

Another major hitch relating to the traditional optimisation process pertains to the definition of household utility function. Basically, the utility function is modelled solely based on a material wealth concept of life. In practice, happiness is not confined to monetary benefits. A person may be deriving happiness when he feels happy with his inner self, while another person may derive happiness through donations. Despite it being difficult to model these heterogeneous issues, it is nonetheless imperative to factor these elements in, since happiness can never be solely attributed to material wealth.

h. Integrated Flow Concept as the medium to enhance productivity at work

There is still poor human capital management around the world. The reason is that performance management systems are considered by many governments as the best way to link efforts to remuneration. However, I believe that the best channel to boost productivity is to render it natural via the Flow Concept of Mihaly Csikszentmihalyi (1991) whereby as individuals get focused on their respective tasks, they start to forget everything, even the time factor, so that they naturally give of their best. Such an approach to human capital management is beneficial since it not only induces instant productivity but also reduces stress levels at work, which can later manifest in terms of diseases that would call for a higher demand for health services. The need for higher productivity is underscored based on the accumulated debt states of countries worldwide, so that higher growth is imperative to accommodate for a sustainable debt level.

i.   Perpetual check on the fictitious/artificial economy: Establishing the Artificial-Real Economy Ratio of 0.75:1

The missing check that regulatory authorities failed to implement pertained to their utter ignorance of linking the financial/fictitious/artificial economy to the real economy.[7] Intuitively speaking, a healthy financial system requires aligned dynamics between the fictitious side and the real side. Should the fictitious side of the economy outgrow the real economy, this would be symptomatic with the formation of bubbles, with absorption of funds into speculative investments in lieu of productive activities. As a rule of thumb, it would be considerate to cling towards an Artificial-Real Economy Ratio of 0.75:1, based on a 25 per cent margin cover. Hence, if the real economy grows by 1%, the artificial economy should not grow by more than 0.75 per cent. The irony is that, whereby data from Bank for International Settlement shows that derivatives grew from $100 trillion in 2002 to $516 trillion in 2007, a more than 400 per cent growth ample enough to trigger any crisis while US GDP rose by only 32 per cent from $10.59 trillion to $13.96 for the same period under consideration.

Another instance includes the case of Switzerland whereby the combined balance sheets of UBS bank and Credit Suisse represent around four times of the country's GDP. To weaken systemic risk, big banks should be subject to vigorous regulation to mitigate any adverse contagion effects that can filter down into different veins of the economy. However, overregulation should be avoided as it can create distortions in the system so that optimal balance should be struck between deregulation and overregulation. The culture of responsible finance should also be instilled among bankers. Similarly, rating agencies should be subject to robust regulations.

One important aspect that the crisis created and was not mentioned by the authorities pertains to the extent of the crowding out effect generated by the artificial economy after the crisis. As a matter of fact, in the post-crisis period, declines in asset prices undermined the wealth of people, and had the effect of scaling down the level of potential investments. This also explained the fall in remittances, aid flows, portfolio investments and foreign direct investments to developing countries. Therefore, by properly controlling the artificial economy, the authorities ensure both the avoidance of any financial crisis and the associated negative effects in terms of reduced availability of funds.

---

[7] This is where Computational General Equilibrium Models come to the fore, on the basis of no consideration given to inflation and financial markets; everything is based on real economic activities.

j.   Unfairness in remuneration system: Call for limits on salaries
A fund manager produces nothing concrete yet obtains a higher salary
relative to factory workers who toil night and day to produce tangible
goods. Since the fund manager has sacrificed part of his life in studies to
enhance his human capital, his higher salary is undeniably justified.
However, the salary difference is huge in some cases, chiefly for those
working in the financial sector, and this has been the foundation stone of
the crisis, since part of the remuneration was based on the return of the
portfolio that consisted of financial assets which were subject to
speculative forces. Indeed, in view of maximising their income, the
managers speculated far beyond the true fundamentals as to create a
burgeoning artificial economy which, when pricked, jeopardised the global
financial system. Subsequently, remuneration mechanisms should be
established to mitigate against excessive speculative forces likely to
induce crisis.

**k. Reliance on sustainable policies and not inflation for reducing
public debt level**
Many countries resorted to stimulus packages and injections of money into
their bruised economies. It is anticipated that upside risks to inflation loom
large on the economic horizon. In addition, there is widespread belief that
inflation constitutes an important ingredient in reducing the debt level of
the economies, since it scales down the real value of public debt. Besides,
this brings about important seigniorage income to central banks, which not
only consolidates their income base but also implicitly scales down
government borrowings. However, merely relying on inflation is not
recommended as this would signify no concrete measures taken in
reducing public debt like curtailing unnecessary costs and inefficiencies in
most governments.

7.3 Conclusion

The US subprime crisis has shown that greed does not lead to bliss but to
bleed. However, the world is currently also facing an ageing population
and the detrimental effects of climate change. Consequently, short sighted
policies geared solely towards reducing the adverse effects of only the
financial/debt crisis are likely to backfire when assessed from the angle of
climate change. Policy coordination is of paramount significance to ensure
a sustainable growth path. This chapter probes into solutions geared
towards ensuring such policy coordination.

In essence, social banks promote capital in a more moral manner via focus on value-oriented channels, with substantial emphasis being laid on customer relationships stretching beyond financial returns into long-term social relationships. A good mixture of social and commercial banks would set the proper foundation stone for a more stable and comforting financial environment. Moreover, money, per se, has no real value for social banks; value is built chiefly when money fosters mutual trust, cooperation, humane development in its global perspective, i.e., catering for people, the environment, nature, climate change, poverty needs, ethics motivations, edge touching viewpoints that integrate realism with idealism, among others. Besides, man also needs to feed his inner soul since spiritual wealth has utterly been overlooked in most economic models. Recourse towards network optimisation, use of sustainable long-term policies, proper check on the artificial economy via 0.75:1 rule of thumb, inciting the flow concept at work and promotion of green finance, are all expected to not only undermine the detrimental impacts of the trident crises, but also establish an environment that deters prevalence of crises.

Finally, governments should be aware that growth, per se, has no real significance; it is the quality of growth that matters. For instance, although India is on a track of higher economic growth than most developed countries, there is still the problem of farmers committing suicide due to crop failures that make them insolvent. Checked growth is better than vigorous growth, as only the former safeguards the values and non-material nature of man, let alone its inherent sustainable nature.

References

1. Akerlof, George A., 1970, The Market for Lemons: Quality Uncertainty and the Market Mechanism, *Quarterly Journal of Economics*, 84(3), 488-500.
2. Chorofas, Dimistris N., 2009, Capitalism without Capital. Palgrave MacMillan.
3. Csikszentmihalyi, M., 1991, Flow: The Psychology of Optimal Experience. New York: Harper Collins.
4. Ehrlich, Isaac. and Francis T. Lui, 1991, Intergenerational Trade, Longevity, and Economic Growth, *Journal of Political Economy*, University of Chicago Press, 99(5), 1029-1059.
5. Engle, R. F., 1982, Autoregressive Conditional Heteroskedasticity with Estimates of the Variance of UK Inflation, Econometrica, 50(4), 987-1008.

6. Intergovernmental Panel on Climate Change Fourth Assessment Report: Climate Change 2007(AR4).
7. Kalemli-Ozcan S., H. E. Ryder and D. N. Weil, 2000, Mortality decline, human capital investment and economic growth, *Journal of Development Economics*, 62(1), 1-23.
8. Keynes, J. M., 1936, The General Theory of Employment, Interest and Money. Macmillan, London.
9. Kotlikoff, Laurence J. and Lawrence H. Summers, 1981, The Role of Intergenerational Transfers in Aggregate Capital Accumulation, *Journal of Political Economy*, University of Chicago Press, 89(4), 706-32.
10. Malthus, T. R., 1798, An Essay on the Principle of Population. J. Johnson, in St. Paul's Church-Yard, London, UK.
11. Shiller, Robert J., 2005, Irrational Exuberance, Second Edition: Princeton University Press.